Keech.

BLACK FACES, BLACK INTERESTS

2/24/93

Bill

I deeply appreciate your support and encouragement. You were one of the very first to recognize my talent and believe in my potential. You will always have a special place in my life.

Carol

BLACK FACES, BLACK INTERESTS

The Representation of African Americans in Congress

Carol M. Swain

Harvard University Press
Cambridge, Massachusetts
London, England 1993

Library of Congress Cataloging-in-Publication Data

Swain, Carol M. (Carol Miller)
  Black faces, black interests : the representation of African Americans
in Congress / Carol M. Swain.
      p. cm.
  Includes bibliographical references and index.
  ISBN 0–674–07615–X
  1. United States. Congress. House. 2. United States. Congress. House—Election
districts. 3. Afro-American legislators. 4. Legislators—United States. 5. Afro-
Americans—Politics and government. 6. Representative government and representation—United States. I. Title.
JK1323 1993
328.73'0089'96073—dc20
92–21837
    CIP

For my sons
Benjamin and Reginald

Contents

Preface

How do the members of the House of Representatives represent the interests of African Americans? In this book I examine what is distinctive about black representation of blacks, how white members of Congress fit into the picture, and how black representation can be increased.

Journalistic accounts of the late 1980s asserted that black politicians would soon claim the last few congressional districts with black majorities that were still represented by white incumbents. There was some speculation that black representation in Congress would then stagnate, given that black politicians were thought to need black majorities to get elected. I wanted to test this assumption. In a growing number of cases, after all, black politicians had been victorious in political units with white majorities. I was repeatedly told by voting rights strategists, however, that those elections either were flukes or involved politicians who had sold out the interests of blacks to get themselves elected.

This book therefore takes a close look at black representatives in a variety of districts—historically black, newly black, heterogeneous, and majority white—and at white representatives in districts with either a significant black minority or a black majority. After evaluating representatives in these diverse environments, I conclude that effective representation of black interests is in no danger of being diminished by either demographic changes or "sell-out" black politicians. Redrawing boundaries to create additional districts with large black majorities, however, appears not to be the most effective way to increase the representation of black interests. The potential exists for the election of additional black representatives in other types of congressional districts, including those with white majorities. In addition, white representatives are an underutilized and perhaps underappreciated alternative source of support for many of the issues that are of greatest interest to African Americans.

The representation of black interests depends on more than the shared skin color of the representative and the electorate.

In studying the representation of black interests in Congress, I have relied on a variety of sources. Most important were numerous interviews with members of Congress and their staffs, both in Washington, D.C., and in their districts, and observations in the field. I have also made extensive use of roll-call analysis and historical data. I have used these sources to examine the careers of members of the 100th Congress (1987–1989); my broader discussion considers the issue of African American representation through the spring of 1992 (the 102nd Congress).

Some portions of Chapter 2 appeared in an earlier draft in "Changing Patterns of African-American Representation in Congress," *The Atomistic Congress*, edited by Allen D. Hertzke and Ronald Peters, Jr. (Armonk, N.Y.: M. E. Sharpe, 1991), and are reprinted with permission. Figure 9.1 is redrawn with permission from a version that appeared in the *Wall Street Journal*, October 18, 1991.

This book could not have been written without the cooperation of numerous people. I am deeply indebted to the members of Congress and their staffs who were most generous in extending to me their time and interest. Being a female attempting to interview a group of mostly male representatives both helped and complicated my work in various ways. One member of Congress offered me a job on his staff, another took me home to meet his parents, and a third introduced me at a party as the woman writing a book about his personal life. Some politicians tried to impress me in their male-dominated world; others did not want to be seen traveling with a woman not known to people in the district. Despite some difficulties, the fieldwork proved to be very valuable, and most of the time it was conducted in a friendly and relaxed atmosphere. Some of the members who were initially the most reserved and cautious later became frank and open during my visit to their district; one even outlined the strategy that a potential opponent should use to defeat him.

Many others deserve special acknowledgment. Merle Black, Paula Hall, Lawrence Hamlar, David Hillman, William Keech, Richard Shingles, and Deil Wright are among the good friends and, in some cases, former teachers who have encouraged, inspired, and challenged me over the years. More recently I have benefited from the generous attention of my friends and colleagues at Princeton University, especially Fred I. Greenstein. In addition, R. Douglas Arnold, John DiIulio, and Stanley Kelley, Jr., commented on significant portions of the manuscript, and

Jennifer Hochschild and Donald Stokes read an early draft. Iris Hunter provided excellent assistance. Susan Perzel and Patricia Trinity helped with the tables and the preparation of the manuscript and provided other forms of support as well. Yao Azibu, Jesse Borges, George Flint, Mark Lopez, and Erika Nystrom provided research assistance at different stages.

Richard Fenno, Jr., a pioneer in this type of research, has been especially supportive of this project. His enthusiasm, encouragement, and friendship have meant a great deal to me. Chandler Davidson, Charles V. Hamilton, Matthew Holden, Martin Kilson, John Kingdon, Glenn Loury, Russell Nieli, Robert C. Smith, Hanes Walton, and Alan Wheat commented on various portions of different drafts. I would also like to thank Aida Donald, Elizabeth Suttell, and Elizabeth Gretz of Harvard University Press and the Press's readers for their comments and suggestions. Auriel Pilgrim and the staff at the Joint Center for Political Studies in Washington, D.C., were especially helpful. Finally, the research for this book could not have been conducted without the generous financial support of the National Science Foundation (SES-8723080), the Ford Foundation, the American Association of University Women, Princeton University, and the Graduate School at the University of North Carolina at Chapel Hill. But I alone, of course, take full responsibility for the book's content.

May 1992

I · THE CONTEXT

1 · The Representation of Black Interests in Congress

The political interests of African Americans are varied and complex.[1] Although the black middle class is increasing in size and some of its members are politically conservative, an alarming proportion of blacks remain at the bottom of the economic ladder, in need of the type of assistance likely to be offered by a liberal government and yet deeply distrustful of all government. The ability of the political system to address the needs of its black citizens is a test of representative democracy. More than two decades after the passage of civil rights legislation, African Americans are still underrepresented in political office, particularly at the federal level. They have sought to increase their congressional representation by challenging white incumbents in majority-black districts and by demanding that courts and state legislatures create new districts with black majorities. But often this way of proceeding has limited black politicians to two choices: to wait in the wings for retirement, death, or crippling scandal to remove white incumbents, or to fight among themselves for those seats made available in newly created black districts. And in recent years, the prospects for getting more blacks into Congress by using these two strategies have decreased dramatically. The retirement in 1990 of Louisiana's Lindy Boggs left no white politicians representing majority-black congressional districts, and 1990 census data initially revealed few areas where new districts with black majorities could be drawn. This situation occurred at a time when the percentage of blacks in Congress, although greater than it had ever been before, was far smaller than the percentage of blacks nationally. In 1991, when blacks held 25 of the 435 seats in the House of Representatives and constituted roughly 6 percent of the House, African Americans made up 12 percent of the U.S. population.

The magnitude of the unsolved problems facing black communities throughout America raises troubling questions for people who equate black representation with more black faces in Congress. What will happen to black representation when courts and state legislatures can no longer draw new majority-black congressional districts? Do blacks have any alternatives for increasing their congressional representation? Can more black politicians be elected in majority-white congressional districts? Can white politicians represent black interests?

In this book I explore some of the answers to these questions. Using quantitative analysis of roll-call data, detailed interviews, and observation of the constituency relations of black and white members of Congress from a variety of districts, I have found additional sources of representation, different strategies for achieving true representation, and different expectations about what representation entails.

This book is divided into four parts. Part I establishes the context for the study. After defining the key concepts "black interests" and "black representation" in the balance of this chapter, in Chapter 2 I briefly trace the history of black representation from the ill-fated and largely ineffective efforts of the Reconstruction era through the relative improvements of the twentieth century. Parts II and III present case studies of thirteen black and white representatives. In Part II, I focus on black representatives in four types of congressional districts: historically black, newly black, heterogeneous, and majority-white. "Historically black" districts are districts with black majorities that have consistently elected blacks to Congress for ten or more years. "Newly black" districts have acquired black majorities more recently. These districts are usually the product of court-ordered redistricting plans, and the percentage of blacks in them is, on the whole, much lower. "Heterogeneous" districts are composed of three or more racial groups and lack a single racial majority. In the terminology that I use, "majority-white" districts are those that are at least 50 percent white and have black congressional representatives. For the next few decades, at least, heterogeneous and majority-white districts must be the source of any significant growth in the number of new black faces in Congress.

Part III examines white representatives of minority-black and majority-black districts. These are districts in which the black voting-age populations, those blacks who are eighteen years of age or older, constitute 35–39 percent and 50 percent or more, respectively, of the total voting-age population. White representatives prove to be an important and often undervalued force in what I call the "substantive representation" of African Americans. Part IV considers the implications of the study: Chapter 9 discusses the relevance of the findings to issues of congressional redistricting, and Chapter 10 concludes with some observations about representation and the general outlook for the future.

What Is Representation?

What, indeed, is representation? And what is so special about black representation? Of the many analyses of the concept, Hannah Pitkin's is the most useful. Pitkin distinguishes between "descriptive representation," the statistical correspondence of the demographic characteristics of representatives with those of their constituents, and more "substantive representation," the correspondence between representatives' goals and those of their constituents.[2]

Descriptive representation can be examined by comparing the incidence of particular demographic characteristics in the population—for example, race, gender, religion, occupation, or age—with those of the representative. I define descriptive representation for African Americans as representation by black officeholders; that is, for this kind of representation the match between the race of the representative and his or her constituents is paramount. But a shared racial or ethnic heritage is not necessary for substantive representation and says little about a politician's actual performance. Bernard Grofman notes: "Being typical may be roughly synonymous with being representative, but it is neither a sufficient nor necessary condition for effective representation."[3] The extent and quality of substantive representation can be determined by examining the responsiveness of the representative to his or her constituency.

More black faces in political office (that is, more descriptive representation for African Americans) will not necessarily lead to more representation of the tangible interests of blacks. Robert Smith, Dianne Pinderhughes, and Mack Jones have used the term "symbolic representation" to refer to the failure of black (and, by extension, any) elected officials to advance the policy interests of their constituency.[4] In effect, they refer to descriptive representation that is *not* accompanied by substantive representation. Whenever we consider the descriptive representation of blacks in Congress, we must always ask whether substantive representation is also present.

What Are Black Interests?

Because representation involves a relationship between constituents and elected officials, the question of interests immediately arises. What is it that is being represented? W. B. Gallie describes "interest" as an essentially contested concept—one that is used differently by different writers and that can therefore lead to empty debates in which semantic confusion obscures real issues.[5] But here it is sufficient to note that interests can have both objective and subjective components, which can at times conflict with each other for a given individual or group.[6] One may treat observable phenomena, such as level of income, physical well-being, or employment status, as indicators or clues to an individual's or group's objective interests. It is possible, however, for objective interests to be wrongly attributed to an individual or group. We may assume, for example, that two-parent families are "better" than one-parent families, that employment is better than unemployment, and that good health is preferable to poor health; but some individuals and groups may not share the values of, or agree with, those who attempt to define what their objective interests are. Thus what certain researchers consider "deviant" in some black families may only appear so because of the tendency of American society to judge black behavior by the cultural norms of whites.

Subjective interests are less observable because they are so closely connected with the feelings, emotions, and temperaments of the people involved. Usually subjective interests are, in fact, related to objective conditions and circumstances—but they do not have to be. The perception of subjective interests may be influenced by cultural and psychological needs that lie outside the range of normal political activity—for example, the need of African Americans to feel that their contributions as a group are valued by society at large. Whenever an individual or a group defines an issue or concern as an interest, then that interest becomes at least to some extent legitimized as a worthwhile pursuit and should be taken seriously by anyone who purports to represent that individual or group on the issue in question.

If one accepts both objective and subjective indicators of interests as valid, what happens when these interests diverge? The conclusion is often that the individual or group is a victim of a false consciousness or, perhaps, of a consciousness that has not been raised. Those who seek to advance their own notion of the interests of a particular group commonly reach this conclusion. Having defined what is in the group's objective interest, they argue that it should be in its subjective interest as well, and, if it is not, they claim that the group is (for whatever reason) unaware of its "true" interests. The question of whether or not a group or individual is evincing a false consciousness is a normative one—it cannot be resolved empirically. For the present purposes, therefore, it is sufficient to identify objective and subjective indicators of the interests of American blacks and then to ask whether and to what extent these are represented in Congress.

No one can argue that African Americans are monolithic. Some are capitalists; others are socialists. Most live in the South, but some reside in the Northeast, Midwest, and other sections of the country. Some are doctors, lawyers, and engineers; others are sanitation workers, street cleaners, and domestics. Owing to these differences the interests of blacks must vary in important ways; still, it would be a mistake to place more emphasis on the variations within American black society than on the commonalities. Broad patterns of objective circumstances and subjective orientations characterize American blacks, and striking differences continue to exist between black and white Americans well over a century after abolition and a quarter of a century after the enactment of civil rights legislation.

Indicators of Objective Interests

Indicators of the objective interests of blacks paint a stark picture of the daily reality in which so many African Americans find themselves. On virtually every indicator of objective well-being, black Americans fall below the white majority.

Unemployment disproportionately affects African Americans: labor statistics regularly show the black unemployment rate to be double and often triple the white rate.[7] Even when minorities are gainfully employed, their income does not equal that of whites. Furthermore, blacks have lost ground since 1970, when their median income was 61.3 percent of that for whites; by 1989 this figure had fallen to 56.2 percent (see Table 1.1).

Almost forty years after *Brown v. Board of Education,* disparities exist with regard to the quality of schools and the educational achievement rates of blacks and whites.[8] Despite widespread efforts to achieve school desegregation, a large number of black children still attend predominantly black schools, which are often grossly inferior to those attended by most white children. Some of the persistent inequities are a manifestation of problems alluded to earlier: black children are likely to be of a lower socioeconomic status than white children. As a consequence, they drop out of school at a higher rate than do their white counterparts and perform more poorly on standardized achievement tests.[9]

Table 1.1. Median family income, 1970–1989

Year	Blacks	Whites	Ratio of black income to white
1970	$20,067	$32,713	61.3
1975	20,234	32,885	61.5
1980	19,073	32,962	57.9
1985	19,344	33,595	57.6
1987	20,091	35,350	56.8
1988	20,260	35,549	57.0
1989	20,209	35,975	56.2

Source: U.S. Department of Commerce, Bureau of the Census, Money Income and Poverty Status in the United States, 1989 (Washington, D.C.: U.S. Government Printing Office, 1990), table 8, p. 36.

Health care continues to pose a serious problem for blacks. The life span for black adults has decreased from 69.7 years in 1982 to 69.4 in 1988. Over the same period, the life span of whites increased slightly, from 75.3 to 75.4 years.[10] A wide disparity exists in the infant mortality rate of blacks and whites; the black rate is 19.2 percent, that of whites 9.7 percent.[11] In addition, a high incidence of HIV infection among African Americans is wreaking havoc in some communities; blacks constitute a fourth of all cases of AIDS reported between 1981 and 1986.[12] Blacks also suffer disproportionately from a host of other physical ailments, including hypertension, heart disease, and cancer. Data on health care indicate that blacks are far less likely than whites to receive quality care, and they are more likely to be underinsured and to rely on hospitals, rather than private physicians, for their primary care. Thus it appears that African Americans would benefit from a national health care system, which liberal Democrats have sought to establish for years.[13]

Both criminal activity and victimization reach alarming proportions in many black communities. In 1984, one in four persons arrested for homicide or non-negligent manslaughter was black. In 1987, 51 percent of all homicide victims were black males.[14] For over four decades homicide has been the leading cause of death among black males aged fifteen to thirty-four.[15] More stringent laws and victimization programs would affect blacks more than whites, because blacks are more likely to be either victims or perpetrators. They are also more likely to suffer from discrimination during arrest and sentencing and to be unable to afford adequate legal defense. Indeed, although the videotape of the brutal beating of a black, handcuffed suspect named Rodney King by members of the Los Angeles police force shocked the nation in 1991, African Americans had spoken out about police brutality and other forms of harassment for years. The riots that then devastated south central Los Angeles in 1992 after a jury acquitted the officers involved of almost all charges were the product of far more frustration and rage than that generated solely by the King incident.

Statistics thus show that, compared with whites, blacks suffer disproportionately from unemployment, poverty, inferior educational opportunities, poor health care, and the scourge of drugs. Because these problems are to some extent objectively measurable, and because there is little doubt that conditions are indeed bad, we can say that blacks have an objective interest in change in these areas. In 1989 a committee on the status of blacks, commissioned by the National Academy of Sciences, reached the following conclusions about policy options that would improve the quality of African Americans' lives: that society (or the government) should provide education, health care, and services to enhance people's skills and productive capabilities, and that the government should strive for national economic growth and full employment, the reduction of discrimination and involuntary segregation, and improvements in income maintenance and other family assistance programs to avoid long-term poverty.[16] In essence, these scholars examined the objective conditions and circumstances affecting African Americans and concluded that these conditions called for the increased involvement of government and society at large—they supported an expanded welfare state and more spending on social programs. Other equally concerned observers, however, might interpret the same data either as an indicator of "spiritual poverty" on the part of some African Americans or as evidence that blacks should withdraw from the traditional two-party system and form a third party or engage in civil disobedience.

The situation of blacks in America is complex, and there are no easy answers. At the same time that black communities are plagued with problems, there exists a growing black middle and professional class whose members often live apart from poorer blacks. Ironically, the percentage of black families earning $50,000 a year or more has increased alongside the percentage of blacks whose earnings place them below the poverty line (see Table 1.2). These income disparities highlight differences both between and within ethnic groups.

Indicators of Subjective Interests

What do African Americans actually think and want? Public opinion polls provide indicators for assessing the subjective interests of blacks and whites, and a variety of notable racial differences in policy preferences exist. Blacks, more than whites, favor increased government spending on health care (84 percent of blacks versus 64 percent of whites), on education (86 versus 63 percent), and food programs for low-income families (65 versus 41 percent). Significant proportions of both races favor school prayer (82 percent of blacks and 68 percent of whites), a seven-day waiting period for the purchase of a handgun (86 and 91 percent), and pollution controls (53 and 70 percent). Blacks as well as whites have opposed U.S. assistance to Nicaragua (63 percent of blacks and 57 percent of whites), increases in military spending (43 and 41 percent), and expenditures on the space program (29 and 42 percent). Blacks and whites are divided evenly against abortion restrictions on rape and incest victims (47 percent of blacks and 46 percent of whites) and have been equally supportive of tax increases to reduce the budget deficit (70 and 67 percent) and the introduction of an Equal Rights Amendment (85 and 70 percent).[17]

That blacks tend to favor redistributive programs more than whites is one of the most important differences between the two races. Surveys show that black Americans disagree with white Americans about

Table 1.2. Percentage of families in selected income ranges by race

Income range	1970		1980		1989	
	Black	White	Black	White	Black	White
Under $10,000	23.0%	8.3%	25.9%	8.3%	25.9%	7.7%
$10,000–$24,999	38.4	25.4	36.0	26.8	32.1	23.9
$25,000–$49,999	30.7	45.5	29.0	41.7	28.1	37.5
$50,000 or more	8.9	20.8	9.2	23.3	13.8	30.9

Source: U.S. Department of Commerce, Bureau of the Census, *Money Income and Poverty Status in the United States, 1989* (Washington, D.C.: U.S. Government Printing Office, 1990), p. 36.

whether the economic situation has improved for blacks, whether there are more opportunities now, whether the competition for jobs is fairly handled, and whether racism in this country has decreased. Blacks are more ideologically liberal than whites on economic issues and are particularly supportive of guaranteed jobs and a government-ensured standard of living.[18] Blacks feel that government has a moral obligation to provide entitlement programs.[19] Because they believe that an activist federal government best serves their needs, they are much more likely than white Americans to favor the redistributive policies historically associated with the Democratic party.[20]

Yet despite all this, a strand of social conservatism runs through black America. More blacks than whites disapprove of abortions on demand (41 versus 28 percent). Fewer blacks than whites approve of married women working (70 versus 76 percent) or like the idea of female politicians (65 versus 75 percent).[21] For representation on issues of this type, blacks may have to look beyond the Democratic party.

Even though blacks rely on the government to improve the quality of their lives, they do not trust it. A 1990 *New York Times* poll found that 77 percent of blacks (in contrast with 34 percent of whites) think that it is true, or most likely true, that the government singles out black politicians for investigations to discredit them. An alarming 60 percent (in contrast with 16 percent of whites) believe that the government makes drugs easily available in poor black neighborhoods to harm black people. Moreover, 29 percent of blacks (but only 5 percent of whites) thought that it was true, or possibly true, that the AIDS virus was deliberately created to decimate the black population.[22] As long as blacks distrust the government—which they perceive to be white-run—to such an extent, they are not likely to have much faith in the politicians on whom they must depend to enact the liberal economic legislation they prefer.

Organized Groups and Black Interests

Organizations such as the National Association for the Advancement of Colored People (NAACP), the National Urban League, and the Congressional Black Caucus have taken the lead in promoting policies that they hold to be in the interest of blacks and other disadvantaged Americans. Over the years these groups have favored legislation designed to improve opportunities for education and health care, reduce unemployment, and provide better housing and childcare for the poor and the working class in the United States.[23] The Black Caucus also takes positions bearing on the interests of people elsewhere in the world—for example, it opposes apartheid in South Africa and speaks out for international human rights, and some of its members have lobbied for Congress to listen to representatives of the Palestine Liberation Organization.

Although the stances such groups adopt are probably supported by many African Americans, it would be simplistic to equate the positions of these organizations with the black interest as a whole. These groups, for instance, are more liberal than the rank-and-file black population on many noneconomic issues, especially on issues of criminal justice. A majority of African Americans, for example, support the death penalty (55 percent), whereas the majority of black interest-group leaders (67 percent) oppose it.[24] This difference may exist because, as Glenn Loury notes, black congressmen interested in criminal justice issues have focused almost exclusively on police brutality, while inner-city black communities have become increasingly dangerous places to live in as a result of crimes committed by blacks against blacks.[25] Some blacks who are forced to live in ghetto areas have come to view the death penalty as a way of improving the security of their neighborhoods.

Affirmative action is another issue on which opinions diverge. Although black interest groups strongly support preferential treatment of minorities in hiring for jobs and in college admissions, an opinion poll conducted for the American Enterprise Institute by Linda Lichter found vast differences between the attitudes of the black public and black interest-group leaders. Seventy-seven percent of black leaders supported preferential treatment of minorities, yet only 23 percent of the black public did.[26] The same poll revealed similar patterns in the perceptions of the black public with regard to the magnitude of job discrimination (74 percent of the black leaders, as opposed to only 40 percent of the black public, believed there to be substantial discrimination). The question of whether or not African Americans were improving in economic status was also divisive: 39 percent of the leaders did not think so, compared with 66 percent of the public; and 61 percent of the black leaders saw a deterioration in black living standards, compared with 34 percent of the black public.[27] It is important to be aware that perceptions of black leaders and the black public may vary on critical social issues.[28]

African Americans also disagreed with most of their leaders on the fitness of Judge Clarence Thomas to serve on the Supreme Court of the United States. A surprising majority of African Americans (60 percent) supported the confirmation of Thomas, even though individuals such as Jesse Jackson and groups such as the NAACP, claimed by a majority of African Americans (54 and 56 percent, respectively) to represent their interests, strongly opposed him.[29]

In addition to the issues on which the black public seems to disagree with the black leadership, there is also an increasingly visible group of black conservatives and moderates who do not automatically accept the positions of the leading black and liberal interest groups. This said, the positions of the liberal groups are widely accepted by over 50 percent of African Americans, and these positions are as close as we can come to a unified black interest. In any event, the positions of organized black interest groups warrant our careful consideration.

Other interest groups that support legislation likely to be beneficial to blacks and poor people are the American Federation of Labor–Congress of Industrial Organizations' (AFL-CIO) Committee on Political Education (COPE) and the Leadership Conference on Civil Rights (LCCR). The Leadership Conference on Civil Rights is an umbrella organization for almost two hundred different groups representing women, workers, the disabled, various religious denominations, senior citizens, and blacks. The LCCR pays particular attention to legislation affecting its membership and issues a biennial report card on each legislator's record on civil rights and on certain social and economic issues. COPE, which issues annual ratings for members of Congress, takes on an even broader range of issues. It monitors legislation on defense and foreign policy as well as on domestic issues and concerns itself with a greater number of issues of low salience for blacks than does the LCCR. Nevertheless, both groups' policy positions provide practical indicators of black interests, and black Democrats score high on the endorsement scales of both.

Who Supports the Interests of Blacks on Capitol Hill?

How well do the Democrats and Republicans on Capitol Hill represent black interests? Which party gives the best substantive representation to blacks? Before tackling these questions, I must stress again the impossibility of positing a single set of interests for a population group as diverse as blacks in America. What we can do, however, is examine the congruence between the policy preferences of the majority of blacks and the voting behavior of their representatives. From these data we can draw inferences about representation.

To determine who on Capitol Hill represents the articulated interests of the majority of African Americans, I use the LCCR and COPE rating scales and two others of my own devising. During the 100th Congress (1987–1989), the LCCR rating scale included votes on the Civil Rights Restoration Act (and on amendments to it), the Hate Crime Statistics, the Japanese Reparations Act, and bills on establishing programs for low-income families, fair housing, and equitable pay. The COPE scale included many of the same bills, plus the Omnibus Trade Bill, which provided that workers be given a sixty-day advance notice of plant closings; the Catastrophic Health Insurance Bill, which placed a cap on out-of-pocket Medicare expenses; a bill placing limits on imports; prohibitions against trading with South Africa; a bill banning the use of lie-detector tests; and legislation requiring that foreign citizens report their controlling interests in U.S. businesses.

Because both of these organizations back legislation not relevant to this book and their support in the black community is uncertain, and because their scales may sometimes overlap, I have also developed alternative rating scales, which exclude a number of the items on the COPE and LCCR scales, for the 100th Congress. My alternative civil rights index (ACRI) includes votes on amendments to and the final passage of the Civil Rights Restoration Act, the Hate Crime Statistics, and the Fair Housing Amendments. It excludes the Japanese Reparations Act, which does not really affect the black community in a clear way and which many southern white representatives, who otherwise support civil rights for blacks, had little incentive to support. I also excluded legislation authorizing publicly financed abortions in the District of Columbia, as did the LCCR and COPE scales, largely because black support for this legislation is unclear. My alternative redistributive index (ARI) includes the Omnibus Trade Bill override veto, the Catastrophic Health Insurance Bill, a welfare reform package (not included by LCCR and COPE), and programs for low-income families.

The bar graph in Figure 1.1 illustrates the extent to which Democrats and Republicans of the 100th Congress supported black interests as measured by the LCCR, COPE, ACRI, and ARI scales (100 percent indicates total support). Although the specific legislation used to construct interest-group scales varies from congress to congress, representatives have fairly consistent scores across time. No rating scale is without problems, of course.[30] There is, however, considerable evidence to suggest that the LCCR and COPE scales work quite well for measuring a representative's support for public policies preferred by blacks.[31] The

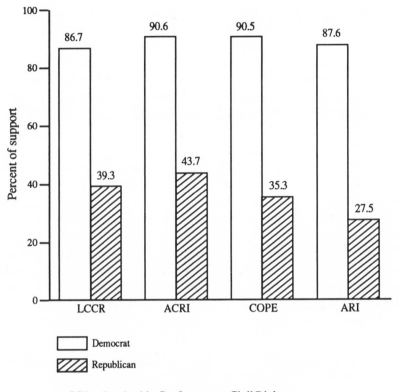

LCCR = Leadership Conference on Civil Rights
ACRI = Alternative Civil Rights Index calculated by author
COPE = AFL-CIO Committee on Political Education
ARI = Alternative Redistributive Index calculated by author

Figure 1.1. Partisan support on the four indicators of black interests, 100th Congress. Data compiled from U.S. Census, roll-call votes, and published reports of the Leadership Conference on Civil Rights and the AFL-CIO Committee on Political Education.

ACRI scale provides a relatively good indicator for civil rights support on black-related issues, and the ARI scale measures support for redistribution and workers' rights.

The data indicate that Democrats and Republicans differ considerably in their support for black interests. Democrats are always more supportive of civil rights and redistributive social welfare policies than are Republicans. As expected, representatives from both parties perform better on the ACRI than they do on the LCCR scale. They do slightly worse on the ARI, however, than they do on COPE's index. Republicans are more supportive of civil rights for blacks than they are of broad redistributive measures and initiatives to protect workers.

Using multiple regression, we may examine the possible influences on a representative's support of black interests (see Table 1.3). The partisan differences are strong and persistent even when we consider other factors that have proved relevant for explaining support of black interests in other studies—region, urbanization, and the proportion of blacks in a district.[32] Next to party, region (South versus non-South) exerts the largest influence on a member's support of black interests, followed by the size of the district's black population.[33] The strong effect of party affiliation is consistent with earlier research that shows it to have an unmistakable impact on a representative's voting behavior. Also consistent with past research is the finding that southerners from both parties are less supportive of the whole range of issues discussed above than are their colleagues from other parts of the nation. Another factor is the size of the district's black population: the higher the percentage of blacks, the greater the support for redistributive policies. This relationship maintains its strength whether we examine it alone or as it interacts with urbanization.[34]

Table 1.3. Multivariate analysis of possible influences on representatives' support of black interests

Variables	Indicators measuring support			
	LCCR	ACRI	COPE	ARI
Party	48**	48**	55**	59**
	(2.1)	(2.3)	(2.0)	(3.0)
Region	–18**	–17**	–17**	–13**
	(2.5)	(2.8)	(2.4)	(2.3)
Percentage urban	5	–4	–1	–2
	(4.7)	(5.1)	(4.4)	(4.4)
Percentage black	7	8	18*	21*
	(8)	(8)	(7.2)	(7.2)
R^2	.58	.52	.67	.70

$*p \leq .05.$ $**p \leq .01.$

Note: The regression coefficients are unstandardized. The numbers in parentheses are standard errors.

LCCR = Leadership Conference on Civil Rights rating; ACRI = Alternative Civil Rights Index; COPE = AFL-CIO Committee on Political Education rating; ARI = Alternative Redistributive Index.

It is possible, however, that Democrats only represent black interests when blacks constitute a high percentage of their district's population. To evaluate how much the voting behavior of white Democrats and Republicans is influenced by the overall percentage of blacks in their districts, I examined their support for black interests at population levels ranging from 0 to 40 percent or more (see Figure 1.2). Only three white Democrats, and no white Republicans, represented districts that were 40 or more percent black during the 100th Congress.[35]

The resulting data reveal strong partisan differences. Regardless of the percentage of blacks in their districts, almost all white Democrats are supportive of black interests. For the Republicans, it is their party and not the number of their black constituents that guides them politically. Further evidence for this proposition can be found in the careers of two white Democrats, Tommy Robinson (AR) and Bill Grant (FL), who had a low proportion of blacks in their districts and who both switched to the Republican party in 1988. (They were subsequently defeated in the next election.) Prior to their party switch both had the voting records of progressive Democrats, Robinson scoring 86 and 80 percent on the COPE and LCCR scales, Grant 70 and 73 percent. After they switched, both voted like conservative southern Republicans, scoring less than 30 percent on both scales. On average, Republicans are least supportive of black interests when the percentage of blacks in their districts is less than 20 percent (see Figure 1.2). Only six southern Republicans and no northern Republicans had black populations exceeding 30 percent; and this, of course, suggests that higher proportions of blacks indeed help Democrats get elected.[36]

When we look specifically at white support for the issues included on the COPE and ARI scales, we find a similar pattern—Democrats are closer to blacks than are Republicans. Southern Democrats, unlike northern Democrats, are most supportive when the percentage of blacks in their districts is either low—less than 30 percent—or particularly high, 40 percent and above. This high-low pattern of support is, in fact, the same curvilinear pattern noted in the older literature on southern politics.[37] It has a new twist, however: southern Democrats never sink to the low levels of support they displayed before blacks started exercising their rights under the 1965 Voting Rights Act and its various extensions. Although most southern white Democrats call themselves fiscal conservatives, they vote like progressive Democrats on many issues that are important to blacks.[38] This pattern is encouraging for African Americans concerned about congressional representation.

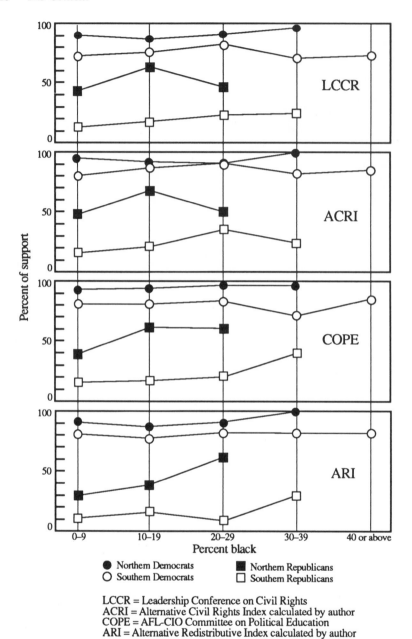

Northern Democrats
Southern Democrats
Northern Republicans
Southern Republicans

LCCR = Leadership Conference on Civil Rights
ACRI = Alternative Civil Rights Index calculated by author
COPE = AFL-CIO Committee on Political Education
ARI = Alternative Redistributive Index calculated by author

Figure 1.2. White representatives' support of black interests by party, region, and percentage of black population in district, 100th Congress. Data compiled from U.S. Census, roll-call votes, and published reports of the Leadership Conference on Civil Rights and the AFL-CIO Committee on Political Education.

Black interests on Capitol Hill, at least as measured by the policy congruence between the representative and his or her black population, are better looked after by the Democratic congressional party. On every indicator, Republicans are less responsive to black interests than are Democrats. Black representatives are thus not the only source of black representation in Congress—white Democrats also appear to represent blacks well. If the Democrats continue to be the more responsive of the two major parties, black interests will be best served by the election of more Democrats. On the one hand, that the Democrats represent black interests, or at least the policy preferences of a large number of blacks, should be reassuring for most African Americans. It suggests that black interests will certainly be represented in Congress, even if the number of black faces remains low. On the other hand, black influence would be substantially reduced if the Republicans were to win control of the House. This is not to say that voting on issues is the only way members of Congress can represent their constituents. As we shall see, black representation means more than policy congruence between black interests and roll-call votes.

2 · Tracing the Footsteps of Blacks on the Hill

Twenty years ago, black members couldn't even eat in the House dining room. It was an unwritten rule. . . . Now I'm chairman of the committee that has jurisdiction over that dining room.

—REPRESENTATIVE AUGUSTUS HAWKINS, *quoted in the* New York Times, *March 11, 1983*

In 1870 the first African Americans, after centuries of slavery, took their seats in Congress. Since then vast changes have taken place in the political status of African Americans on and beyond Capitol Hill, and especially in the House of Representatives. By 1989 the majority whip was black, five blacks chaired full committees, and seventeen chaired subcommittees. The penetration of blacks into the power structure of the House is a dramatic change for a race whose representation was virtually nonexistent until Reconstruction and after that still often far from adequate. Progress has been slow and unsteady, punctuated by regressions and resurgences.[1]

During the 1980s the number of blacks in Congress, along with the diversity of the districts from which they were elected, increased at a greater rate than ever before. As a consequence, there were new views on policy and on ways of fulfilling the responsibilities of a representative. In particular, more and more blacks were elected from districts that were not predominantly black, and some of these representatives were following the traditional congressional pattern of giving the interests of their districts priority over the collective representation of a prescribed black agenda.

The Reconstruction Era

The Reconstruction era began in 1868 and is traditionally viewed as having ended with the Compromise of 1876 (although it can be extended until 1901, when the last black representative left Congress). In 1876, disputed electoral votes in the presidential contest resulted in a constitutional crisis that ended when the Democratic candidate Samuel Tilden, who had 184 of the 185 electoral votes necessary to win, conceded to Rutherford Hayes, the Republican candidate, who was then declared President. In exchange for the needed electoral votes, the Republican party abandoned its attempts to advance the interests of blacks and in effect left the South to deal with its black population as it saw fit.[2]

Twenty-two blacks served in Congress between 1869 and 1901—twenty in the House of Representatives and two in the Senate (see Tables 2.1 and 2.2). The influence of Abraham Lincoln and emancipation was evident in their party affiliations: all were Republicans. Black Americans served in Congress for three decades in the post–Civil War period. The initial breakthrough came in the 41st Congress (1869–1871): three black

Table 2.1. Number of black members by year and congress, Reconstruction era

Year	Congress	Number of black members of Congress
1869–1871	41st	3
1871–1873	42nd	5
1873–1875	43rd	7
1875–1877	44th	8
1877–1879	45th	4
1879–1881	46th	1
1881–1883	47th	2
1883–1885	48th	2
1885–1887	49th	2
1887–1889	50th	0
1889–1891	51st	3
1891–1893	52nd	1
1893–1895	53rd	1
1895–1897	54th	1
1897–1899	55th	1
1899–1901	56th	1

Source: "CRS Report for Congress: Black Members of the United States Congress, 1789–1989," Congressional Research Service, Library of Congress, August 10, 1989.

Table 2.2. Black members of Congress by party, state, and congress, Reconstruction era

Member of Congress	Party and state	Congress
Senate		
Hiram R. Revels	(R-MS)	41st
Blanche K. Bruce	(R-MS)	44th, 45th, 46th
House		
John H. Rainey	(R-SC)	41st, 42nd, 43rd, 44th, 45th
Jefferson F. Long	(R-GA)	41st
Robert C. Delarge	(R-SC)	42nd
Robert B. Elliot	(R-SC)	42nd, 43rd
Benjamin S. Turner	(R-AL)	42nd
Josiah T. Walls	(R-FL)	42nd, 43rd, 44th
Robert H. Cain	(R-SC)	43rd, 45th
John R. Lynch	(R-MS)	43rd, 44th, 47th
Alonzo J. Ransier	(R-SC)	43rd
James T. Rapier	(R-AL)	43rd
Jeremiah Haralson	(R-AL)	44th
John A. Hymann	(R-NC)	44th
Charles E. Nash	(R-LA)	44th
Robert Smalls	(R-SC)	45th, 47th, 48th, 49th
James E. O'Hara	(R-NC)	48th, 49th
Henry P. Cheatham	(R-NC)	51st, 52nd
John M. Langston	(R-VA)	51st
Thomas E. Miller	(R-SC)	51st
George W. Murray	(R-SC)	53rd, 54th
George White	(R-NC)	55th, 56th

Source: "CRS Report for Congress: Black Members of the United States Congress, 1789–1989," Congressional Research Service, Library of Congress, August 10, 1989.

members were elected, though they were not seated until 1870. The number of black legislators grew rapidly for a few years but peaked in the 44th Congress (1875) with eight members. After 1875 Congress was characterized by the sporadic and dwindling presence of blacks. No blacks served during the 50th Congress (1887–1889), three served during the 51st (1889–1891), and between the 52nd and 56th Congresses (1891–1901), there was one black member per session.

As might be expected, the first black representatives came from states with high black populations—the former slave states of the South (see Table 2.3). No state outside the South elected African-American repre-

Table 2.3. Correlation between states' percentage of black population, 1870, and number of black members of Congress

State	% black in population	Congress		Total
		Senate	House	
South Carolina	59%	0	8	8
Mississippi	54	2	1	3
Louisiana	50	0	1	1
Florida	49	0	1	1
Alabama	48	0	3	3
Georgia	46	0	1	1
Virginia	42	0	1	1
North Carolina	37	0	4	4
Total				22
r				−.0006

Sources: *Historical Statistics of the States, Colonial Times to 1970, Bicentennial Edition* (Washington, D.C.: U.S. Government Printing Office, 1975), series 195–209, pp. 24–37; "CRS Report for Congress: Black Members of the United States Congress, 1789–1989," Congressional Research Service, Library of Congress, August 10, 1989.

sentatives until well into the twentieth century. Between 1870 and 1897, South Carolina (59 percent black) elected eight blacks to the House. Mississippi (54 percent black) and Louisiana (50 percent black) each elected one black. Mississippi also sent two blacks to the Senate. Five other states with sizable black populations—Alabama, Florida, Georgia, North Carolina, and Virginia—elected ten black representatives among them. Although blacks were elected to Congress only in states with high percentages of African Americans, the exact overall percentage in the state was not strongly related to the number of blacks elected. Far more important was the percentage of blacks within each electoral district. In the Reconstruction era over 92 percent of black representatives were elected from districts with black majorities.[3]

Despite the large black populations of the South, black voters elected few politicians of their own race. Four former slave states—Arkansas, Tennessee, Texas, and West Virginia—never elected black representatives during Reconstruction. Far fewer blacks served in Congress than might be expected from the size of the total black population, and this was true for politics at the state level as well.

Although their numbers were small, the high visibility of black politicians during this period led many white southerners to view blacks as one component of an "unholy triumvirate" that included "scalawags" and "carpetbaggers," the white southerners and relocated northerners who took part in the Reconstruction era governments.[4] The electoral success of blacks during the first three decades after the Civil War is traceable partially to structural changes and efforts of the federal government to empower the newly freed slaves and partially to black mobilization and coalition building with sympathetic whites. But these successes were remarkably limited: few African Americans were elected.

Eric Foner writes that during the Reconstruction era, African Americans embraced "an affirmation of Americanism that insisted that blacks formed an integral part of the nation and were entitled to the same rights and opportunities that white citizens enjoyed."[5] Although the majority of blacks who emerged from slavery were illiterate and few qualified as voters,[6] by 1867 many had joined with whites in political organizations such as the Friends for Universal Suffrage, National Equal Rights League, and Union Free State party.[7] Blacks studied the Declaration of Independence, eagerly embracing its tenets that "all men are created equal . . . [and] are endowed by their creator with certain inalienable rights."[8] Through the Freedmen's Aid organizations the federal government provided the newly freed slaves with access to voting registrars, who instructed them in American history and gave them lessons about government.[9]

The earliest biracial coalitions resulted in the election of sympathetic white politicians from the ranks of the scalawags and carpetbaggers, but growing frustration with the tendency of these coalition strategies to cast blacks as "junior partners" led African Americans to demand more representation in the descriptive sense. In 1870, blacks in South Carolina demanded a fairer share of political offices. They gained concessions that resulted in the election of African Americans to four of the eight state executive offices and three of the five congressional seats, and the placement of one black on the state supreme court.[10] An observer at the 1873 South Carolina state legislative session noted: "The Speaker is black, the clerk is black, the doorkeepers are black, the little pages are black, the chairman of the Ways and Means Committee is black, and the chaplain is coal-black."[11]

In Mississippi, blacks were in part responsible for the election of the two black senators of the Reconstruction era. The first breakthrough occurred when delegates to that state's Republican convention demanded that the legislature select an African American to fill the unexpired term of Jefferson Davis, the former president of the Confederacy. Hiram Revels, who thus became the first black senator, explained the circumstances surrounding his nomination:

> An opportunity of electing a Republican to the United States Senate to fill an unexpired term occurred, and the colored members, after consulting together on the subject, agreed to give their influence and votes for one of their own race for that position, as it would be in their judgement a weakening blow against color line prejudice, and they unanimously elected me for their nominee. Some of the [Democrats] . . . favored it because they thought it would seriously damage the Republican Party. When the election was held everything connected with it was quiet and peaceable and I [was] elected by a large majority.[12]

Galvanized by their success, black delegates at Mississippi's 1873 Republican state convention moved that three of seven state-level vacancies be filled by blacks. In introducing this motion, the delegates argued that they were entitled to a proper share of state offices and were tired of voting for white men.[13] Black voter strength in the state eventually led the first governor of the reconstructed Mississippi, a white, to declare his intent to "vote with the Negro, discuss politics with him, sit, if need be, in council with him, and form a platform acceptable to both."[14] The nature of the political participation of the newly emancipated blacks demonstrated their belief that they were entitled to the same rights enjoyed by white men, including the right to elect members of their own race. They made it evident that they believed that democratic principles guaranteed them a right to share in governance.

A majority of the blacks who served in Congress between 1870 and 1901 were former slaves, but they were not illiterate. Half had attended college and five were graduates. Their colleges and universities included Oberlin (Ohio), Howard (District of Columbia), Knox (Illinois), Shaw (North Carolina), the University of South Carolina, and Wilberforce (Iowa). Only of Benjamin S. Turner (R-AL) was it said that "he could write his name and nothing more."[15] The historian Terry Seip, who closely examined their performance, concluded that "most demonstrated a command of the language equal to that of their white peers."[16] As a group, they had a remarkable amount of political experience: seventeen of the twenty-two blacks who served in Congress following emancipation had previously held an elective office such as tax assessor, sheriff, or state legislator.

Nor were black representatives poor. Seip reports only one with an estate less than $1,000, and five had estates ranging from $5,000 to $20,000, respectable fortunes in those times.[17] Among the wealthiest were Josiah Walls, who was able to use his salary to buy a huge estate from a former Confederate general, and Blanche K. Bruce, a man who was said to have acquired a fortune in real estate.[18] African-American representatives thus had economic interests more like those of whites than those of other blacks.[19] Perhaps as a consequence, black representatives did not seek an economic revolution. Indeed, many worked to return lost economic power to white southerners.[20]

Although the majority of blacks met the legal definition (one-eighth black ancestry) and were technically providing descriptive representation, many were not representative of African Americans in appearance. Many were mulattoes. Photographs published in *Black Americans in Congress* show twelve with marked Caucasian features—light complexions and straight hair—which suggests that some of them may have identified more with whites than blacks.[21] Some of them may have felt the ambivalence at being of mixed racial ancestry that was expressed by one black candidate for a South Carolina office. He declared in 1868: "I never ought to have been a slave, for my father was a gentleman. . . . If there ever is a nigger government—an unmixed nigger government . . . I shall move."[22]

The *Congressional Globe* of the era shows petition after petition introduced by black representatives seeking the return of the lost political rights of the former rebels. In general, the freed slaves who took part in Reconstruction era politics displayed little vindictiveness. Even in states such as South Carolina, where blacks had substantial political power, they made no concerted efforts to subjugate whites. In a speech in 1871 before the House, Representative Joseph Rainey brought this to the attention of his colleagues when he asked whether blacks had "presumed to take improper advantage of the majority they hold in the state by disregarding the interests of the minority." "They have not," he replied. "Our convention which met in 1868, and in which the Negroes were in a large majority, did not pass any prescriptive or disfranchising acts, but adopted a liberal constitution, securing equal rights to all citizens, white and black, male and female. . . . Mark you we did not discriminate, although we had a majority. Our constitution towers up in its majesty with provisions for the equal protection of all citizens."[23]

Most of the twenty-two blacks in Congress served on at least one committee. Six served on Education and Labor,[24] four on Agriculture,[25] and four on Public Expenditures.[26] Blacks were also represented on the

District of Columbia, Library of Congress, Manufactures, Mining, Militia, Pensions, and War Claims committees. There was only one black chairman, Senator Blanche Bruce, and he served on a minor committee, Levees and Dikes of the Mississippi River.

Black representatives sought to advance national policies affecting their states and districts—for example, public education and protective tariffs for local products—as well as dealing with more specifically black issues such as relief for depositors of the failed Freedmen's Savings and Trust Company. They also worked for the interests of native Americans.[27] Their successes, however, were confined to procuring easily obtained political patronage appointments such as postmaster, customs inspector, and internal revenue agent for some of their constituents. They had few legislative accomplishments: most of their bills languished in committee.[28] Not all blacks even pursued the interests of their African-American constituents. Manning Marable notes that although the black Republicans were in favor of suffrage for black males, many advocated the denial of voting rights to the poor and illiterate of all races.[29] For example, John Langston (R-VA), who served on the House Committee on Education between 1890 and 1891, introduced a measure that would have disenfranchised a significant proportion of the former slaves by requiring that all voters be able to read and write before voting in federal elections.[30]

Alert to their minority status, African-American politicians presented their legislative goals as measures affecting both races in order to garner white support. Congressman Rainey, for example, in a speech in support of civil rights legislation, acknowledged "a certain degree of truth" to the claim that the legislation was "for the protection of colored people" but declared that it would also protect "those loyal whites, some to the manor born . . . who, in the exercise of their rights as American citizens, have seen fit to move thither from other sections of the states, and who are now undergoing persecution simply on account of their activity in carrying out Union principle and loyal sentiments in the South."[31]

The constraints on what black Reconstruction era representatives could accomplish are suggested by their own poignant references to personal experiences with discrimination. Each of the seven blacks in the 43rd Congress gave a speech in support of the Civil Rights Bill of 1875. Many of them shared a litany of public humiliations: one spoke of being ousted from a Virginia streetcar, another of being forced to sit in a railroad smoking car with undesirables, others of being denied service in inns and restaurants.[32]

A number of events and forces brought an end to Reconstruction and black representation in Congress: the Hayes-Tilden compromise, Supreme Court decisions that negated the effect of the Fourteenth Amendment and the Civil Rights Act of 1875, intimidation of black voters by the Ku Klux Klan, and all the other concomitants of the return to power of the former Confederates and their allies. By the turn of the century black representation seemed about to end, even at the descriptive level. Only one black member, George White of North Carolina, remained.

In a speech in 1899 White observed that he and his compatriots had been modest in their demands: "Our representation is poor. . . . We have kept quiet while numerically and justly we are entitled to fifty-one members of this House; and I am the only one left. We kept quiet when numerically we are entitled to a member of the Supreme Court. We never had a member, and probably never will; but we have kept quiet. . . . We should have the recognition of a place in the President's Cabinet. . . . We are entitled to thirteen United States Senators, according to justice and our numerical strength, but we have not one and possibly will never get another; and yet we keep quiet."[33] In his farewell address in 1901 White expressed a view that must have been shared by other black politicians: "This, Mr. Chairman, is perhaps the Negro's temporary farewell to the American Congress; but let me say Phoenix-like he will rise up someday and come again. These parting words are on behalf of an outraged, heart-broken, bruised and bleeding, but God-fearing, people."[34]

White's departure occurred during the Jim Crow era of white primaries, literacy tests, and grandfather clauses.[35] To leave the House was his voluntary decision in an increasingly hostile environment. The racist climate that led blacks to conclude that staying in Congress was futile was captured in a cartoon published in 1900 in the Raleigh *News and Observer*. It depicted George White as a beast with a human head, a dragon's spine, and an elephant's trunk dipping into a container representing the public till. The caption read: "He doesn't let go, but most people think our Negro Congressman has had it [his salary] long enough."[36]

The first black congressmen were clearly trailblazers, but there is disagreement about their actual impact. W. E. B. Du Bois quotes two commentators with differing interpretations of the representatives' performance. One concluded: "They left no mark on the legislation of their time; none of them, in comparison with their white associates, attained the least distinction." The other made an observation carrying more positive implications: "The colored men who took seats in both Senate and House did not appear ignorant or helpless. They were as a rule studious, earnest, ambitious men, whose public conduct . . . would be honorable to any race."[37] Seip suggests that they did not differ significantly from their white counterparts, and Foner presents a sympathetic and favorable evaluation of their performance.[38]

No matter how responsible these pioneers may have been, the times, the precariousness of their situation, and the attitude of their white colleagues kept them from accomplishing much in the way of substantive representation.[39] They were never able to penetrate the power structure of the House, nor did they learn to use the procedural rules of Congress in a meaningful way. In terms of descriptive representation, their numbers never approximated the ratio of blacks to whites in the population; and, again, many of the representatives had more in common with whites—in education, income, and physical appearance—than with their black constituents.

Yet black representatives may have made an important nonlegislative contribution. Some white colleagues must have been struck by the many petitions blacks introduced on behalf of their former masters. The eloquence of speakers such as Elliot and Rainey, along with their sophistication and reasoning, undoubtedly helped—however modestly—to break down their white colleagues' notions of black inferiority.

The Twentieth Century

The second wave of black electoral activity began in 1928 with the election of Oscar DePriest (R-IL) from an inner-city Chicago district (see Tables 2.4 and 2.5).[40] Like almost all the Reconstruction era blacks before him, DePriest was elected from a majority-black district. He won office after black constituents, tired of voting for white politicians, agitated for a black representative. His election made him a celebrity, and he came to be viewed as the national representative of the then eleven million African Americans. Unfortunately, the modest, merely descriptive representation he provided conveyed little of substance. He introduced no legislation during his first congressional term, and during his second term his performance improved only slightly. He sponsored an unsuccessful bill calling for the integration of the House restaurant.[41] (Real desegregation of the restaurant did not occur until three decades later.) After serving in the 71st, 72nd, and 73rd Congresses (1929–1935), he was defeated by Arthur Mitchell, the first black Democrat elected to Congress. DePriest's defeat was traceable to his failure to represent his

Table 2.4. Black representatives by year and congress, 1901–1993

Year	Congress	Number of black representatives
1901–1929	57th–70th	0
1929–1935	71st–73rd	1
1935–1943	74th–77th	1
1943–1945	78th	1
1945–1955	79th–83rd	2
1955–1957	84th	3
1957–1963	85th–87th	4
1963–1965	85th–95th	5
1965–1967	89th	6
1967–1969	90th	6
1969–1971	91st	10
1971–1973	92nd	13
1973–1975	93rd	16
1975–1977	94th	17
1977–1979	95th	17
1979–1981	96th	16
1981–1983	97th	18
1983–1985	98th	20
1985–1987	99th	20
1987–1989	100th	22
1989–1991	101st	23
1991–1993	102nd	25

Sources: "CRS Report for Congress: Black Members of the United States Congress, 1789–1989," *Congressional Research Service, Library of Congress*, August 10, 1989; *Congressional Quarterly Weekly Report,* November 10, 1990, pp. 3822–3823.

district's interests, as evidenced by his vote against Roosevelt's emergency legislation, even though its passage would have helped his district.[42] More than five decades were to pass before another black Republican was elected to the House.

Arthur Mitchell's election in 1934 was followed two years later by the

1936 Democratic landslide, part of the New Dealers' electoral realignment in which African Americans transferred their loyalties en masse from the Republican to the Democratic party.[43] Mitchell was considerably more active in Congress than DePriest had been. He supported New Deal legislation and sponsored several bills of his own, covering civil service reform, the abolition of lynching, desegregated interstate travel, and the creation of a Negro exposition. Still, he may have struck some of his black constituents as being overly conciliatory when he declared that 19,000 whites had voted for him and he intended to represent them, too, and when he supported the Supreme Court nomination of Hugo Black, a former Ku Klux Klansman. On that occasion Mitchell told black voters: "It is no more fair . . . to say that because a white man is from the South he is an enemy to the Negro than it is to say because you are a Negro you are worthless as an American citizen. Other Congressmen may draw the color line, but I have not done it."[44]

In 1942, after eight years of service, Mitchell resigned, and William Dawson, another black Democrat, succeeded him. Two years later, Adam Clayton Powell, Jr., was elected congressman in Harlem, New York, and this meant that for the first time since 1891 there was more than one black representative in the House. In 1950 there was another breakthrough for black representation when Dawson gained enough seniority to become the first black to chair a standing committee, the Government Operations Committee. In 1960, Powell became chairman of the more important Education and Labor Committee.[45]

Still another breakthrough came in 1966, when Edward W. Brooke was elected as a Republican senator from Massachusetts, a state with a population less than 3 percent black. Brooke served until his defeat in 1978. Just as race had not earned him his office, it was not a factor in his defeat, which involved political issues entangled with unsavory family matters. Insiders had long considered Brooke vulnerable. He had rarely returned home to look after his state and had sponsored no major legislative initiatives.

Overall the turnover rate for twentieth-century African-American representatives has been extremely low, as is also true for white incumbents. Since the 1950s the reelection rate for House members has rarely dipped below 90 percent. For 1988 and 1990 it was 98.4 and 96.9 percent, respectively.[46] Black representatives almost always get reelected. Only a handful of incumbent blacks have ever been defeated (most in primaries)—Oscar DePriest (1934), Adam Clayton Powell, Jr. (1970), Robert Nix (1978), Katie Hall (1984), Bennett Stewart (1981), Alton Waldon

Table 2.5. Black representatives by party, state, and congress, 1901–1993

Member of Congress	Party and state	Congress
Senate		
Edward Brooke	(R-MA)	90th–95th
House		
Oscar DePriest	(R-IL)	71st–73rd
Arthur W. Mitchell	(D-IL)	74th–77th
William L. Dawson	(D-IL)	78th–91st
Adam C. Powell, Jr.[a]	(D-NY)	79th–90th, 91st
Charles C. Diggs	(D-MI)	84th–96th
Robert C. Nix, Sr.	(D-PA)	85th–95th
Augustus F. Hawkins	(D-CA)	88th–101st
John Conyers	(D-MI)	89th–
Shirley Chisholm	(D-NY)	91st–97th
William L. Clay	(D-MO)	91st–
George W. Collins	(D-IL)	91st–92nd
Louis Stokes	(D-OH)	91st–
Ronald V. Dellums	(D-CA)	92nd–
Ralph H. Metcalfe	(D-IL)	92nd–95th
Parren H. Mitchell	(D-MD)	92nd–99th
Charles B. Rangel	(D-NY)	92nd–
Yvonne B. Burke	(D-CA)	93rd–95th
Cardiss Collins	(D-IL)	92nd–
Barbara Jordan	(D-TX)	93rd–95th
Andrew Young	(D-GA)	93rd–95th
Harold E. Ford	(D-TN)	94th–
Julian C. Dixon	(D-CA)	96th–
William H. Gray III	(D-PA)	96th–102nd
Mickey Leland	(D-TX)	96th–101st
Bennett M. Stewart	(D-IL)	96th
George W. Crockett	(D-MI)	96th–101st
Mervyn Dymally	(D-CA)	97th–102nd
Gus Savage	(D-IL)	97th–102nd
Harold Washington	(D-IL)	97th–98th
Katie Hall	(D-IN)	97th–98th
Alan Wheat	(D-MO)	98th–
Major Owens	(D-NY)	98th–
Edolphus Towns	(D-NY)	98th–
Charles Hayes	(D-IL)	98th–102nd
Alton R. Waldon	(D-NY)	99th
Mike Espy	(D-MS)	100th–
Floyd Flake	(D-NY)	100th–
Kweisi Mfume	(D-MD)	100th–
John Lewis	(D-GA)	100th–
Donald Payne	(D-NJ)	101st–

Table 2.5 (continued).

Member of Congress	Party and state	Congress
Craig Washington	(D-TX)	101st–
Maxine Waters	(D-CA)	102nd–
Gary Franks	(R-CT)	102nd–
William Jefferson	(D-LA)	102nd–
Barbara Rose Collins	(D-MI)	102nd–
Lucian Blackwell	(D-PA)	102nd–

Sources: Bruce A. Ragsdale and Joel D. Treese, *Black Americans in Congress, 1870–1989* (Washington, D.C.: U.S. Government Printing Office, 1990); Congressional Black Caucus Office, Washington, D.C.

a. The 90th Congress refused to seat Powell.

(1986), and more recently Gus Savage (1992) and Charles Hayes (1992). Edward Brooke was defeated in a general election after serving in the Senate for twelve years.

Regardless of their race, members of Congress are better educated, and often come from higher-status jobs and backgrounds, than most of their constituents.[47] During the 101st Congress (1989–1991), for example, only two of the twenty-four black members did not have college degrees. Five held law degrees and listed "attorney" as their previous occupation; another five held master's degrees; one had a Ph.D., and another was in a Ph.D. program. This educational level contrasts strikingly with that of the black population in general: in 1980, only about 8 percent had attended college.[48] Twentieth-century blacks in Congress are thus similar in one respect to black representatives of the Reconstruction era—they are not very typical of the African-American population. As in the Reconstruction era, many of the twentieth-century congressional blacks have already held political office—most often in state legislatures and city councils. Others have served as clergy, teachers, professors, or have been business executives.[49] Such a disparity is not a major problem for black representation; few people would argue that politicians should somehow personify an "average" member of the population they represent.

In all other respects there is a sharp contrast between the two eras of black representation. At the end of the nineteenth century—that is, after 1877—black representation decreased; throughout the twentieth century, it has increased. In the nineteenth century, blacks served short terms; in the twentieth century, they have had continuous service and have risen in seniority. In the nineteenth century, all black representatives were

Republican; in the twentieth century, almost all have been Democrats. In the Reconstruction era, 92 percent of the blacks came from congressional districts with black majorities;[50] in the twentieth century, black candidates have no longer been dependent on black majorities as their only means to reach Congress.

Different Ways of Representing Blacks: The Examples of Powell and Dawson

Substantive representation for African Americans had an unpromising start under Oscar DePriest, but it gained vigor with the passage of time. Arthur Mitchell, William Dawson, and Adam Clayton Powell, Jr., were pioneers in attempting to bring a more substantive form of representation to blacks. DePriest, Mitchell, and Dawson worked within the system to accomplish their goals through coalition building. Powell, however, made himself an outsider with his confrontational style, and he irritated his colleagues.[51]

Largely because of his style, Powell was considered too militant by many whites; in contrast, some blacks found Dawson too conciliatory.[52] Both won recognition, but for very different accomplishments: Dawson for gaining power in the House and winning the respect of his white colleagues, Powell as a source of pride for African Americans, who enjoyed the spectacle of a fearless black man ready to stand up to whites. He fought vigorously for the integration of the U.S. military, and thousands of black and sometimes white servicemen sought his assistance.[53]

It has been said that politicians are strategic calculators of advantage.[54] Dawson and Powell were influenced by the nature of their respective political organizations and resources.[55] Dawson, using the traditional patronage of the Chicago machine and serving the black community within the confines of the Democratic party, was a master politician. He once admonished his black constituents: "We must play the game according to the rules. I always play that way and I play with my team. If you are on a baseball team you stick with your team or you might not be able to play much longer."[56]

Powell, in contrast, relied on his personal charisma and on his constituents' admiration for him. "I've always got my mouth open, sometimes my foot is in it, but it is always open," he once declared. "It serves a purpose; it digs at the white man's conscience."[57] Powell had a devoted following. He saw himself as a representative of the masses with a mandate to fight racism throughout the nation. His strength in his district allowed him to be militant, but his confrontational style eventually led to a multitude of troubles. He was sued by one of his constituents for slander. At one point he was expelled from Congress on charges that he "padded" his payroll. When the Supreme Court ruled that Congress had used illegal procedures to oust him, he was reseated but stripped of his seniority. Finally, he was defeated in 1970 by Charles Rangel, who was still in Congress in 1992.

Powell was the first black representative to understand and use the procedural rules of Congress to acquire power far beyond his individual vote. Under pressure from the NACCP, which had adopted at its 1949 convention a policy of opposition to any federal support for racially segregated facilities, Powell in 1950 offered the first of a series of amendments aimed at ending segregation. The first Powell Amendment stipulated that federal funds should be distributed without discrimination on account of race or color, but because compliance was totally compatible with continued segregation, the NAACP was not happy with that amendment. Thereafter Powell moved to a more stringent requirement.[58] In 1956, when Democratic party leaders sponsored a bill to get federal funds for the construction of new schools, Powell used the occasion to strike a blow at segregation. He proposed an amendment that funds could go only to schools that desegregated in compliance with the Supreme Court decision in *Brown v. Board of Education*.[59]

The Powell Amendment in effect put civil rights ahead of education. At first conservative Republicans who opposed federal aid to education strategically joined forces with liberal Democrats and voted in favor of the changed bill. In the end, however, the amended bill was defeated when the conservative Republicans, this time aligned with southerners opposed to integration, voted against its final passage. The Powell Amendment became known as a "killer amendment," because it killed the educational assistance bill.

The amendment posed a serious problem for white representatives of northern urban districts who, in principle, favored school aid and who also represented large numbers of black constituents. According to Arthur Denzau, William Riker, and Kenneth Shepsle, these members of the House were placed in an n-person game of prisoner's dilemma.[60] If they voted against the amended bill, it might look to their constituents as if they favored segregation, and this would give any potential challenger in the next election an issue to place before black voters. If they voted in favor of the amended bill, they might be killing school aid altogether, because the amendment made the bill less attractive to southern Democrats. The southern representatives went so far as to defy their party's leadership. The Democratic leadership could have issued sanctions, but only if defections were expected to be low. Members who defied the leadership were safe, therefore, only if a large number of Democrats voted in the same way. Dawson voted with the Democratic leadership and against the Powell Amendment despite his black-majority district. Most white northern representatives with black constituents supported the Powell Amendment, however, knowing full well that it would kill the school aid bill by making it less attractive to the southerners. In this instance Dawson was trying to advance the interests of the nation, because passage of the unamended legislation would have resulted in new schools for blacks as well as for whites. Powell's actions, though putting pressure on whites and drawing attention to school segregation, had the short-term effect of denying better schools to both races.

As chairman of the Education and Labor Committee, Powell was capable of acting within the congressional system, and he presided over much of the legislation that emerged from that committee. According to Richard Fenno, Jr.: "Powell's contribution to decision making consisted mainly in moving subcommittee recommendations through the committee's Democratic caucus and/or the full committee to the House floor as quickly as the ratio of policy partisanship to policy individualism would allow. He wanted his chairmanship to be judged by the large number of bills passed."[61] When it suited his purposes, Powell used his prerogatives as chairman to delay the forwarding of liberal legislation to the Rules Committee if he thought that it did not contain enough concessions for blacks. Until this time, black members had not used the institutional rules to bargain effectively with the white-dominated leadership structure.

A number of events have brought about gradual but significant increases in the number of blacks in Congress. These include urban migration, which made possible the concentration of large numbers of blacks in congressional districts in cities such as Chicago, Philadelphia, Detroit, and New York; court decisions affecting reapportionment and redistricting; and the passage and implementation of the Voting Rights Act of 1965. Safe electoral seats—that is, seats in districts with black majorities—have made it possible for African-American representatives to gain the seniority necessary to rise in power in a way that was not possible during the Reconstruction era. Increasingly, congressional blacks have come to be as favorably situated in the opportunity structure as whites.

The Institutional Aspects of Black Representation

Dawson and Powell operated without the formal organization that African-American representatives were to establish in later years, the Congressional Black Caucus (CBC). The caucus was formed in 1971, when the nine black members of the House got together to coordinate their individual efforts to represent African Americans. According to Marguerite Barnett, "the CBC saw itself as Congressmen at large for 20 million black people." Its creation was in part a response to renewed interest among blacks in electoral politics and in part a response to the Nixon Administration's unofficial policy of "benign neglect" of African-American policy preferences.[62] The organization gathered and disseminated information about black policy preferences, and it helped coordinate activities such as casework for constituents.

The caucus was initially chaired by Charles Diggs (D-MI), but members switched the chairmanship to Louis Stokes (D-OH) when it became clear that Diggs was not sufficiently aggressive. It took until 1990, however, for Ron Dellums to become chairman, although he was very senior, because caucus members had considered him too assertive for the job.[63]

How effective has the Black Caucus been? Some studies imply that the caucus has not been a dominant voting cue for its members and has served more as a social organization than as an effective political institution.[64] Bruce Robeck has concluded that the caucus and the blacks on the Hill have made little difference on policy outcomes. He claims that it would not matter much in legislative outcomes if all black representatives were replaced by white northern Democrats.[65] Charles Jones and Augustus Adair present a much more favorable assessment of the caucus's legislative achievements; but many of the issues they use to evaluate the caucus's effectiveness are, in any case, traditional Democratic initiatives.[66]

Marguerite Barnett's indictment is most severe.[67] She charges that the caucus is failing in its mission to deliver the types of legislation most needed by blacks in America. Barnett characterizes the organization as transforming itself through a series of stages that involved different views of representation. In stage one, caucus members emphasized collective action to advance the interests of a national black constituency. In stage two, caucus members attempted to become "just legislators." According to Congressman Louis Stokes: "Our conclusion was this: if we were to be effective, if we were to make a meaningful contribution to minority citizens in this country, then it must be as legislators. This is the area in which we possess expertise—and it is within the halls of Congress that we must make this expertise felt."[68]

The caucus's third stage blends the strategies of the first and second stages. Barnett argues that the caucus both mobilizes behind legislation and seeks to serve as a national forum. In the early 1990s, the organization appears to be firmly entrenched in the third stage.

In spite of early legislative failures, the Black Caucus has often received national attention, as when, for example, it boycotted Nixon's State of the Union address in 1971 and issued its own message to the nation after Nixon refused to meet with the caucus. In 1972 the caucus sponsored a series of hearings on racism in the media and began a concerted effort to identify and respond to the needs of a "national black constituency." In 1974 it made a major advance by wresting an agreement from the House leadership to place at least one black member on each of the major committees, and by 1990 this had been achieved.

In 1975 the caucus established the Action-Alert Network, aimed at targeting white representatives in districts with populations that are more than 15 percent black. The CBC threatened to mobilize the representatives' black constituency if they voted against legislation favored by the caucus. This "stick" approach was especially controversial given congressional norms of collegiality, and from the start some African-American representatives disagreed with the tactic.[69] Yet to the extent that David Mayhew is correct in describing congressmen as "single-minded seekers of reelection,"[70] the activities of the caucus members in the Action-Alert Network were bound to be threatening to the white representatives they targeted.

In 1988 the Black Caucus supplied the controversial Action-Alert Network with a "carrot." At the urging of Alan Wheat (D-MO), a black representative from a district that was 80 percent white when he was elected, the caucus opened its membership to whites.[71] Forty-one white congressmen immediately joined as nonvoting associate members (they pay $1,000 per year—black members pay $4,000) but are not allowed to attend closed-door meetings. White membership in the caucus makes the organization seem more mainstream and gives the white representatives an easily accessible public forum. The inclusion of white members is a significant change: in 1975 the caucus denied membership to Pete Stark (D-CA), a white representative from a racially mixed district.

The caucus has successfully used its power to negotiate for greater black inclusion in the institutional structure. Indeed, in 1989 one-quarter of all standing committees in the House were chaired by blacks. The caucus has established its own foundation, research group, and political action committee, but there are signs that the organization may be imperiled by its own successes. The sense of relative deprivation that led to its creation is gone, and it may be difficult for individual caucus members to criticize the institutional arrangements of Congress when they themselves are so much a part of the system. Senior black members, such as Ron Dellums (D-CA) and John Conyers (D-MI)—once viewed as militants—now rarely criticize the system. As one observer put it: "There's been a recognition . . . that you can't stand outside the castle and throw rocks anymore."[72]

The behavior of African-American representatives is of course affected by the characteristics of their district.[73] Most blacks in Congress represent majority-black districts, but increasing numbers are now from racially diverse constituencies. Some even represent majority-white districts. Although Black Caucus members come together for issues such as South African sanctions, civil rights, and busing, they are not cohesive in their overall voting behavior. Like white representatives, most respond first to the electoral considerations imposed by their districts and second to their own values, but they also consider the views of the caucus.[74] If there is a conflict between the position of the Black Caucus, on the one hand, and the representative's district and personal values, on the other hand, the representative is likely to follow his own conscience.

Accordingly, in recent years members of the Black Caucus have become more diverse in the issues they have supported as well as in their voting behavior. Representative Mike Espy (D-MS), for example, supports the death penalty and belongs to the National Rifle Association (NRA); Representative Floyd Flake (D-NY) opposes abortion and supports school voucher programs. In the past, African-American representatives unanimously opposed the death penalty and restrictions on abortion, and they traditionally supported tough gun-control laws. Since the election in 1990 of a black conservative Republican, Gary Franks, the caucus now has an anti–affirmative action member among its ranks. Thus far, all black House members elected since the caucus's establishment have chosen to become members. Changes of style and ideology have occurred naturally with the election of new black representatives, because the type of behavior that was appropriate when blacks initially gained power is not necessarily consistent with the requirements of blacks in power. To the extent that Congress is an organization in which one must "go along to get along," black representatives face important trade-offs. If they want to rise in power, then they must play by the rules of the institution. Some blacks will be accommodating to the white majority; others will remain militant and angry. Given the diversity, it is not surprising that the Black Caucus has lost some of its force and impact. Since 1986 it has not been able to get unanimous support from its members for its annual alternative to the national budget. It is difficult to anticipate the future of the caucus, but as more and more African Americans climb the leadership ladder, it seems likely that it will cease being an organization geared primarily toward advancing a black-focused agenda.

Important changes have occurred for blacks with regard to the committee structure. During the 1970s, black representatives joined with other Democrats to pass a series of rule changes permanently altering the relationships between committee chairs and subcommittees. In addition, some northern Democrats have gained the seniority to challenge aging southern Democrats,[75] and blacks especially have benefited from these changes. Moreover, the caucus arrangement whereby blacks are assigned highly prized positions on the exclusive committees represents an important institutional change.[76] Prior to 1974, black representatives sat mostly on nonexclusive and minor constituency committees, such as Public Works. By 1992, however, blacks were well represented in all committees, and high seniority had led to five chairmanships (see Table 2.6).

In 1988 Walter Fauntroy, a black delegate representing the District of Columbia, commented that in the early 1970s, black representatives had complained about the seniority system, but "the longer we stay, the more we like it."[77] Representative Dellums (D-CA) explained one of the reasons, noting that the chairmanship gave him "the opportunity to set the agenda, explore issues, bring in witnesses that have never been presented."[78]

The first real effort by blacks to rise to leadership positions came in 1971, when John Conyers challenged Carl Albert (D-OK) for the post of Speaker of the House. He was dismissed by his colleagues as a prankster and defeated by a vote of 220 to 20.[79] Representative Shirley Chisholm (D-NY) tried to advance in the hierarchy, but the real penetration of African Americans into the power structure of the House of Representatives did not begin until after the election of Pennsylvania's William Gray III in 1978. Gray quickly moved from being co-chairman of the Democratic Leadership Council to Budget Committee chairman, and then to the position of Democratic Caucus chairman, eventually becoming majority whip (see Chapter 3). He resigned his seat in Congress in 1991, but he left behind other African Americans in crucial positions.

During the 101st Congress, Charles Rangel was a deputy whip, while Mike Espy (D-MS), John Lewis (D-GA), and Kweisi Mfume (D-MD), all elected in 1986, were at-large whips. In addition, Harold Ford (D-TN) was a member of the Democratic Steering and Policy Committees, while William Clay (D-MO), Mervyn Dymally (D-CA), and Mike Espy sat on the Democratic Congressional Campaign Committee. Never before had so many African Americans been so close to the core of power.

With insider positions comes a special conflict between individual and collective goals. African-American representatives' quest for reelection and advancement may not always coincide with caucus goals. On the Black Caucus's alternative to the national budget, for example, Representatives Gray and Espy have in recent years voted "present," indicating that although they were there for the roll call, they neither supported nor opposed the proposal. Richard Cohen comments: "This new breed of black legislators bears striking similarities to the relatively independent lawmakers in both parties who have been elected to the House during the last decade. First, they worked painstakingly to build their own organizations to win elections. Once in the House they have become issue activists and coalition builders eager for influence, not necessarily inclined to await the delayed rewards of the seniority system."[80] Gray explained his position by stating: "It's not an issue of [being] black. The issue is: I'm chairman of the Budget Committee, a Democrat. I build a consensus. I walk out with a budget. Now do I vote against my own budget? . . . that doesn't make a lot of sense."[81] His position evoked criticism from other members of the Black Caucus. According to Conyers, members took exception to Gray's refusal to show solidarity, especially when he actively campaigned against caucus initiatives.[82]

It is no less accurate for having been said so often that Congress is a club, where certain norms must be observed for members to advance in rank. Writing before the reforms of the 1970s, Herbert Asher summarized congressional norms as: (1) maintaining friendly relationships; (2) realizing the importance of committee work; (3) knowing procedural rules; (4) avoiding personal attacks during floor debates; (5) being willing to specialize; (6) being willing to trade votes; and (7) being willing

Table 2.6. Black Democratic members of the House: Committee assignments and rankings, 102nd Congress

Committee	Democratic members	Black members	Rank
Exclusive committees			
Appropriations	37	Stokes	7
		Dixon	18
		Gray	22
Rules	9	Wheat	7
Ways and Means	23	Rangel	4
		Ford	7
Semi-exclusive committees			
Agriculture	27	Espy	21
Armed Services	33	Dellums	4
Banking, Finance and Urban Affairs	31	Flake	18
		Mfume	19
		Waters	23
Budget	23	Espy	6
Education and Labor	25	Clay	3
		Owens	9
		Hayes	10
		Payne	13
		Washington	16
Energy and Commerce	27	Collins, C.	7
		Towns	22
Foreign Affairs	28	Dymally	7
		Payne	26
Judiciary	21	Conyers	3
		Washington	18
Public Works and Transportation	36	Savage	9
		Lewis	16
		Collins, B.	34
Science, Space and Technology	32	Collins, B.	32
Nonexclusive committees			
District of Columbia	8	Dellums	1*
		Gray	3
		Dymally	4
		Wheat	5
Government Operations	25	Conyers	1*
		Collins, C.	2

Table 2.6 (continued).

Committee	Democratic members	Black members	Rank
Govt. Operations (cont.)		Owens	12
		Towns	13
		Payne	18
House Administration	15	Clay	7
		Gray	13
Interior and Insular Affairs	29	Lewis	19
Merchant Marine and Fisheries	26	—	—
Post Office and Civil Service	15	Clay	1*
		Dymally	8
		Hayes	11
Small Business	27	Savage	9
		Conyers	14
		Mfume	16
		Flake	17
Standards of Official Conduct	7	Stokes	1*
Veterans' Affairs	21	Waters	17
Select committees			
Aging	42	Ford	3
		Lewis	34
Children, Youth and Families	22	Wheat	11
		Collins, B.	18
Hunger	22	Espy	9
		Flake	10
		Wheat	18
Intelligence	12	Dellums	9
Narcotics Abuse and Control	21	Rangel	1*
		Collins, C.	5
		Towns	12
		Mfume	14
		Payne	16
		Washington	20
Joint committees			
Economic	5	Mfume	5

Source: Phil Duncan, ed., *Politics in America, 1992: The 102nd Congress* (Washington, D.C.: Congressional Quarterly, 1991).
*A seniority ranking of 1 indicates chairmanship of the committee.

to serve apprenticeships.[83] Black representatives of the past have not always observed these norms, but more recently they appear to have had no difficulty adhering to them.

African-American representatives are assimilating, just as other ethnic representatives have. One does not have to be a prophet to see the direction of the changes that are happening. Black representatives are increasingly becoming more like white liberal Democrats. They no longer automatically seek the traditional constituency committees, such as Education and Labor, Public Works, and Post Office. They have taken part in a range of committees, including Rules, Ways and Means, and Appropriations. In these new positions, most seek to advance the legislative agenda advocated by black groups such as the NAACP and the National Urban League. Depending on their constituencies, however, they may depart from the positions taken by such groups. Mike Espy, for example, maintains that his support for the death penalty and opposition to tough gun control is consistent with the preferences of his conservative, rural Mississippi constituency (see Chapter 4). This suggests that in order to understand fully the different forms of black representation, we also need to study it at the district level.

As blacks have become more experienced in Congress, they have become more effective. Their ability to provide substantive representation for their constituents has increased with their understanding of the procedural rules of Congress: the amendment process, bill drafting, timing, and logrolling. Representatives who know the institutional rules of Congress have power far beyond their individual vote. Representative Parren Mitchell (D-MD), for example, was able to use the amendment process to obtain passage of several programs requiring special set-asides for members of minority groups. Similarly, both John Lewis and Mike Espy got legislation passed during their first term in Congress. Black representatives no longer simply drop their bills into the hopper (the collection box for new bills) and pray for action. Rather, they are using specific strategies—such as persuasion, procedural modification, and coalition building[84]—to their advantage. With a combination of strategies, black representatives are achieving many of their individual and collective goals.

II · BLACK
REPRESENTATIVES

3 · Black Representatives of Historically Black Districts

We're not legislators, we're not politicians. Every time we vote on a bill, I sign it if it will help the poor, the elderly, the disadvantaged. I'm about housing legislation, putting people in decent housing. . . . We have a ministry to carry out in Washington—to do what is right.

—REPRESENTATIVE PARREN MITCHELL (D-MD), *quoted in the* Philadelphia Tribune, *November 8, 1983*

"Historically black districts," as here defined, are congressional districts with black voting-age populations of over 50 percent that have had black representation in Congress for ten years or more. During the 1980s, eleven congressional districts qualified as historically black (see Table 3.1). Regardless of where they are located, historically black districts are united by a common set of problems. Each of these districts includes within its boundaries blighted inner-city areas that are racked by poverty, high unemployment, homelessness, crime, and other indicators of social and economic dislocation. Despite this common set of problems, however, the political leadership of historically black districts varies enormously in the way the representatives approach their roles. Historically black districts have produced both docile and militant black representatives, and they have also rejected representatives of both types. Of the four kinds of black-represented districts defined in this book, historically black districts seem to be the least constraining for black representatives. In most of these districts, large black populations mean that white voters are essentially irrelevant to the election process. The representative alone decides whether or not he or she will represent the district's white minority.

Among the congressional districts that have had black representation

Table 3.1. Black representatives of historically black districts

District	Principal city	Representative	Years served	BVAP 1980s	HVAP 1980s
CA-29	Los Angeles	Augustus Hawkins	1963–1990	51%	32%
		Maxine Waters	1991–		
TN-9	Memphis	Harold Ford	1975–	51	1
OH-21	Cleveland	Louis Stokes	1969–	58	1
IL-7	Chicago	George Collins	1969–1971		
		Cardiss Collins	1971–	60	4
IL-2	Chicago	Gus Savage	1981–1992	66	7
MI-1	Detroit	John Conyers	1965–	66	2
MI-13	Detroit	Charles Diggs	1955–1980	67	3
		George Crockett	1981–1990	67	3
		Barbara Collins	1991–		
MD-7	Baltimore	Parren Mitchell	1971–1986	70	1
		Kweisi Mfume	1987–	70	1
NY-12	Brooklyn	Shirley Chisholm	1969–1982	78	9
		Major Owens	1983–	78	9
PA-2	Philadelphia	Robert Nix, Sr.	1958–1978		
		William Gray III	1979–1991	76	1
		Lucian Blackwell	1991–		
IL-1	Chicago	Oscar DePriest	1929–1934		
		Arthur Mitchell	1935–1942		
		William Dawson	1943–1970		
		Ralph Metcalfe	1971–1978		
		Bennett Stewart	1979–1980		
		Harold Washington	1981–1983	90	1
		Charles Hayes	1983–1992	90	1

Sources: Linda Williams, ed., The JCPS Congressional District Fact Book, 3rd ed. (Washington, D.C.: Joint Center for Political Studies, 1988); Congressional Quarterly Weekly Report, November 10, 1990, pp. 3822–3823; "The 101st Congress, 1989–1990," Congressional Black Caucus Foundation, September 1990.

Note: BVAP = Black voting-age percentage of district population; HVAP = Hispanic voting-age percentage of district population.

for not just one but more than two decades are Michigan's thirteenth district, located in Detroit, and Pennsylvania's second district, located in Philadelphia. Both districts have overall black populations of 70 percent or greater. Each has had black elected officials at different levels of government for many decades. Their most recent long-term black representatives are George Crockett (D-MI, 1981–1991) and William Gray III (D-PA, 1979–1991).

The Thirteenth District of Michigan: George Crockett

Recent History

The thirteenth district of Michigan is an inner-city congressional district located in central Detroit. Of Michigan's eighteen congressional districts, it has the smallest number of college-educated constituents and owner-occupied homes.[1] The district's problems are intertwined with those of the city. Until other cities surpassed it in the late 1980s, Detroit had the highest murder rate in the country, and in 1991 it was second (behind Washington, D.C.) in infant mortality.[2] In 1954 the district elected its first black member of Congress when Charles Diggs, Jr., defeated a white incumbent in what was then listed as a district with a white majority. He proudly told his black supporters: "Joyous as the occasion is and important as it is to our race, we must . . . [not] forget for one moment that I am here to represent all of the people of my district."[3] Diggs's election increased the number of blacks in Congress from two to three. Diggs left Congress in 1980 because of a scandal that resulted in a House censure and eventually in a conviction for fraud for taking $66,000 in payoffs from his congressional staff; he was sentenced to three years in federal prison. Before his election to Congress, Diggs had served in the state senate seat that his father had vacated upon a conviction and imprisonment for bribery.[4] Corruption has long been and continues to be a problem for the district and the city. In 1991 William Hart, the city's first black police chief, was indicted along with a white accomplice for embezzling $1.3 million from the city.[5]

In 1964 Michigan became the first state, and Detroit the first city, to have two black members of Congress: John Conyers (D-MI) was elected as its second black representative. At a time when cries for black power reverberated among blacks from around the country, however, the presence of the two black representatives did not prevent the city from having one of the worst race riots of 1967. When the representatives tried to quell the violence personally, they were booed by the crowd. The riot straddled the first and thirteenth districts, lasted four days, resulted in forty-three deaths and thousands of dollars worth of property damage, and did not end until President Johnson dispatched 4,700 troops to the city.[6] White flight characterized the decade following the devastating riots, making Detroit the second large U.S. city to go from majority white to majority black (Washington, D.C., was the first). The thirteenth district lost about 40 percent of its population after the riot, dropping from 800,000 in 1960 to 444,000 in 1986. Its population is still dropping in the 1990s. From 1980 to 1990, the thirteenth district lost over 185,000 people—more than any other congressional district in the nation. Many of the city's white residents have fled to form some of the most racially segregated suburbs in America.[7] Over the years, the white residents have been replaced by Arab Americans: by 1991 Detroit had the nation's largest concentration of Syrians, Palestinians, and Chaldeans.

The Expansionist Stage: George Crockett's Electoral Strategy

Richard Fenno, Jr., has introduced the concept of a constituency career, with identifiable "expansionist" and "protectionist" stages, for members of Congress. The expansionist stage occurs early in a politician's career, when he or she is attempting to build a base and solidify support in the district. After serving in Congress for a certain period of time, a representative enters a protectionist stage, in which the goal is to protect the existing political base.[8] The expansionist stage of George Crockett's career started long before he was elected to Congress. A long-time friend of Charles Diggs, Jr., Crockett entered the Democratic primary in 1980. He was already seventy years old, older by far than most first-time congressional candidates. His campaign style was influenced by his long record of service to the black community and the prominence he had earned himself by his radicalism. A 1934 graduate of the University of Michigan Law School, Crockett arrived in Detroit in 1943 to open a fair employment practices office for the United Automobile Workers (UAW). He was one of the left-wing officials whom Walter Reuther eliminated from the UAW when he took control during the 1940s. In 1949 Crockett achieved national prominence by serving as a defense attorney for eleven members of the American Communist Party in the Foley-Square case. Because of the harshness of his criticisms of the judge in the case, he received a four-month jail sentence for contempt of court and a recommendation for disbarment. Continuing his left-wing path into the McCarthy era, he defended Coleman Young, the future mayor of Detroit, before the House Committee on Un-American Activities. Throughout his career, Crockett publicly expressed socialist convictions that led some to label him a communist or a radical.

In announcing his congressional bid, Crockett told his supporters: "I take second to no one as far as my loyalty to our present congressman. . . . But I think we have to be realistic and realism dictates that we have lost effective representation in Washington."[9] He quickly garnered the support of the United Automobile Workers, Mayor Coleman Young, the *Free Press,* and the *Chronicle.* The local Democratic party's endorsement, however, went to David Holmes, Jr., a state senator, and Crockett did not get the endorsement of the district's major newspaper. An editorial in the *Detroit News* argued that the district needed a representative "less cumbersome and ideological" than Crockett, and criticized him for saying that the automobile industry needed to accept lower profit margins. The night before the primary Crockett received Diggs's endorsement. Crockett went on to win the Democratic nomination with 42 percent of the vote in a crowded field of twelve, and then received 92 percent of the general election vote (see Table 3.2). Compared with other representatives' campaign costs during the eighties, Crockett's campaigns have been low-budget affairs (see Appendix B).

Table 3.2. The election history of George Crockett

Year	Primary election opponents	Vote total (percentage)		General election opponents	Vote total (percentage)	
1980	Crockett	8,810	(41%)	Crockett	79,719	(92%)
	Holmes, Jr.	4,187	(20)	Hurd	6,473	(7)
	Cleveland	3,373	(16)			
	Hood III	3,364	(16)			
	eight others	1,767	(8)			
1982	Crockett	Unopposed		Crockett	108,351	(88)
				Gupta	13,732	(11)
1984	Crockett	22,923	(87)	Crockett	132,222	(87)
	Barber	3,400	(13)	Murphy	20,416	(13)
1986	Crockett	26,784	(75)	Crockett	76,435	(85)
	Bates	4,746	(13)	Griffin	12,395	(14)
	Randolph	2,079	(6)			
1988	Crockett	18,250	(51)	Crockett	99,751	(87)
	Collins	15,438	(43)	Savage II	13,196	(12)
	others	21,045	(6)			

Sources: Michael Barone, Grant Ujifusa, and Douglas Matthews, *The Almanac of American Politics* (New York: E. P. Dutton, 1978, 1980); Barone and Ujifusa, *The Almanac of American Politics* (Washington, D.C.: National Journal, 1984–1990 biennial eds.).

Crockett's relationship with the white minority in the district was shaky from the very beginning. He was accused of polarizing the city in 1969, while it was still recovering from the 1967 riot. Crockett, who was then a recorder's judge, angered whites by releasing a group of black prisoners—men, women, and children. They had been arrested in a black church after militants holding a conference in the church clashed with police, killing one white officer and wounding another. Crockett held hearings in the middle of the night and released all the prisoners except two on the grounds that they were being illegally detained. However much his actions may have antagonized white voters, Crockett understood that he did not need white support to win either the primary or the general election. Although many of his district's white voters and some of the black voters have viewed him as a communist, Crockett does not believe that he was too radical for his district's black voters: "What the white press regards as a radical, the black man regards as in his interests. To the extent that a black opponent identifies with the white press and calls another black candidate names similar to those that the white press is using, he's really driving more blacks into their camp."[10]

Crockett served in Congress for eight years, generating very little primary opposition until 1988, when Barbara Rose Collins, a city councilwoman, was able to get the endorsement of a major black political organization (Black Slate) and win 43 percent of the primary vote. Collins criticized Crockett's failure to endorse Jesse Jackson's 1988 presidential bid and his reluctance to retire. The major issue in the campaign, however, was who could best preserve the district's black majority during the next round of redistricting.[11] After Crockett announced his retirement in March 1990, Collins easily won the Democratic nomination and the seat.

Interactions with Constituents: Satisfying a Homogeneous Constituency

For ten years, Crockett shared the representation of Detroit with John Conyers and two other Democratic representatives. Crockett and Conyers had the vast majority of the city's black voters, while the neighboring two districts (the fourteenth and seventeenth) had white representatives, with black populations of 5 and 10 percent, respectively. Although Conyers's district is more middle class than Crockett's was and has fewer pressing problems, Conyers often finds himself trading constituents with the thirteenth district's representative when the district lines change after each decennial census. As it happens, the two congressional district offices are located in the downtown section of the city, where constituents can most easily reach them by public transportation. As a result, one member's constituents will often request service in the other's district. Whenever a constituent walks into either district office, the staffers quickly check street addresses before tackling the problem. Unless the constituent is a special friend of one of the representatives or has a long history with the district office, he or she is referred to the representative whose district includes the address in question.

Both of Detroit's black representatives have had staffs that were overwhelmingly black, but an occasional white face does appear. Like other black representatives from historically black districts, Crockett felt that the high rates of unemployment among blacks, the high percentage of blacks in his districts, and what he viewed as employment discrimination on the part of his white colleagues were sufficient reasons for hiring more black than white staffers. Black representatives who do otherwise are likely to be criticized by other blacks both in Congress and from their districts. Thus one disgruntled black staffer accused several black representatives of racism because white staffers held the highest-ranking office positions, which to him reflected the black representatives' "lack of faith in black expertise."

When I asked Crockett how his district had changed over the years, his voice reflected a certain sadness as he spoke of the conditions in his district and their continuing deterioration. He said: "The district has become poorer. The economic problems have become more intense. There is an even greater need for housing; the number of homeless has increased. In other words, my district reflects the common ailment of the city of Detroit. When the automobile industry began its retrenchment program and we had massive unemployment, most of the blacks who were affected lived in the thirteenth congressional district, and they have never fully recovered from that unemployment."[12] He had witnessed significant losses in his district's black population: "The more affluent blacks are moving out of the city into the suburbs. There's one community called Southfield that's just outside of Detroit, across Three Mile Road. Within the past ten years the high school in Southfield has become predominantly black. Ten years ago I doubt if you had more than one hundred black children going to Southfield High School."[13]

In addition to the movement of affluent blacks from the inner-city areas to the suburbs, Crockett noted that many blacks had left Detroit and gone back to the South. Blacks have also been affected by urban planning decisions that have displaced them. "Some fairly large areas of land were taken over in Detroit for purposes other than housing," Crockett said, "so people have had to move out and find living accommodations in other places."

Decades of population losses have forced redistricters to add white communities: "Following the 1980 election, a rather large number of whites were added to my district because they redrew the district lines to include Grosse Point Park and the city of Grosse Point, and both of those communities are overwhelmingly white. I doubt if there were more than ten black households in Grosse Point Park, and I would be surprised if there were more than five in the city of Grosse Point."[14] "Most of the newly added voters were Republicans who are the owners and leaders of Detroit area businesses," Crockett said. "Nevertheless," he added, "my district remains overwhelmingly black. It's probably 71 or 72 percent black, maybe higher. I have a substantial Hispanic population, which I would put at maybe about 3 percent, and I have a fairly large Arab population, which I would put at about 2 percent of the district. So, roughly speaking, about 10 percent of my district is white."[15]

The addition of more white voters after the 1980 census caused Crockett to express strong views about redistricting: "We should carve districts according to geographical and sociological interests. You don't go around creating a split personality. I've got the richest section of Michigan. I've got the poorest section of Michigan. I've got the major business establishment in Michigan."[16] Because he rarely heard from the mostly white community of Grosse Point, Crockett interpreted their silence as a sign of self-sufficiency. "As I tell them," he explained to me, "maybe they don't need a congressman because they are so affluent. They can go directly to the President or to a member of his Cabinet to present their problems."[17] Although he did not acknowledge this, the location of his district office might have been one reason for the lack of traffic from white constituents; many whites are afraid to venture into the downtown area.[18] The lack of requests from his white constituents did not bother him because he was consumed with the need to represent the downtrodden, and they mostly happened to be minorities, a category in which he includes the Arabs in his district as well as the blacks and the Hispanics.

Crockett was not sure that he adequately represented his district. Reflecting on his ten years in Congress, he told me: "If I had to do it all over again, I probably would try to get on one of the committees that has a greater impact on the appropriations process [rather than Foreign Affairs, Judiciary, and Aging]. That way I could do more in the way of getting projects for my district. I haven't been able to do much in that regard. What I have been able to do, I did by speaking to my friends on the relevant committees."[19] He did not, however, consider himself to have been totally unsuccessful in aiding his constituents. In particular, he believed his actions were instrumental in winning the authorization for a new veterans' hospital that would provide a limited number of new jobs for the district.

Representation through Legislation: The Outsider

Crockett's legislative style was characterized by the same bold, controversial stances that marked his early career as a lawyer and a judge. During his first term in Congress he filed a suit (along with ten co-plaintiffs) against President Reagan, Secretary of State Alexander Haig, and Defense Secretary Caspar Weinberger, demanding that they end the United States's involvement in El Salvador. Crockett later participated in another suit against Reagan that charged illegalities in the U.S. invasion of Grenada.[20] He was among the national leaders arrested in 1984 while protesting South Africa's policy of apartheid outside that country's embassy in Washington.

Crockett's vigorous representation of his Arab constituents ensured that he would not get contributions from what he called "Pro-Israeli Political Action Committees." In 1985, for example, he invited Zehdi Terzi, the Palestine Liberation Organization (PLO) observer at the United Nations, to come to Washington and brief the House Foreign Affairs Committee on the PLO's views. He was unsuccessful because Mark Silijander, another Michigan representative and a member of the committee, persuaded others to oppose the visit. Three years later, Crockett issued a statement condemning the State Department for refusing to grant Yasir Arafat, the chairman of the PLO, an entry visa.

Crockett's attitude toward U.S. foreign policy made him one of the most radical members of Congress. When the Soviet Union shot down a Korean airliner over Soviet airspace, he refused to join the 416 House members who condemned that action (he says that the plane was later found to be spying). On another occasion he refrained from protesting the shooting of a member of the U.S. armed forces by Soviet troops inside a restricted Soviet military area. "There was a hue and cry for a resolution condemning the death," he later recollected. "I said to my colleagues, 'Here again I don't think you have all the facts. What was the officer doing over there in the first place? Wouldn't our reaction be the same if we found a Soviet officer in our restricted area?'"[21]

Crockett's stances on domestic issues were no less controversial. He told his constituents that he had never supported foreign military assistance measures, because of their adverse impact on taxpayers. He voted against legislation mandating the death penalty for certain drug dealers because, in his view, the death penalty is irrevocable and judges do make mistakes. After charging that the "War on Drugs" was essentially a war on young black men, he became the first member of Congress to advocate legalization of the private possession of drugs. In an article written primarily for his constituents, Crockett explained his position:

> As I understand it, I am the first member of Congress to publicly advocate decriminalization. I hope I am not the last. . . . When I was a judge of the Recorders Court in Detroit for twelve years, I saw hundreds of men and women come before me charged with using drugs. The "drug of choice" at the time was heroin. The "criminals" were mostly poor, mostly black, and mostly shut out of the "American Dream." In most cases their privacy had been invaded by an illegal stop, search, and seizure. . . . I said then— and it is still true—that if drug use were mostly a white, middle-class problem, addicts would be in treatment centers and hospitals instead of jail.[22]

Solutions to the drug crisis and alternatives to incarceration would certainly be in the interests of African Americans, who are over-represented among those incarcerated for drug abuse.

The indexes of the Leadership Conference on Civil Rights and the Committee for Political Education, introduced in Chapter 1, allow us to see how well Crockett represents the interests of blacks on other issues. Consider the interest group and voter participation scores for black members from historically black districts as well as for white and black representatives from other kinds of districts (see Table 3.3). Crockett's voting record was similar to the records of other liberal Democrats. During the 100th Congress, COPE gave him a 97 percent rating and LCCR gave him 100 percent.

Two other indexes that help us to compare representatives' performances are those for the conservative coalition (CC) and for voting participation. The *Congressional Quarterly* uses the term "conservative coalition" to refer to a "voting alliance" of Republicans and southern Democrats against other Democrats in Congress. The more liberal the

Table 3.3. Legislative records of black representatives from historically black districts contrasted with records of representatives from other districts (100th Congress)

Representative and district	COPE rating	LCCR rating	Conservative coalition	Voting participation
Black representatives from historically black districts				
Collins (IL-7)	100	80	1.5	90
Conyers (MI-1)	100	100	4.0	86
Crockett (MI-13)	97	100	6.0	86
Ford (TN-9)	100	53	7.0	70
Gray (PA-2)	100	87	11.5	84
Hawkins (CA-29)	100	100	7.5	84
Hayes (IL-1)	100	73	2.5	92
Mfume (MD-7)	100	100	15.0	98
Owens (NY-12)	100	93	5.0	85
Savage (IL-2)	100	93	5.0	92
Stokes (OH-21)	100	100	4.5	84
Mean score	*99.7*	*89.0*	*6.3*	*86.4*
Black representatives from other types of districts				
Heterogeneous	95.3	96.5	24.8	91.0
Majority white[a]	100.0	88.8	4.5	85.5
Newly black	98.9	97.7	2.8	90.3
Mean score	*98.1*	*94.3*	*10.7*	*88.9*
White representatives by region				
Northern Democrats	92.7	90.3	25	—
Southern Democrats	80.2	72.7	61	—
Northern Republicans	37.5	43.1	56	—
Southern Republicans	14.6	13.1	82	—
Congress	—	—	—	92

Sources: Phil Duncan, ed., *Politics in America: 1990, 101st Congress* (Washington, D.C.: Congressional Quarterly Press, 1989); *Congressional Quarterly Weekly Report,* November 19, 1988, pp. 3321–3376; Leadership Conference on Civil Rights, "A Civil Rights Voting Record for the 100th Congress," January 1989.

Note: COPE = AFL-CIO Committee on Political Education (scores are not lowered by missed votes); LCCR = Leadership Conference on Civil Rights; Conservative coalition = Percentage of votes cast in support of coalition between Republicans and Southern Democrats against other Democrats; Voting participation = Percentage of roll-call votes cast.

a. Scores are below average because of an outlier (Clay, MO-1). See Table 6.1.

member of Congress, the lower the CC score. It is possible, however, to have a high CC score and still be progressive on civil rights and redistributive issues. Voting participation records reveal the percentage of roll calls for which a member was present and voting. District work, illness, and foreign travel can lower voting participation scores. During the 100th Congress, Crockett scored 6 percent with the conservative coalition and his voting participation rate was 86 percent, which is slightly lower than the congressional average of 92, but much better than the record of some other black representatives (see also Appendix C).

Crockett, however, was not among the most active members of the House. After six years in Congress, he acknowledged to an interviewer: "I haven't initiated new legislation." He explained his inactivity by saying that there were enough laws on the books already. He did co-sponsor many bills, however, and in his role as chairman of the Foreign Affairs Committee he introduced legislation calling for relief for Jamaica after it was struck by Hurricane Gilbert.[23]

In a determined effort to represent racial and political minorities, Crockett took bold stances that kept him isolated from the leadership structure. At the time that he became chairman of the Foreign Affairs subcommittee on Western Hemisphere Affairs, which has jurisdiction over legislation affecting Central America, a number of conservatives tried to stop him by portraying him as a communist, but representatives—white and black—came to his defense and spoke of his high integrity. That his supporters included Carl Parcell, a former head of a Detroit police organization who had vehemently opposed Crockett during his years as a recorder's judge, is evidence that he had gradually come to be recognized as a legitimate figure in mainstream politics.[24] In the process Crockett had been able to win over some of his former opponents.

Although Crockett believed that he could not have taken the same personal and political positions or cast the same votes if he had represented a district with a lower percentage of blacks, he may have underestimated his own tenacity. He told me: "If I had a more diverse constituency they would not agree with me, and representation would probably present a greater challenge for me to really stand and vote my convictions. I've had many of my colleagues come to me after a controversial vote and say: 'Boy, I wish I had the kind of constituency that would go along with me voting the way I'd like to vote on some of these issues.'"[25] Whatever such colleagues may have thought in private, however, few supported him in public. The support he did get usually came from liberal white Democrats and outspoken liberal black representatives such as Ron Dellums, Mervyn Dymally, and Mickey Leland.

Interestingly, many of the issues on which Crockett spoke most forcefully did not bear on black or Arab interests. Instead, they were more broadly related to his own ideological convictions, as in the case of his defense of the Soviet Union at a time when such a position was highly controversial. The success of Crockett's individualistic style is consistent with the more general proposition that representatives from historically black districts have great freedom to advance their own personal political agendas.

The Second District of Pennsylvania: William Gray III

Recent History

The second district of Pennsylvania is located in Philadelphia, along with four other congressional districts (the first, third, seventh, and thirteenth). As in other majority-black political units, poverty permeates the district, and it suffers from the population decline that affects most of the Northeast. In 1988 it ranked in the bottom 10 percent of the nation's congressional districts in terms of poverty.[26] Twenty-eight percent of its families were below the poverty line and 29 percent were headed by females. Between 1970 and 1980 the city of Philadelphia lost 13.4 percent of its population, which dropped from 1.9 million to 1.7 million. The losses were greatest in north Philadelphia where, according to the journalist Mike Mallowe, a major change has occurred: "[North Philadelphia] has become a hostile province, a savage satrapy where banks, supermarkets, chain stores, factories, offices, theaters, bakeries, physicians, deliverymen, taxis, a major league baseball team, mortgages, insurance coverage, schools, Catholic parishes, synagogues, pharmacies, thousands of people and entire city blocks have vanished."[27]

The second district has had its black population preserved, despite four decades of reapportionments (1950–1990) during which Pennsylvania lost seven congressional seats. In 1991, it continued to be the state's only district with a black majority and it had elected the state's only black representative. The district has a distinctive, old, black middle class that traces its roots back to the colonial era, when its growth was nurtured by William Penn, a Quaker, who never allowed slavery to flourish in his state.[28] Income and neighborhood characteristics vary widely. Part of the district contains the ruins of north Philadelphia, an area which exploded during the urban race riots of the 1960s and which for decades before that had been called "the jungle" by white Philadelphians. Another part includes the black working-class sections of west Philadelphia and the wealthy white areas toward the south side of the district. West Philadelphia received national attention in May 1985 when the city's black mayor, Wilson Goode, appeared to authorize the police bombing of a house occupied by members of a black cult who called themselves MOVE. Eleven people died and sixty homes were destroyed in the resulting fire.

The district has had a black representative in Congress since 1958, when Earl Chudoff, the white Democratic incumbent, died and was replaced by Robert Nix, Sr. This breakthrough for African Americans came about after the leaders of the local Democratic organization decided that the majority-black district should have a black representative. The party leaders bestowed the honor of completing Chudoff's unexpired term upon Nix, a ward leader, who had spent much of his life getting out his party's black vote on election days. Nix represented the district until he was defeated in 1978. He was, unfortunately, a lethargic representative, and throughout his long congressional career his poor performance invited criticism from around the country and from a string of challengers at home. He was repeatedly accused of not pushing civil rights legislation and of simply voting the way that Representative William Green, the leader of the state Democratic party, told him.[29] His voting participation scores were often dismally low, and he did not earn the respect of his colleagues. Michael Barone, Grant Ujifusa, and Douglas Matthews have described him as an inactive chairman of the subcommittee on Asian and Pacific Affairs who was allowed to rise to the chairmanship of the Post Office and Civil Service Committee because "no one wanted to challenge a black's right to be Chairman."[30] On the explosive issue of the Vietnam War, he followed the lead of President Johnson and the leaders of the Philadelphia delegation despite widespread misgivings among blacks and other groups in his district.

Nix served as a representative for twenty years despite the fact that he rarely campaigned, rarely returned to his district, and rarely participated in Black Caucus functions; his detractors dubbed him "the Phantom."[31] Attesting both to the enormous power of incumbency and to the electoral security of black representatives from historically black districts, Nix's constituents dutifully reelected him many times. The voters returned him to Congress with less and less conviction, however, until

William Gray III, one of Nix's former Capitol Hill interns, eventually defeated him in the 1978 Democratic primary. Nix had shown himself vulnerable long before: in 1972, he won reelection with only 47 percent of the Democratic primary votes in a crowded field of four. In 1974, he faced another strong challenge and won renomination with 56 percent of the vote (his opponent got 39 percent). In 1976, his opponent was Gray, and Nix defeated him by the razor-thin margin of 48 to 47 percent, which encouraged Gray's successful second bid.

The Expansionist Stage: William Gray's Electoral Strategy

When William Gray III, a Baptist minister without any prior political experience, challenged Nix in 1976 and came within 339 votes of defeating him, he described himself to reporters as a "political upstart," who would soon defeat "the Phantom."[32] Nix did not take Gray's challenges lightly, as his decision to campaign actively in 1976 shows. In the past he had relied on the party's ward leaders to ensure his reelection. But Nix knew that a small number of the district's voters would decide the outcome of the Democratic primary, and he was aware that this time his opponent was the minister of a church with 3,000 members where his father and grandfather had once served as ministers. Responding appropriately to the magnitude of the threat, Nix mounted an active person-to-person campaign, used endorsements from then Speaker of the House Carl Albert, and aired a series of radio commercials. It was said that in these commercials many of his constituents heard his voice for the first time. Mustering all the resources of his incumbency, he just managed to get reelected.

By the time of the 1978 Democratic primary, however, Gray had picked up the backing of more ward leaders, ministers, and labor unions, and he had endorsements from Coretta Scott King, Martin Luther King, Sr., and Mayor Richard Hatcher of Gary, Indiana. Gray also benefited from a political action committee (PAC) formed shortly after his loss in 1976. Named "The 339 Club" to symbolize the closeness of the 1976 race, each member contributed $339 to start a war chest for the 1978 primary.[33] Nix, however, had endorsements from Sam Evans, the leader of a major black organization in the city, the black columnist Chuck Stone, Muhammad Ali, and others.[34] Nix's supporters also included Frank Rizzo, who was perhaps more of a liability than an asset. As Philadelphia's mayor, Rizzo, who was white, was especially controversial among blacks because of his emphasis on law and order, which extended to a notorious episode in which he ordered that a group of black radical activists be publicly strip-searched.[35] In response to Nix's advertisements emphasizing his seniority and his chairmanship of the Post Office and Civil Service Committee, Gray urged voters to make a retrospective evaluation, telling them to "walk around your neighborhood and find out what seniority has done for you."[36] Gray easily won the Democratic primary and then defeated Roland Atkins, his Republican opponent, in the general election (see Table 3.4).

In 1980, Gray had only token opposition in the Democratic primary and no Republican challenger for the general election. In the 1982 general election, however, a black state representative named Milton Street ran against him. Two years before challenging Gray, Street had

Table 3.4. The election history of William Gray III

Year	Primary election opponents	Vote total (percentage)		General election opponents	Vote total (percentage)	
1976	Gray	27,261	(47%)			
	Nix, Sr. (incumbent)	27,700	(48)			
1978	Gray	36,506	(58)	Gray	132,594	(82%)
	Nix, Sr. (incumbent)	24,855	(40)	Atkins	25,785	(16)
	one other	1,482	(2)			
1980	Gray	Unopposed		Gray	127,106	(96)
				two others	5,865	(4)
1982	Gray	50,428	(88)	Gray	120,744	(76)
	Britt	6,964	(12)	Street	35,205	(22)
1984	Gray	65,754	(84)	Gray	200,484	(91)
	Bowen	12,112	(16)	Sharper	18,244	(8)
1986	Gray	75,829	(97)	Gray	128,399	(98)
	Henderson	2,455	(3)	one other	2,620	(2)
1988	Gray	Unopposed		Gray	184,322	(94)
				Harsh	12,365	(6)
1990	Gray	Unopposed		Gray	94,584	(92)
				Bakove	8,118	(8)

Sources: Michael Barone, Grant Ujifusa, and Douglas Matthews, The Almanac of American Politics (New York: E. P. Dutton, 1978, 1980); Barone and Ujifusa, The Almanac of American Politics (Washington, D.C.: National Journal, 1984–1990 biennial eds.).

switched his party affiliation from Democrat to Republican, seeking to give the Republican party control of the state's senate in exchange for their removing from the district the majority-white precincts that supported Gray. But when Street's efforts to remove the white precincts failed and he could not find anyone else willing to run against Gray, Street mounted his own bid, ran as an Independent (because he had missed the Republican party's filing date) and received 22 percent of the vote.[37]

Street's decision to challenge Gray was fueled by divisions in the black community over Gray's style of representation and his close connections with white constituents and wealthy business leaders. (Several local polls showed that the district's white minority was more enthusiastic about Gray than were the district's black voters.)[38] Bitter name-calling erupted during that campaign. Street said of Bill Gray: "The man is known as an Uncle Tom and a house nigger in my community. He is controlled by white people, by the big corporations downtown. . . . He has clergyman's syndrome. [He says] I am the anointed! What I say goes! Do not question me! I am the interpreter! . . . He uses political power to destroy people."[39] Gray responded in kind by saying: "Milton Street is driven by an insatiable lust for power. . . . He will do whatever is expedient for him, whatever is going to aggrandize him. That is his political philosophy. His role in the Republican Party is to be the divisive force that keeps the black community in Philadelphia from coming together."[40] It became public during the course of that heated primary that a prominent black business leader was claiming to have been offered $15,000 by Gray's administrative assistant to switch his support from another candidate (presumably Street) to Gray.[41] Street was soundly defeated, but he and his family continued to be an important force in Philadelphia politics, and they were still antagonistic toward Gray when he resigned from Congress in 1991.

Prior to Street's unsuccessful bid, Chuck Stone, a prominent black journalist, contemplated running against Gray. Stone declined to run, however, after a poll conducted by the Republican city committee showed him losing almost all the white vote and splitting the black vote evenly with Gray.[42] Several years previously, Stone had endorsed Gray for the general election, stating: "If ever a candidate has shown the promise of excellence and dedication, this man does."[43] By 1981, however, his opinion had changed so much that in July he published a derisive newspaper editorial entitled "Ma, He's Pickin' on Me," in which he ran a picture of Gray alongside the black actor Steppin Fetchit and repeated Street's charges against Gray. Stone went on to maintain that "few black elected officials in Philadelphia have done more to spark bitter disunity in the black community than Bill Gray." Gray has responded to such charges with exasperation: "I'm tired of people talking about black unity," he says. "Show me white unity. . . . Don't ask the black community to do what you don't ask the white community."[44]

Between 1982 and 1990, Gray did not have any strong challengers. He was reelected by wide margins, and he was unopposed in the 1990 general election. Seventy-six percent of the voting-age population in his district was black. Comfortable with that proportion, Gray did not show any inclination to support either a reduction or an increase in his district's black population. He stayed out of the 1990 redistricting debate in Congress, except to voice his support for "safe" black districts.

Although Gray was easily reelected in 1990 and he was active in local politics, his support at home was not transferable to other candidates. When Wilson Goode prepared to step down as mayor of Philadelphia in 1991, Gray endorsed, and fervently campaigned for, the former city councilman George Burrell to succeed Goode (Goode also endorsed Burrell). Gray's support for Burrell was so pronounced that the latter became known as Gray's candidate for mayor. Burrell suffered a stunning defeat in the Democratic primary, however, winning a mere 13 percent of the vote and trailing behind Lucian Blackwell, another black councilman, who, as a rival of Gray, was the choice of the Street family and the city's black working classes.[45] In the general election, the city's heavily black population elected a white mayor, Edward Rendell. The split in the black community between middle-class and working-class elements and the disgust of some black voters with the candidates offered led to the selection of the white Democrat. Burrell's rejection by most of the electorate was widely interpreted as a repudiation of Gray. Ironically, Lucian Blackwell now serves in the congressional seat that Gray vacated in 1991.

Interactions with Constituents: Satisfying a Homogeneous Constituency

Gray's expansionist stage appears to have started long before he ran for Congress. He had been a local minister for many years before his first congressional bid. During his campaigns in 1976 and 1978, he greatly expanded his support network. He told voters that he would be an active representative, protecting their interests in Washington but also living among them. He did live for several years in the district before moving his family to the District of Columbia. Gray's move corresponded with his rise in power and signaled the beginning of the protectionist stage of his career, in which he sought to maintain his base.

Gray maintained three district offices strategically located to correspond with the diversity of his constituents. Staffed by eleven congressional aides, these offices were located in Germantown, north Philadelphia, and west Philadelphia. They provided the typical kinds of constituency service, the nature of which varied according to the location of the office. The north Philadelphia office, for example, concerned itself with helping the district's poorest citizens receive what they needed for survival, and large amounts of federal aid were brought to the area to rehabilitate the barren neighborhoods and the dilapidated schools.

While in Congress, Gray kept his ministerial position at Bright Hope Church in Philadelphia, where he preached two or three Sundays a month and from which he received free use of a house that his congregation purchased from him to facilitate his move to Washington. The free rent, the congregational purchase of the house, and the timing of his subsequent large donations of excess honoraria to the church and to a charity organization that employed his wife led to raised eyebrows in Washington and triggered an FBI investigation.[46] Gray, who viewed his work for the church and his close relationship with it as an important part of his constituency service, once said: "If preachers, lawyers, business entrepreneurs, and teachers can engage in politics, why not a Baptist minister?"[47]

During his first few years in office Gray advertised extensively about his activities. Among other things, he claimed credit for getting his district $24 million in federal funds for SEPTA's takeover of Conrail commuter lines, $8.4 million for senior citizen housing, $633,000 for professional assistance to minority businesses, $400,000 for the House of Umoja (home for boys), and funding for other projects. In addition, a press release entitled "Bill Gray's Record" began with his accomplishments within Congress and made much of the fact that as early as 1980 he was well on his way to earning a national reputation.

As is true of congressional districts around the country, voter turnout was low in Gray's district: 20 percent during the 1990 general election and 38 percent during the 1988 presidential election year. It is therefore difficult to gauge accurately the constituents' interest in and support of Gray. Almost all black members of Congress, unless they represent nonblack districts, are returned to office with high reelection margins that come from a tiny fraction of the electorate.

Gray was a widely known and controversial figure among his constituents, many of whom held strong opinions about him. A young social worker said: "Being from North Philly, just seeing [Gray] progress is a positive statement in itself." Another man observed that "[Gray is] effective, he seems to get what he wants from the white man. What he wants, not what we want. I'm not criticizing him. I'm saying he's smart. He's an opportunist, but I would vote for him again." One of Gray's district office managers commented that "[Gray's] gonna be our first black president." Still another observer said: "Gray is not militant enough for me. He doesn't let those rednecks in Congress know he's representing us."[48]

Some constituents charged that Gray was not accessible to them, which is very different from accusing him of not bringing home the bacon.[49] One elderly black lady told an interviewer, "Don't blame us for not voting. We're sick and tired of these no account leaders. That Mayor Green, all he does is grin, and nobody can find Mr. Gray [a reference to Gray's frequent foreign trips]."[50] Gray was also criticized for sending six different letters recommending six different individuals for the same important city job, and for supporting white candidates over black.[51]

Apparently, Gray was not militant enough for some of his constituents. Often his signals were ambiguous. In March 1990 he, with Representative Charles Rangel (D-NY), traveled to Chicago to campaign for Representative Gus Savage, who was facing a tough primary challenge from a former Rhodes Scholar named Mel Reynolds. Gray's and Rangel's presence at the rally was surprising, because Savage's career was seeped in controversy.[52] Savage was always challenged in his Democratic primaries, but was reelected—until 1992, when Reynolds challenged him successfully—despite low voter attendance rates, charges of sexual harassment, numerous anti-Semitic comments, close association with the Nation of Islam leader Louis Farrakhan, and his attendance at the 1988 Democratic Convention with Steve Cokely, a black activist who advanced the theory that some Jewish doctors deliberately infected black infants with the virus that causes AIDS. During the rally, Savage made anti-Semitic comments. The resulting public furor, largely from outside of Gray's congressional district, caused first Rangel and then, several days later, Gray to denounce Savage's language as "unacceptable, divisive, and bigoted."[53] Although both representatives claimed ignorance of Savage's intentions, his past performances might have led them to anticipate the outcome. Gray may have viewed the rally as an opportunity to improve his image among more militant black leaders; however, the unexpected press coverage spoiled what might have been a low-key visit before a mostly black audience.[54]

Gray may have been placed at a disadvantage because he was not a racial militant. Frequently, black politicians who are not militant toward whites are viewed by other blacks with suspicion. The fiery black representative Shirley Chisholm, who represented a 90 percent black Brooklyn district from 1968 to 1982, once complained: "They've said I like whitey, that I'm too close to Hispanics, that I'm not black enough. . . . When you have black racists and white racists it is very difficult to build bridges between the communities."[55] There are benefits for blacks who blame the system and white people for society's injustices.[56] These benefits, however, are not likely to help them to attain the heights that Gray reached in the power structure of the House.

Representation through Legislation: Gray's Route to Power

Although Gray entered Congress with no prior political experience in an elective office, he showed evidence from the very beginning of being a shrewd politician. To obtain an influential committee assignment, he enlisted the assistance of John Murtha, a more senior member of his state delegation, and ended up on the Appropriations Committee. He rose quickly in the leadership structure. As a freshman he was named to head the 1978 freshman group and was elected to the Democratic Steering and Policy Group. The next year he became vice chairman of the Black Caucus. Shortly after his reelection he won a seat on the Budget Committee, and in 1985 he was elected as chair. In 1989 he was elected majority whip after controversies over alleged ethical transgressions forced Speaker Jim Wright (D-TX) and Majority Whip Tony Coelho (D-CA) to resign from their posts. A series of strategic moves were associated with Gray's success. In the 1984 contest for the budget chairmanship, all eyes were focused on James Jones (D-OK) and Leon Panetta (D-CA), both of whom wanted the job but were barred from serving owing to a restriction limiting tenure on the committee. Both contenders sought a change in the rules. While others were involved in the Jones-Panetta debate, Gray lined up support for himself and convinced Speaker Tip O'Neill to oppose changing the three-year term limitation on Budget Committee membership. O'Neill in turn convinced the Democratic Caucus to maintain the status quo. When the dust settled, a solid majority of Democrats had committed themselves to supporting Gray.[57]

In 1988, when his budget chairmanship was about to expire, Gray successfully ran for the Democratic Caucus chairmanship previously held by Richard Gephardt (D-MO). Again he followed a strategic game plan. Imitating the examples of earlier power brokers such as Representative Henry Waxman of California, Gray donated large sums of money to his colleagues' campaigns. He followed the same pattern in his pursuit of the majority whip post, and it came easily to him despite a Justice Department leak, shortly before the election, that his office was under investigation. Throughout the whip contest, rumors had surfaced: one of them, for example, alleged that Gray had cut a deal with Martin Frost (D-TX) to deliver the votes of Black Caucus members in exchange for support from the Texas delegation. Gray denied the charge.[58]

Gray raised large amounts of campaign money that he used for a variety of purposes, including paying his legal fees. Some journalists have suggested that Gray was "buying votes," because he had donated as much as $6,000 to certain of his colleagues' campaigns. They cited Federal Election Commission records that showed that Gray was more generous to his colleagues in 1988 than in any previous year: $119,750 to ninety colleagues, as opposed to $24,550 spread among thirty-seven in 1985 and 1986.[59] More eyebrows were raised when Gray sponsored a thousand-dollar-a-plate dinner for his colleagues with an invitation letter stating: "This is the first 1,000-dollar-a-plate dinner where only the food gets the bite put on it. If you come to the dinner, you get a thousand dollars for your campaign."[60] Gray's actions may have seemed bold and perhaps imprudent, but he was following the path of white power brokers who have personal Political Action Committees and who use part of their funds to pay personal expenses and to help them gain influence in the House. In 1990 alone, Gray raised over $700,000, with 71 percent ($516,953) coming from PACs around the country.[61]

By downplaying the role of race, that is, by presenting himself as an individual who just happened to be black, Gray may well have benefited from the desire of Democratic party leaders to find a more acceptable black presidential candidate than the Reverend Jesse Jackson. Before the rise of Governor Douglas Wilder of Virginia, Gray was the black political figure most frequently mentioned as presidential and vice presidential material.[62] In comparing him with Jackson, Representative Marvin Leath

(D-TX) stated: "[Gray] brings a great deal more to the table than Jesse Jackson." Similarly, the former Budget Committee chairman James Jones explained: "When an audience hears Jesse Jackson, they feel threatened that he will alter the institutions. When they hear Bill Gray, they don't feel threatened."[63] A white representative from a southern district told me: "I love that Bill Gray. He's a congressman's congressman. He's not like the others. Whenever he sees me in the hallway he always takes the time to say hello."[64]

Some members of Congress, however, were critical of Gray and his performance. One Black Caucus member told me: "Study Bill Gray. Which constituency does he represent? Is it the one who elects him, or is it the one that keeps him in power?" Representative George Miller, a liberal Democrat from California, told a reporter that Gray was "moving and bobbing and weaving so fast, he's not always taking everybody with him. . . . Along the way he's offended some people."[65] A *Wall Street Journal* article reported some opinions of Gray's congressional colleagues: "He is sometimes short on facts but quick to take credit for things that were really a team effort. He can be quick-tempered, especially with his own staff, and has riled members of his own committee by his frequent tardiness and tendency to talk at great length without listening."[66] At home some of the criticisms leveled against Gray were similar to those that Nix heard. "He won't trouble the waters," said Charles Bowser, a prominent black Philadelphia leader. "If you don't want to trouble the waters, don't jump in the pool."[67]

To achieve his goals, Gray needed substantial white support at home and in Washington. Although he publicly recognized the existence of racism, he often chose to ignore the signs or at least not to make them an issue. In this regard, he approached his white colleagues in the manner of Martin Luther King, Jr. He decided to appeal to the better nature of those from whom he needed support: "I face what all blacks go through. People see your skin before they see anything else, and sometimes that's all they see. But you've got to keep on truckin' and hope that you have the chance to demonstrate excellence. If I do an effective job as [Budget] chairman, I will break down a barrier and demonstrate that race is not an obstacle to heading a major committee or winning a leadership post."[68]

All of his moves appear to have been carefully planned. He angered some blacks and confused others by waiting until four days before the Democratic Convention to endorse Jesse Jackson's 1984 candidacy.[69] In

1988, however, Gray, along with most black leaders in the country, found it politically expedient to endorse Jackson's candidacy early on. The considerable negative constituency opinion about Gray did not matter much politically: grumblings alone are unlikely to cost black representatives from historically black districts many votes. Disapproving black constituents are more likely to stay at home than go to the polls and "vote the rascal out." One proof of Gray's independence from his district came when he vowed to the House leadership that as Budget chairman he would place institutional responsibilities above any political responsibilities to his district.[70] That Gray could say this and be reelected attests to the exceptional freedom enjoyed by black representatives from historically black districts. It may also indicate that black voters understand the need for black politicians to prove themselves to whites, and that proving themselves may require them to reassure their suspicious and jittery white colleagues that they will not merely use their leadership positions to help their own race.

Gray's voting record did not differ significantly from the records of other black representatives (see Table 3.3 and Appendix C). All Democrats are high scorers on the COPE scale. During the 100th Congress, Gray was among the twenty-one southern Democrats, 109 northern Democrats, and four Republicans who were listed as perfect scorers on that index. The LCCR, however, gave him a score of 87 percent after he missed two of the organization's targeted votes on the Fair Housing Bill. One was an amendment that sought to delete a provision barring discrimination against families with small children; the other vote concerned the rights of people with AIDS. Unlike the COPE index, the LCCR counts absences against a member's score. On votes in which the conservative coalition (CC) mobilized, Gray and most of the other black members scored well below the average for Democrats from both regions. Among representatives from historically black districts, Kweisi Mfume (D-MD) was the highest scorer on the CC scale (15 percent), and Mike Espy (D-MS) was highest for newly black districts (41 percent). Gray's voting participation score (84 percent) was lower than the average for the Congress (92 percent) and lower than the scores of three-quarters of the black members.

Gray was not particularly forceful on the domestic issues affecting black communities in his district or throughout the nation. What was Gray's legislative focus? Issues relating to Africa consumed much of his time. Gray advanced the interests of Africa in much the same way that

Jewish representatives advance the interests of Israel. He was one of the early voices against apartheid in South Africa. He proposed an amendment to the Export Administration Act calling for penalties against companies making new investments in South Africa. He also initiated an emergency appropriation of $90 million for drought relief in Africa. Among his national legislative successes was the decision of the House leadership to support his South African sanctions bill rather than a stronger measure authored by the black congressman Ron Dellums (D-CA). Although Dellums's bill was successful in passing on the House floor, the Senate eventually adopted a plan that was closer to Gray's original bill than to Dellums's bill.

Walking Away from Power in the House

After successfully pursuing power in Congress and breaking many actual and perceived racial barriers, Gray resigned from the House in 1991 to become the head of the United Negro College Fund, an important but less glamorous position. Some observers saw his resignation as an attempt to avoid an investigation and political stigma.[71] Congressional insiders say that not only was Gray being investigated by the Justice Department because of his handling of excess honoraria, but that there was talk of a pending House investigation of his finances.[72] His resignation ended discussions of an internal investigation. Gray explained his decision to resign in altruistic terms, focusing on his family legacy and the good he could achieve: "I come from a family where my father was president of two historically black colleges. My mother was dean of students at a black college, and my sister teaches now at a black college. So, that's really my roots." He told a commentator on ABC's "Good Morning America" show that he was "giving up political power to have a big impact on the education of black young people throughout the decade. . . . And to me that's very important."[73]

An article in the *Wall Street Journal* based on interviews with his congressional colleagues explained: "Mr. Gray has grown bored with life in the House and, with college-age and teenage children, increasingly concerned about financial questions. At the fund, he will probably double his congressional salary of $125,000. He will also be able to sit on corporate boards."[74] One member jokingly said that Gray had given up life in a fishbowl for a $250,000-a-year job that would allow him to keep the thousands of dollars that he could earn from his speeches.[75]

Regardless of why he resigned, it must be said in conclusion that no other black representative has come close to achieving Gray's power and stature. He rose in power while supporting the liberal agenda that most black leaders see as being in the interests of African Americans. His voting record was no less liberal than that of the average northern Democrat or the average black representative. What made him different was his Washington style, his way of interacting with his colleagues, his willingness to bargain and negotiate to get what he wanted, and his skill at doing so. This shrewd and calculated approach took him far on Capitol Hill and, as he used his power to bring thousands of federal dollars to his district, benefited his constituents as well.

Historically Black Districts and Electoral Security

Historically black districts have produced black representatives who vary enormously in style, goals, and temperament. George Crockett was very different from Charles Diggs. William Gray's low-key, conciliatory manner did not differ significantly from Robert Nix's habit of not "muddying the waters," but Lucian Blackwell, who followed Gray, has a very different style from that of his predecessor—he is an outspoken champion of the underclass. A close look at representatives from historically black districts reveals militants and moderates as well as individuals whose styles defy simple characterization. The freedom this kind of district gives them means that great variety in what Fenno calls "home styles" is possible, and representatives are not fettered by the styles of those who precede them.

The same electoral security that benefits representatives from historically black districts can have a negative effect on the caliber of their representation. Representatives from such districts sometimes appear to become complacent, not consulting their constituents as frequently as representatives from other kinds of districts do. In adopting this pattern they appear to embrace the point of view of Fenno's Congressman F, who told him: "When I vote my conscience as a black man, I necessarily represent the black community. I don't have any trouble knowing what the black community thinks or wants."[76] Such a position ignores the growing diversity among African Americans, and it points to the problem of elite domination in black communities, where black politicians often see themselves as "trustees" for a proscribed legislative agenda.

White politicians, however, are more likely to see themselves as "delegates" for interests to be derived and then represented.[77]

Electoral accountability is so weak in some historically black districts that one black representative told me unabashedly: "One of the advantages, and disadvantages, of representing blacks is their shameless loyalty to their incumbents. You can almost get away with raping babies and be forgiven. You don't have *any* vigilance about your performance."[78] Nonetheless, the eventual defeats of Oscar DePriest (1934), Robert Nix (1978), Adam Clayton Powell, Jr. (1970), Charles Hayes (1992), and Gus Savage (1992) by other black candidates and the pressure on Diggs to resign even before his conviction illustrate that no congressional district is truly safe. Vigilance is indeed warranted.[79]

4 · Black Representatives of Newly Black Districts

We're in an era that the blacks are going to get what they want, and I'm going to ride the tide and get it too.
—*Comment by a middle-aged white woman about her support for Mike Espy's reelection, January 1988*

Unlike historically black districts, newly black districts are usually the product of court-ordered redistricting plans. Because these districts have voting-age populations that are usually less than 65 percent black, white voters play a decisive role in determining which of several black candidates gets the nomination and, ultimately, the congressional seat. As of 1991, four districts qualified as newly black (see Table 4.1). None of these districts has a black population large enough for the representative to have much of a choice about whether to appeal to white voters: because whites are the swing voters in each of these districts, they are courted assiduously. What are the resulting implications for the representation of the black constituents? What influence, if any, does a black candidate's need to represent a large number of whites have on his or her style of representation?

Mike Espy and John Lewis represent new majority-black districts located in Mississippi and Georgia, respectively. Both men were elected in 1986. Their cases illustrate the enormous power of white voters in districts in which black candidates compete either with each other or against less attractive white candidates.

Table 4.1. Black representatives of newly black districts

District	Principal city	Representative	Years served	BVAP 1980s	HVAP 1980s
LA-2	New Orleans	William Jefferson	1991–	52%	3%
MS-2	Greenville	Mike Espy	1987–	53	1
NJ-10	Newark	Donald Payne	1989–	54	12
GA-5	Atlanta	Andrew Young[a]	1971–1977		
		John Lewis	1987–	60	1

Sources: Linda Williams, ed., *The JCPS Congressional District Fact Book,* 3rd ed. (Washington, D.C.: Joint Center for Political Studies, 1988), p. 20; *Congressional Quarterly Weekly Report,* November 10, 1990, pp. 3822–3823; "The 101st Congress, 1989–1990," Congressional Black Caucus Foundation, September 1990.

Note: BVAP = Black voting-age percentage of district population; HVAP = Hispanic voting-age percentage of district population.

a. Resigned from the House on January 29, 1977, to become U.S. ambassador to the United Nations. The district was 59 percent white, 40 percent black, and 1 percent Hispanic at that time.

The Second District of Mississippi: Mike Espy

Recent History

Mississippi's second congressional district, which has the Mississippi River as its western border, is contained mostly in the Delta region, where annual floods deposit the nutrient-enriched soil that has made the area perfect for agriculture. Once this was an international cotton center, maintained by sharecroppers who were dependent on wealthy white landlords for their basic needs.[1] During the Reconstruction era the heavily black district elected a black congressman, John Lynch, who served from 1873 until his defeat in 1877. Memories of this long-lost black power flourished in 1986, when the district elected Mike Espy, its second black representative. The significance of Espy's election can only be appreciated when set against Mississippi's long history of repression of black people and their interests.[2]

For more than a century, Mississippi has had the highest percentage of African Americans in the nation—59 percent during the Reconstruction, 42 percent in 1960, 35 percent in 1989. Nevertheless, before the passage of the 1965 Voting Rights Act the state had among the lowest rates of black voter registration (6.5 percent). White fear of black domination has been prevalent in the district since Reconstruction, when a court decision defined "Negro domination" as any election in which "white men may be divided" and "the Negro vote would be sufficiently decisive to be potential in determining the result"—thus making it clear that the dreaded "Negro domination" could occur even if a white candidate were elected.[3]

Mississippi has long ranked at the bottom of the nation on a wide variety of economic and social indicators. As the journalist Peter Boyer noted, Mississippi has endured "for generations as the national symbol of racial prejudice and cultural backwardness—last in the nation in per capita income, last in employment rate, last in literacy rate, last to mandate kindergartens and compulsory education." There have been periodic, if uneven, signs of change: in 1988, for example, Governor Ray Maubus took office, calling for "basic change, drastic change" and declaring that "Mississippi will never be last again."[4] But Maubus's administration was short-lived, and in 1991 he was defeated by a conservative Republican.

The civil rights attorney Frank Parker provides an overview of how and why Mississippi has changed for African-American voters in his book *Black Votes Count*.[5] Focusing on white resistance to the 1965 Voting Rights Act and on recent changes, he analyzes the court cases that have had such an impact on the state and on the nation. The most important of these cases are *Allen v. State Board of Election*,[6] which led to a Justice Department review of annexations, redistricting, and any changes that might have an adverse effect on black voting strength, and *Connor v. Johnson*,[7] first filed in 1966 and resolved fourteen years later under the name *State of Mississippi v. United States*.[8]

The latter case forced the state to eliminate at-large voting in multi-member districts and made an argument for the establishment of electoral districts that were 65 percent black (or had a black voting-age population that was at least 60 percent black):

> Low Black voter registration and voter turnout combined with racial bloc voting make it necessary for an electoral district in Mississippi to contain a substantial majority of Black eligible voters in order to provide Black voters with an opportunity to elect a candidate of choice. . . . Barring exceptional circumstances such as two White candidates splitting the vote, a district should contain a Black population of at least 65% or a Black voting age population of at least 60 percent to provide Black voters with an opportunity to elect a candidate of their choice.[9]

Nevertheless, when Mike Espy was elected to Congress in 1986, the Bureau of Census listed the black population in his district as constituting only 58 percent of the aggregate population. Espy believes that the actual percentage was even lower than that: "I think the numbers are incorrect. We had lost about 70,000 people when I ran in 1986. The Census even admits that we lost 70,000 people in its pre-estimate. I think that's the low end of it. I believe we lost a lot more people than that, and most of them have been black, so if I just had to say, I'd put the white-black population at 50–50."[10]

Robert Clark, who ran unsuccessfully in the district in 1982 and 1984, would have certainly agreed with the court's decision in *State of Mississippi v. United States* to encourage the creation of districts that were at least 65 percent black. Although he had served sixteen years in the state legislature, which should have placed him at a strategic advantage as a career politician, he could not win the second district.[11] He failed despite in 1968 having been the first black elected to the Mississippi state legislature since 1894, an achievement that had gained him significant recognition in the state.

Mississippi's requirement that the winner of the Democratic nomination compete in a second primary, a runoff, if he or she does not get 50 percent or more of the vote was not a handicap for Clark. When he ran for Congress in 1982, he won the Democratic nomination with 57 percent of the vote, and he easily defeated his three white opponents. But he lost the general election, despite the strong support of his party and black political organizations such as the Student Nonviolent Coordinating Committee (SNCC) and the Mississippi Freedom Democratic Party.

The strategy that Clark's white Republican opponent, Webb Franklin, used to defeat him is interesting. Franklin and Clark initially opposed each other in an open-seat contest that occurred after the district had been redrawn to have a black majority. Franklin won, and Clark challenged him again in 1984. Franklin, encouraging white voters to "protect their heritage," made Clark's race an issue in both campaigns. One of Franklin's tactics was to remind white voters that Clark was black by placing Clark's picture on fliers. Clark unwittingly aided Franklin by attempting to conduct a dual campaign: he played up his race in the black community, but at the same time he tried to avoid drawing attention to it in his dealings with the district's white voters. Franklin also used television advertisements as a subtle reminder of the importance of race. One commercial pictured him in front of a Confederate monument, stating: "You know, there's something about Mississippi that outsiders will never understand. The way we feel about our family and God, and the traditions we have. There is a new Mississippi, a Mississippi of new jobs and a new opportunity for our citizens. We welcome the new, but we must never, ever forget what has gone before. We cannot forget a heritage that has been sacred through generations."[12] Another advertisement showed photographs of the two candidates with the slogan "Vote for Franklin because 'he is one of us.'" On election day, Franklin's radio announcements mobilized white voters by warning that Clark's supporters were going to the polls in "droves."[13]

We will never know the impact of any specific appeal to race, but in 1982 the election was extremely close—Franklin defeated Clark by a margin of 50 percent to 48 percent. In 1984, with President Reagan heading the Republican ticket, Clark—not surprisingly—did worse. According to Mary Coleman and Leslie McLemore: "In 1982, [he] won four of seven counties, in 1984 he won three and lost four, including majority black Washington and Sunflower counties. From 1982 to 1984, Clark lost 9 percent of the vote he received in the same counties in 1982."[14]

Some observers have criticized Clark's decision to downplay his race in order to appeal to white voters rather than publicizing it in order to mobilize black voters by stirring their racial pride. When he campaigned before white voters, Clark focused on economic issues, attacking Reaganomics in particular. This strategy was a sensible one given the economic level of the district, which has the dubious distinction of being one of the poorest in the nation, but Clark seemed to have overestimated the potential of issue appeal and underestimated the importance of voter mobilization.

No black candidate could have won in the second district of Mississippi without some white support. Nor could a white candidate have won without black support. Franklin's Democratic predecessor, David Bowen, relied on a biracial coalition and performed a delicate balancing act between the conservative whites and the poor blacks in the district. He explained his winning strategy:

> I had a lot of very conservative white people supporting me, a lot of conservative farmers and businessmen, people like that. And at the same time a large bloc of the black community. . . . I just didn't do anything to alienate either of those two blocs that I had put together. . . . Take things like food stamps. . . . Theoretically, a lot of the people who do not receive food stamps are against them. Of course, almost all of the black community is for them as well as a lot of whites. I'm on the Agriculture Committee

and I have to write food stamp legislation. Of course, blacks stayed with me because I voted for food stamps. And [to] the whites, I was able to explain that I was tightening up the legislation, improving it. And it would have been a lot more costly and less efficient if I were not in there trying to put amendments in there to improve it—conditions that require recipients to register for work and accept work if it is offered and to make sure that people don't draw food stamps who are able-bodied and willing to work. So, generally, those conservatives who would cuss and holler about food stamps all the time would say, "Well David's doing a good job trying to improve the program. . . . He's in there trying to improve it, trying to tighten it up, trying to cut out the fraud and waste."[15]

When the district was redrawn to create a black majority, Bowen stepped aside after having served for five terms.

Political commentators suggested several reasons for Franklin's defeat of Clark. Much of the speculation centered on Clark's history of civil rights involvement, which may have alienated some white voters, his lack of sophistication when speaking before white audiences, and his failure to mobilize the black electorate. Although all of these are plausible explanations, the evidence is not available to test them and establish their relative importance. Whatever the case, Clark did not establish the kind of bond with the district that Fenno claims is essential to get elected to Congress.[16] Coleman and McLemore write, "In the process of gaining white acceptance [Clark] did not develop in blacks the perception of his legitimacy as a black leader."[17] Mike Espy's experience is in marked contrast to Clark's.

The Expansionist Stage: Mike Espy's Electoral Strategy

Mike Espy, a thirty-two-year-old Yazoo, Mississippi, native with a bachelor's degree from Howard University and a law degree from Santa Clara University, showed that a black could win in the second district when he defeated Webb Franklin by 5,000 votes in November 1986 (see Table 4.2). Unlike Clark, Espy was not well known, and he had no prior political record. He did have administrative experience, having been the assistant secretary of state (1980–1984) and assistant attorney general (1984–1985), but these are both relatively low profile positions. Espy is ambitious and goal-oriented. He had known for some time that he would eventually run for Congress, and he felt that his home state provided the best career opportunities for educated young blacks. His

Table 4.2. The election history of Mike Espy

Year	Primary election opponents	Vote total (percentage)	General election opponents	Vote total (percentage)
1986	Espy	29,724 (50%)	Espy	73,119 (52%)
	Johnson	15,335 (26)	Franklin	68,292 (48)
	Eastland	14,229 (24)		
1988	Espy	59,801 (88)	Espy	112,401 (65)
	Clark (Boja)	8,250 (12)	Coleman	59,827 (34)
			Benford	1,403 (1)
1990	Espy	Unopposed	Espy	59,393 (84)
			Benford	11,224 (16)

Sources: Michael Barone, Grant Ujifusa, and Douglas Matthews, *The Almanac of American Politics* (New York: E. P. Dutton, 1978, 1980); Barone and Ujifusa, *The Almanac of American Politics* (Washington, D.C.: National Journal, 1984–1990 biennial eds.).

bid for Congress marked the beginning of the expansionist stage of his constituency career.

Espy's electoral strategy depended on generating a high black turnout and concomitantly increasing his white support. He described how he did so: "I went into every nook and cranny of the district. There were people who questioned my judgment. But I went everywhere I was invited—even places where I wasn't."[18] He studied the precincts that Clark had lost and saw the potential for victory. Instrumental to his success was a field organization of 750 precinct captains, 1,500 block captains and biracial co-chairmanships in twenty-two counties that helped him reach and mobilize potential voters, both white and black.[19]

Espy adopted an approach frequently used in the past by black politicians who needed white support. He ran a modified dual campaign, with some elements geared toward blacks and some toward whites. His campaign to gain white support focused on personal contact, endorsements from prominent white Democrats, criticism of the Reagan Administration's farm policy, and the effect of budget cuts on the district's economy. Interestingly, the issue-based strategy Espy used to gain white votes was similar to Clark's unsuccessful strategy. The difference was that Espy rejected the portion of dual campaign strategy that involved attempting to hide one's race by relying primarily on radio commercials and advertisements without photographs. Such a strategy gives the candidate's opponent an incentive to provide the voters with the missing information (as Franklin did with Clark), and can make the candidate seem dishonest.

Espy's use of personal contact served to let black voters know that a black candidate was in the race. He made a concerted effort to go into the backwoods of the district to ask individuals for their support personally. Political consultants have found that people are more likely to vote when a candidate makes a personal request.[20] These findings are consistent with the observation of Robert Bush, the field coordinator for Espy in 1986 and 1988, that Mississippi blacks expect to be asked directly for their vote and will otherwise stay home on election day.[21] Espy established a wide circle of personal contacts by using hundreds of volunteers, many of whom came from other states to help him with his voter mobilization effort.

Espy campaign workers tried especially hard to combat the apathy of black voters. They confronted masses of blacks with the fact that they had never been registered and had, therefore, never voted despite the removal of overt barriers to their participation. Using drivers' license lists, broken down by race, to identify unregistered black voters, they made an attempt to register the unregistered and get them all to the polls. Espy says that black community leaders were lukewarm to his candidacy. Some felt that whites would never allow a black to be elected in Mississippi; others claimed that the seat ought to be Robert Clark's to win or lose. As a result, local black leaders in the district did little to help Espy. Clark himself refused to endorse him and gave his support to Espy's white opponent. This lack of enthusiasm from black leaders caught Espy by surprise. He said: "I thought that if I became the only black candidate in the primary that I could win the support of the party and civil rights leaders. I was mistaken. . . . There was a generational jealousy."[22]

Gaining the support of white voters was not easy. Espy ran television and radio advertisements featuring his endorsement by several white county sheriffs, the secretary of state, and the Mississippi attorney general. The contrast between Clark and Espy was one of Espy's assets. Espy was too young to have the history of civil rights involvement that may have been a liability for Clark. Espy's education and social class were also on his side. Espy's success is illustrated by statements from his white supporters: "We have so many black politicians who cater to the black more than they do to the white. . . . I don't think Mike is like that." "Most blacks get in office and the first thing they do is start talking about racial things. Topics. But Espy is not like that. He seems to grasp the concerns of all the people, I think. Not just the blacks, but whites, too. He is refreshing for that." Espy is the antithesis of Jesse Jackson: he is known for his low-key style of interacting with people (he has been nicknamed Clark Kent). As an attorney and a member of a prominent black family, whose grandfather built Mississippi's first black hospital and whose family owned a chain of funeral homes, he is definitely a member of the middle class and is more similar to the district's white elites.

Espy won the 1986 election by mobilizing a slightly greater percentage of black voters than Clark had (1 percent more) and by gaining a small but crucial portion of the white vote (12 percent). Furthermore, his campaign did not mobilize white voters to turn out in large numbers to vote against him. He won with 52 percent of the vote. Over 20,000 registered white voters and 19,000 black voters did not vote in the 1986 election. Espy believes that many of the whites who did not vote deliberately helped him by staying at home, whereas in the past they had actively opposed Clark.[23] Ehrenhalt writes that "in the end . . . it was his organization in the black community that fueled his victory,"[24] but it is also important to remember that he went to great lengths to cultivate the district's white voters. Since his 1986 election, Espy's reelection margins have increased dramatically (see Table 4.2) and he has raised a large campaign war chest for himself (see Appendix B). Espy is now in the protectionist stage of his constituency career.

The racial makeup of the district that elected Espy did not differ substantially from the district that Clark lost. What was different were the candidates, their strategies, and their respective appeal to whites. The comments of white voters suggest that they were only prepared to support a certain type of black candidate—one whom they could feel good about, that is, one able to convince them that he was sufficiently qualified in terms of their criteria to hold office. One woman said: "Espy is qualified, and he is not the stereotype that so many people think of the blacks from Mississippi. He's a cut above." Another admitted, "I was worried about how he would appear in public. Say, he made a speech, I wanted to make sure he would use good grammar. That sort of thing. I wanted to make sure he would present a positive, intelligent image." A young man commented: "There's almost a certainty that you're going to have a black representative. I'm just glad it's a good one."[25]

Image was important to the white voters—both their own image and that of the representative they would help elect. In particular, white Mississippians feared that a black representative might be elected who would further damage the state's already tarnished reputation. How could they ever live down the past, the murder of the three civil rights workers? One man talked about his frustrations about being a white Mississippian: "We all have this other image of how the rest of the country sees us. . . . We're treated as rednecks, as if everyone walks around in white sheets at night with crosses." By voting for Espy, white voters elected a representative of whom they could be proud and who would help change Mississippi's reputation for backwardness.

A test of Espy's strength came in 1988 when he was opposed in the general election by both a white Republican, Jack Coleman, and a black Independent, Dorothy Benford. Coleman made four negative charges against Espy:

1. "Mike Espy voted in favor of the third pay raise in one year for congressmen, raising his own salary to $92,000."
2. "Mike Espy is the darling of some of the most immoral and anti-family organizations in this country. For example, last year he received money, $7,675, from the National Gay Rights Political Committee, more than anyone else in the country. Last year he also received more than $8,000 from national pro-abortion organizations. His acceptance of these donations is a disgrace to all Mississippians."
3. "Last year Mike Espy accepted almost $200,000 in campaign contributions from labor unions."
4. "Mike Espy voted against President Reagan's aid request for $100 million for the Contra Rebels fighting to overthrow the communist government of Nicaragua."[26]

Espy did not lose significant white support as a result of Coleman's charges, however, and he won despite the candidacy of another African American.

Benford has run against Espy in every race since he was first elected. She is a former campaign worker and party activist whom Espy refused to hire as a permanent staffer. In 1988 the strength of her campaign generated speculation that her benefactors were Republicans. Concerns were raised that she might receive as much as 10 percent of the black vote, thereby causing Espy to lose the election. But in the general election she received only 1 percent of the vote, and Espy was reelected with 65 percent of the vote, compared with 52 percent in 1986. In 1990 Benford ran on the Republican ticket and received 16 percent of the vote. Espy's continuing electoral success demonstrates that even in a state with a history of minority repression, voters can move beyond their racial differences.

Interactions with Constituents: Forging a Biracial Coalition

The size of Espy's winning coalition influenced his interactions with his constituents. His initial election margin of 52 percent was so low that expansion of his base was crucial to his hopes of reelection. His first gesture toward white voters was to win a seat on the Agricultural Committee and allow district farmers to select his agricultural assistant.[27] This hiring decision addressed their fears and criticisms that he was not a farmer and had no experience in agricultural issues. In taking this seat, he became the first black to sit on the Agricultural Committee since Reconstruction; Shirley Chisholm (D-NY) had refused the assignment some twenty years earlier.

The need to expand his constituency encouraged him to adopt an active home style. After his election he established four district offices, left his family in the district, and made a policy of returning home most weekends. Regular newsletters flow from his office. In these letters he has claimed credit for millions of dollars that have come to the district. He was responsible for the creation of a National Catfish Day, which aids the catfish farmers in his district, and for legislation exploring ways to develop the Mississippi River. During trips around the country, he has personally signed up deals for orders of catfish, soybeans, and cotton worth thousands of dollars. Both constituents and journalists have contrasted his style with that of his predecessor Webb Franklin, who supported Reagan's farm policies and was not known for his activism.[28] Constituents have stated that Espy attends twice as many functions as did Franklin. Whites have come to view him as a hard worker who is approachable.

Since 1988 Espy has made important changes in the racial makeup of his staff. He has hired substantially more white staffers. I remember my surprise in 1988, when I first visited his Washington and district offices and saw the large number of blacks on his staff: eighteen staff members, sixteen blacks and only two whites; four were non-Mississippians. In most districts I had visited, the racial makeup of the district had been proportionally reflected in the staff, and I had expected to see this trend in Espy's district as well. Given the nature of Espy's district, it is not surprising that his staff has become more white with the passage of time. When I asked him about his staff in 1990, then about half black and half white, Espy responded: "You try to be sensitive to racial balance. I don't have to tell you—white female here, black male there. I try to remain sensitive to the makeup of the whole district but there's no mandate, there's no quota."[29] As we shall see, a racially diverse staff is especially prevalent in more competitive districts, in which the representative needs the votes of racial groups other than his or her own.

Espy's casework has been an essential factor in his ability to increase support among whites. In 1989 he reported having worked on approximately 6,380 individual cases since he took office in 1987, and his support among whites had skyrocketed. When asked to explain why, he commented:

> The short answer is through service—effective service. I think the greatest part to all of it is that the white community, when faced with the prospect of a black representative, feels a lot of fear, a lot of trepidation—a lot of concern that this individual won't represent them as zealously as he might another group. So you have to prove yourself, that you will open your door, answer that phone call, answer that letter just as quickly and heartily as you will for another group. I think a lot of that fear is relaxing. They know that the sun is going to shine, the sun is going to rise as surely as it rose the day before, whether there's a black or white in office.[30]

Espy faces a problem common to many black representatives: how to retain black support and enthusiasm while at the same time expanding his political base into white territory. Espy has described his policies as nonracial: "I have performed for everybody, regardless of race." Most of his statements seem designed to refute the state's image as a place of racial oppression. He said during the same interview that "the attitudes of overt racism in Mississippi are no longer prevalent."[31] This angered black leaders in the state who still see significant institutional racism, and some even accuse him of selling out black interests. Others say that he has spent a large amount of his time in the white community, sometimes to the apparent neglect of his black constituents. Black leaders were especially offended when Espy sent a staffer to represent him at an annual NAACP banquet.[32] The decision was viewed as a serious affront to the blacks who helped him get elected.

Espy has described his balancing act as a "tightrope." In 1988 some whites criticized him for voting for Jesse Jackson at the Democratic National Convention (Jackson had carried Mississippi on Super Tuesday), whereas black constituents criticized him for supporting the "predominantly white-owned catfish industry."[33] Much of his success has to do with the ease with which he interacts with whites. Most white constituents address him by his first name, which is part of the southern tradition. Calling him "Mike," rather than "Congressman Espy" or "Mr. Espy," seems offensive, however, to some of his black staffers, who feel he should be addressed with a title. Southern whites and blacks interpret the signals differently. In another southern district, one with a white representative, a white staffer commented: "Listen to them call the congressman by his first name—that shows they really like him."

On one spring day, Espy spoke to a largely white audience, mostly members of a local garden club. The ladies, looking like true Daughters of the Confederacy, were clad in antebellum-style southern dresses. The invitation to speak was his first before this particular group. The topic they had given him was "Preserving Our Mississippi Heritage," one that might have been a difficult assignment for a black congressman representing a southern district. Espy, however, handled the matter by discussing the need to "preserve our heritage" while not forgetting the "lessons of history" and the "need to create opportunities for those who will otherwise leave the state."[34]

Espy has said that each time he speaks before a mixed group, some whites come up to him, introduce themselves, and say: "I didn't vote for you last time but you have my vote in the next election."[35] In Espy's case, greater exposure is enough to expand his base. Similar exposure may have hurt Clark. The excitement in Espy's voice is unmistakable as he speaks of his invitations to garden clubs, Baptist conventions, Boy Scout groups, and other institutions that in the past have avoided black politicians. When Mike Espy says, "I believe in the State of Mississippi and its people," he sounds utterly convincing.

Representation through Legislation: Serving Diverse Interests

Espy serves on the Agriculture and Budget committees and on the Select Committee on Hunger. He is considerably less liberal on legislative issues than other black members of Congress and northern white Democrats, but he is more liberal than most southern whites. In this regard he does not provide a consistent and reliable vote for a progressive legislative agenda. He is more concerned about representing the concerns of his geographical constituency than a broader set of interests.

Espy's conservative coalition score is the highest ever for a black Democrat (see Table 3.3 and Appendix C). During the 100th Congress, his CC agreement score of 41 percent was much higher than Harold Ford's 7 percent and John Lewis's 8.5 percent, and it was two points higher than the 39 percent of Lindy Boggs (see Table 7.2). In the 101st Congress he scored 50 percent, compared with 6 percent for Ford and Lewis and 35 percent for Boggs. Nevertheless he is by far the most liberal member of his state's delegation, where the mean conservative coalition score (excluding his) is 85 percent. His COPE score was 90.5 percent during the 100th Congress, and he had an 86 percent voting participation rate.

Espy entered Congress as something of a celebrity because of his election from Mississippi—a state famous for lacking black representation. Members of the Democratic leadership have supported his style and independence. He has been called a "crony" of Bill Gray's, and has been criticized, along with Gray, for voting "present" on the Black Caucus's alternative to the national budget. In 1990, however, Espy supported the caucus budget, because he felt that "it was the right thing to do."[36]

At home, Espy has been instrumental in the establishment of a commission to study poverty in the Mississippi Delta; he has brought modernization and running water to poor, predominantly black communities; he has gone far around the country for food and other donations for Mississippi's poor blacks; and he has sponsored legislation benefiting minority farmers. Through his ability to transcend race and represent broad interests, Espy has established himself as a "professional politician." He has more moderate and conservative constituents than most black representatives, and he gives them a type of representation that contemporary black representatives have rarely provided for their constituencies.

His reelection margin of 65 percent in 1988 against an attractive white Republican conservative in a district with a black voter turnout of 40 percent suggests that he has indeed managed to get many white Mississippians to look beyond his race to the values he holds in common with them. In an advertisement for the National Rifle Association he says: "Unlike most kids from Mississippi, I didn't grow up hunting. . . . But I understand that freedom to own a firearm—for recreation or self-protection—is a constitutional issue. And when government tries to infringe upon a constitutional right, we must be extremely wary and cautious. . . . People tend to see all black congressmen as liberals with an urban twist: they're all for gun control and against the death penalty. It's not true, and it shouldn't be true. Our communities are different. Don't look to me to support urban mass transit. There are no subways in my district."[37]

In 1990, as the keynote speaker at the NRA's annual convention, he challenged the group to reach out to other groups who are suspicious of it.[38] He has stuck firmly to his anti–gun control position, even to the point of voting against the 1991 Brady Bill that would have required a seven-day waiting period before the purchase of a handgun. He also came out in support of Republican programs such as Jack Kemp's Home Ownership for People Everywhere (HOPE) program, and he co-sponsored legislation with Representative Jim Kolbe (R-AZ) that would shift $151 million–one-half of one percent of the Housing and Urban Development (HUD) budget—from traditional housing programs to project HOPE.[39] Espy explained his actions: "A lot of people describe me as conservative based on my views regarding gun control, prayer in school, and tax increases. I would reply by saying that my views cut across racial lines. I think both blacks and whites in my district, if you asked them, say that they would rather have an unfettered right to bear arms. I think most of them do believe in the death penalty and prayer in school. And you tell me anybody who believes in raising taxes! The burden is already too high. So when I vote against or for these things, I would rather people say I'm representing my district."[40]

Representatives who adopt the "delegate style" of representation seek very close counsel with their constituents. Espy's more conservative voting record is based on his decision to act as a "delegate" rather than to use the "trustee style," which relies mainly on personal judgment and is more common among black politicians representing black districts, or a "politico style," which is a mixture of the two.[41] In this regard, Espy demonstrates that blacks can represent moderate, and even conservative, whites, as well as blacks. On economic and civil rights issues, he is a stable vote for the progressive agenda that most blacks prefer. Espy's success in representing whites does not imply, however, that black representatives must become more conservative to gain white support. The legislative records of Alan Wheat (D-MO) and Ron Dellums (D-CA) demonstrate that this is not necessarily true. Legislators can move in many different ways in a policy space.[42] Accordingly, there is no single best voting strategy for black representatives seeking white support; best strategies may vary between, for example, Berkeley, California, and Greenville, Mississippi.

The Fifth District of Georgia: John Lewis

Recent History

Atlanta, a city with an overall population that is 65 percent black, forms the heart of the fifth district of Georgia. The district suffers from some of the same social and health problems that affect other metropolitan areas: crime, unemployment, teenage pregnancy, and a high rate of HIV infection. Like the second district of Mississippi, it is the product of court-ordered redistricting, but there are major differences between the two southern districts, both demographically and in the area of race relations.[43] The fifth district of Georgia has, on the one hand, a large affluent black community and, on the other hand, an even larger poor black community, and provides a good example of the differing interests of middle-class and poor blacks. Considering Atlanta's history of race relations, it is no surprise that it was the first majority-white city in the South to elect an African American to Congress. Unlike the second district of Mississippi, Atlanta has rarely been considered a place of racial oppression. As the "commercial capital of the South," the city developed the slogan "too busy to hate,"[44] and its history of biracial coalitions extends back into the 1940s.[45] In 1974, when the fifth district was 59 percent white, it elected Andrew Young to Congress; a year later Maynard Jackson, another black, became mayor of Atlanta. Like the seventh district of Illinois and the ninth district of Tennessee, Georgia's fifth is an example of a majority-white district that was redrawn to ensure a safe black seat despite the fact that it already had a record of electing black representatives.

The district's new boundaries were set in federal court when a judge ordered the creation of a 65 percent black district in 1980. The effect of the new districting was minimal, however, in that it did not result in the election of a black representative. Senator Wyche Fowler, Jr., a white man who once represented the district, said:

> This federal judge made a determination to take the district up to 70 percent black because he didn't think 58 percent black was adequate to elect a black representative. . . . I tried to tell him, stuck in his racial stereotypical thinking, that the great tribute of the city of Atlanta was not my election or Andy Young's, but the people of Atlanta who refuted stereotypical racial thinking when, as a majority-white district [59 percent], the voters rejected a qualified white man for an equally qualified black. And, when the district was made overwhelmingly black [65 percent] and the voters had an op-

portunity to elect a black representative, either Ralph Abernathy, John Lewis, or Julian Bond, they elected me.[46]

The Expansionist Stage: John Lewis's Electoral Strategy

John Lewis, a native of Troy, Alabama, holds two Bachelor of Arts degrees: one in religion from American Baptist Seminary and one in philosophy from Fisk University. Along with Whitney Young, A. Philip Randolph, James Farmer, Roy Wilkins, and Martin Luther King, Jr., Lewis was known in the 1960s as one of the "Big Six" leaders of the civil rights movement. In 1986, although no one expected him to advance beyond the primary, he was elected to represent the fifth district in Congress.

Lewis, then forty-eight, was making his second bid for the seat; he had been defeated in 1977 by Wyche Fowler. In 1986 he was the unmistakable underdog, because the candidate most favored by liberal whites and the black elite was State Senator Julian Bond, an African American with twenty years of legislative experience. Bond indeed beat Lewis in the Democratic primary, gaining 47 percent of the vote to Lewis's 35 percent, but in the runoff primary Lewis gained significant support and defeated Bond. To the surprise of many, he won 52 percent of the vote to Bond's 48 percent and thus became the party's nominee (see Table 4.3). He then easily won the general election.

Once good friends, the two nationally recognized leaders became enemies during the course of the campaign. Bond was a member of an influential Atlanta family. His father had been dean of Atlanta University, and his campaign supporters included Mayor Andrew Young (the district's former congressman) and Coretta Scott King as well as other leaders from around the country. The fifth district seat was thought to be Bond's to win. Preelection polls indicated that he would win the election by garnering the support of the black middle and upper classes, splitting the vote of lower-income blacks, and taking the majority of all white votes. In the runoff, however, one portion of the white electorate cast the decisive vote between the two candidates, and Lewis won. Post-election polls revealed that upper-income whites had not been particularly supportive of Bond. Precincts composed of affluent white voters rarely gave him more than 10 percent of their vote.[47]

Bond had already gained international attention in 1966, when the Georgia state senate refused to seat him because of his support for the Student Nonviolent Coordinating Committee's anti-Vietnam policy. It

Table 4.3. The election history of John Lewis

Year	Primary election opponents	Vote total (percentage)		General election opponents	Vote total (percentage)	
1977	Lewis	21,531	(29%)			
	Fowler, Jr.	29,898	(40)			
	Coverdell	16,509	(22)			
	Abernathy	3,614	(5)			
	eight others	3,848	(5)			
Runoff	Fowler, Jr.[a]	54,378	(62)			
	Lewis	32,732	(38)			
1986	Lewis	23,622	(35)			
	Johnson	5,756	(8)			
	Bond	31,911	(47)			
	four others	6,693	(8)			
Runoff	Lewis	35,142	(52)	Lewis	93,229	(75%)
	Bond	32,447	(48)	Scott	30,562	(25)
1988	Lewis	Unopposed		Lewis	135,194	(78)
				Tibbs, Jr.	37,693	(22)
1990	Lewis	Unopposed		Lewis	86,037	(76)
				Tibbs, Jr.	27,781	(24)

Sources: Michael Barone, Grant Ujifusa, and Douglas Matthews, *The Almanac of American Politics* (New York: E. P. Dutton, 1978, 1980); Barone and Ujifusa, *The Almanac of American Politics* (Washington, D.C.: National Journal, 1984–1990 biennial eds.).
a. Wyche Fowler, Jr., won the runoff and the general election.

took a legal fight for him to be seated. Once in the legislature, he clashed frequently with conservative whites, earning their contempt. The publicity over the senate seat and Bond's eloquence as a speaker kept him in the national eye. In 1968, at the Democratic Convention in Chicago, his name was placed into nomination for the vice presidency, and he won forty-eight votes. He became a much sought after public speaker and something of a celebrity, once guest-hosting NBC's "Saturday Night Live" show.[48] That Bond has been described by some Atlantians as a snob with a penchant for driving fancy sports cars indicates that his style may have proved alienating to the district's white voters.

Lewis's background can be contrasted with Bond's. Lewis was the son of an Alabama sharecropper and was one of ten children to rise above poverty. He was closely associated with Martin Luther King, Jr., and even after the heyday of the civil rights movement he continued to work for the cause. In 1963 Lewis gained national attention during the March on Washington when he was reprimanded by black leaders for a public statement considered too strong for the times. In 1965 he was among those severely beaten by the police in an attack on the Edmund Pettus Bridge during the march from Selma to Montgomery. Later he headed the Southern Regional Council's Voter Education Project. He held a series of public service jobs until 1981, when he was elected to the Atlanta city council. Lewis stayed on the council until he retired to make his second bid for Congress. He was generally popular with the white establishment: in 1977, when he ran and lost to Fowler, the *Atlanta Constitution* endorsed him, and it did so again in 1986.[49]

By contrast, Bond's detractors have portrayed him as a person who sat in an air-conditioned office during the civil rights movement writing press releases. Charles King, a consultant on racial relations, has argued that white voters were intimidated by Bond because they resented a smart black man who was quick on his feet.[50] However, the support that white Atlantians gave Andrew Young and Maynard Jackson, both well-educated blacks, would seem to refute King's argument. It was more likely that Bond was hurt by his poor performance in the state legislature than by his privileged background. He was inaccessible to constituents and had already nearly been defeated by a relatively unknown candidate in one of his state senate races. Many phone calls to his home were answered by a telephone answering machine advising callers to try again at another time.[51] Moreover, as the front-runner in the race against Lewis, he was the target of every candidate. A radio spot claimed that he was delinquent in federal taxes. He was portrayed as a racist, and he was characterized as lazy and difficult to motivate.[52] In general, Bond did not seem to demonstrate the qualities that constituents normally expect in their representative. It was easy for voters to see John Lewis as a work horse and Bond as a show horse.[53]

The differences in the candidates were also reflected in their speech patterns and in what Fenno refers to as their "presentations of self."[54] During their debates Bond was said to have "talked circles" around Lewis. According to commentators, Lewis's "slow and sometimes miscast speech became an issue in the campaign," but not necessarily a negative one—it pointed up differences between the black elite and the working class and helped establish him as an underdog. Some observers have described Lewis as being "more like the vast majority of black Atlantians whose families moved here from the country and who remain working-class or poor," and it has been said that "lower-class blacks could . . . identify with his poor speech."[55] Lewis's slow speech and

Bond's "silver tongue" provided voters with a strong contrast that did not hurt Lewis.[56]

The two candidates did not differ on major issues. Both supported sanctions against South Africa, opposed interventions in Central America, and were critical of the Reagan Administration. As a consequence, what would have ordinarily been nonissues became much more salient. Material in a book written by Bond almost fifteen years earlier, for instance, was used by his opponents in the primary to support accusations that his election would result in racial divisions.[57] It was easy to exploit the fears of white voters, because whites knew that a black would represent the district. For them, it was simply a question of who among several blacks was the most palatable.

Another important issue, especially for Lewis, was drug testing. In a controversy that was eventually picked up by the nationally syndicated Doonesbury comic strip, Lewis repeatedly challenged Bond to take a urine test. The issue carried over into the runoff: Lewis was able to present himself as the more conservative of the candidates and thus create a more negative image of Bond.

Lewis used his image as a hard worker to his advantage. While campaigning for office he walked the length of the district, wearing out three pairs of sneakers. Many nights he campaigned all night long, camping at twenty-four-hour grocery stores. At 6:00 A.M. he was often stationed at local subway stations. Lewis later said: "I sensed that we were going to win when small children would run for their parents, shouting, 'Here comes Mr. Lewis. Here comes the man we saw on television.'"[58] This image of a hard worker had its roots in his days as a civil rights activist and had been maintained during his terms on the city council.

He used television advertisements extensively during the campaign. One commercial showed a lit room in a dark office building, while a voice gave the time as 11:00 P.M.: John Lewis was still working. Another commercial showed a senior citizen speaking of how helpful the councilman had been to her. Some commercials focused on a *Time* magazine article from the 1960s in which Lewis was called a "living saint." It mentioned his long participation in the civil rights movement.

There has been much speculation about Lewis's victory. Lewis himself said: "I think the black and white electorate said that we are not going to be dictated to by the power structure. They saw me as a worker and a doer. They saw this guy walking from door to door, at shopping malls, theaters, and churches. They said that John Lewis really wants the job.

... The black leadership structure had the idea that they could endorse someone and that black people would flock to that person. They were mistaken."[59]

Lewis forged an unusual coalition of two very different disaffected groups to win his congressional seat—poor blacks and rich whites. Both groups felt equally left out of the black political establishment.[60] He was able to stir black consciousness because of his background and at the same time gain the support of white voters, many of whom found him the more likable of the two candidates.

Interactions with Constituents: Satisfying a Multiracial Coalition

Lewis was initially elected with 75 percent of the vote in a district with a 65 percent black population, where 60 percent of the blacks are of voting age. His reelection margins have steadily increased, and he has attracted no strong opposition. Much like black representatives from historically black districts, whether to represent the whites in his district has been a matter of choice rather than a requirement for reelection, and Lewis has chosen to maintain the biracial coalition that led to his initial election. His efforts to establish himself as a "humanitarian" have met with a mixed response from his constituents. Some resent his efforts on behalf of Cubans and Soviet Jews. In one town meeting in a black neighborhood a man rose to express his dissatisfaction with the black congressional delegation and its relationship with Israel. "Our neighborhood is not in support of Israel but our black politicians are voting with the Jewish bloc," the man complained. "They are voting in support of Israel. Too many of our black politicians are taking Jewish dollars. They speak one way in the white community and differently in the black." To this Lewis replied: "I can only speak for myself, John Lewis. I was elected to represent the people of this district, white, black, Hispanic, Asian, and Indian. As long as I am in Congress, I will represent them all."[61]

Lewis's staff was evenly divided between whites and blacks in 1988. Since then the number of blacks has slightly increased. Lewis maintains a large district presence but only one office, located in the downtown section of the city. The district office employs several full-time caseworkers, who specialize in different areas. One handles problems of old age, education, and state and local affairs. Another deals with small business, employment discrimination, and post office employees. Another focuses on the problems of the poor, such as food stamps, evictions, homelessness, and mental health.

The influence of Lewis's philosophy can be seen in his allocation of both personal and public resources. He has been extremely active, showering his district with attention. To communicate with his constituents, he sends newsletters every four months and holds town meetings every three weeks. On a typical constituent day, he sees thirty-five to forty people. They might ask for help with problems of discrimination or for intervention in prison paroles. Regardless of the nature of a constituent's concerns, the congressman and his staff exhibit compassion. As I sat in on office appointments, I saw several constituents who were convinced that people had cast evil spells on them, put things inside their bodies, were plotting to kill them, or steal children they had never had.[62] There was no condescension in the response of Lewis or his aides. According to Michael German, the district manager: "We try to treat each constituent with the respect that we would give our parents."

Often black constituents have unrealistic expectations of a congressman's job, something black representatives from each of the four district types experience over and over again. As Lewis remarked: "Many of my constituents, and especially the black ones, think that we can walk on water. They believe that we can make anything happen. . . . Just the other day I heard this lady use the phrase, 'We need somebody to take care of us.' There is a feeling on the part of many constituents that we, that government, have a moral obligation to take care of their needs, to put a roof over their house. To do something about things that we have no control over."[63] But attempting to intervene in such matters is part of Lewis's style of representation. On one of the days that I was in the district, he was absorbed in efforts to find a suitable solution to the problems of an elderly black woman who, although she had asked only for a new roof, was in need of much more. Her dilapidated house was without indoor plumbing, parts of the structure had rotted and caved in, and boards were strewn across the floor to mark safe stepping places. The congressman's major concern was how to solve the problem without having the city condemn the house and place the lady in a nursing home, where he was afraid she would die.

In expressing his consternation about the nature of the problems confronting the black poor, Lewis said: "It is difficult for the average constituent to understand how Congress operates. You say you are only one of 435, you have only one vote, you can write a letter or make a phone call but you can't do much alone. And that's why I say to my colleagues from time to time that we [black representatives] cannot create this false sense of hope. This false sense of optimism. You do what you can do, but we cannot lead people down a false alley."[64]

The problems of the black poor can be contrasted with the constituency requests from middle-class blacks who are primarily concerned about getting what they consider their "fair share" from programs that set aside contracts for black-owned businesses. Many black organizations also sought the congressman's help and influence with fund raising; college graduates came with résumés and requests for help in finding jobs.

Personal contact is at the heart of Lewis's interactions with constituents. Walking as little as two blocks with him can take as long as thirty minutes, because he stops to shake hands with almost everyone he meets. In speeches, he introduces himself as "the son of a sharecropper" or "a poor boy from Troy, Alabama." He makes a deliberate attempt to distinguish himself from Atlanta's black elites. His efforts in this regard no doubt affect the nature and volume of his casework.

Representation through Legislation: Life on the Hill

Lewis is a member of the Public Works and Transportation Committee and the Interior and Insular Affairs Committee, both of which are committees appropriate for him, given Atlanta's position as a national and international hub. He also co-chairs the Congressional Committee on Soviet Jewry and was named by the Speaker as a deputy whip in 1991. He likes to tell his constituents about how he spends his time in Washington:

> Being in Washington is exciting but hard work. I want to tell you what being a legislator is like. On a given day I see ten, fifteen, maybe twenty groups from all across the state: peanut, tobacco, and chicken farmers. On a typical day I am up by 6:00 A.M., usually by 5:00 A.M. By 6:30 I am in the office, where I leave my briefcase before going to the House gym to work out with other members. Around 8:00 A.M. are the breakfasts involving other people from Georgia. I stop in at each of these to show my face. There are also the committee meetings. I sit on the Public Works and Interior Committees. There are usually several meetings, then I may have to run to the House floor to cast an important vote. There may be several receptions during the evening.[65]

He has taken credit for legislation he called the "Lewis amendment," which allowed for contract set-asides for minority-owned businesses, and he has sponsored legislation to rename the federal building in Atlanta after Martin Luther King, Jr. He says this would make it the first federal building in the country to be named after King.

Lewis's voting record is among the more progressive in Congress. It is closer to that of nonsouthern blacks than it is to that of southern whites (see Table 3.3 and Appendix C). During the 100th Congress, Lewis scored 9 percent with the conservative coalition. His COPE scores are usually 100 percent, and he has a high voting participation record (96 percent). His progressive voting record seems to be consistent with the preferences of his district, which is fairly liberal. Although the fifth district voted for Nixon for President in 1972, it was progressive enough to elect a black congressman in the same year, and later presidential candidates Carter, Mondale, and Dukakis all carried the district.

Lewis has represented the more liberal policy preferences of his constituents. Although he supported drug testing during his 1986 congressional campaign, he has since backed away from that position, and he has cast votes that were not supportive of tobacco interests in the state. His positions are consistent with the preferences of the majority of Atlantians, who have always been more progressive than people in other parts of the South. Given the growing tensions between blacks and Jewish Americans, Lewis's position on issues relating to Israel and other Jewish concerns is controversial among the blacks in his district. Nevertheless, he prefers to rely on his conscience on these matters. He remembers a time when Jewish Americans were the staunchest supporters of civil rights for blacks. He seeks to mend that fractured relationship through his activities on behalf of Jewish causes and through his attempts at consciousness raising among his African-American constituents.

Newly Black Districts and the Need for Biracial Coalitions

The 1990s round of congressional redistricting created a number of newly black districts that black politicians should be able to win. Because the percentage of blacks of voting age in newly black districts is likely to be low, white voters will be the swing voters in each district. Successful candidates must therefore work hard to forge and maintain winning coalitions. Nothing about the representational styles of Mike Espy and John Lewis suggests that their choices diminished their ability to represent all the people in their congressional districts. They have worked much harder than the typical black representative from a historically black district. The performances of Espy and Lewis have shown that black politicians can represent the needs of their white constituents without neglecting the needs of the blacks in their districts.

5 · Black Representatives of Heterogeneous Districts

A mixed district makes my life easier because some ethnic groups will take on leadership roles. I have, for example, a 20 percent Jewish constituency who basically do their own fighting to get things for the district. This makes my life much easier because they can access places that would ordinarily be off-limits to a black representative from a black district.

—INTERVIEW WITH REPRESENTATIVE FLOYD FLAKE, *August 2, 1990*

Heterogeneous districts, as described here, are composed of three or more racial or ethnic groups, with no single group constituting over 50 percent of the population (see Table 5.1).[1] Representatives of racially heterogeneous districts must form biracial and multiracial coalitions. Although it might be assumed that the winning coalitions are between blacks and Hispanics, this is not always the case. Sometimes the coalitions are between black and Jewish voters who vote together to elect a black representative.[2] Because heterogeneous districts are likely to increase in number during the 1990s, they will provide a battleground on which members of various ethnic groups will fight among themselves for political opportunities. The diversity of the districts will mean that, by necessity, their representatives will have to be aware of and responsive to varied interests. These interests will of course conflict at times, when some groups gain, or appear to gain, at the expense of others.

What determines the likelihood that a multiracial coalition will form? How do the representatives of heterogeneous districts construct and maintain their coalitions? What types of representation do representatives of heterogeneous districts provide for the racial subgroups in their districts? We can answer some of these questions by studying two very different kinds of black representatives of heterogeneous districts: Mervyn Dymally (D-CA) and Floyd Flake (D-NY).

Table 5.1. Black representatives of heterogeneous districts

District	Principal city	Representative	Years served	BVAP 1980s	HVAP 1980s
CA-28	Los Angeles	Julian Dixon	1979–	37	24
CA-31	Compton	Mervyn Dymally	1981–1992	31	18
TX-18	Houston	Barbara Jordan	1973–1978	39	27
		Mickey Leland	1979–1989	39	27
		Craig Washington	1990–		
NY-6	Queens	Alton Waldon, Jr.	1986	47	8
		Floyd Flake	1987–	47	8
NY-11	Brooklyn	Edolphus Towns	1983–	47	4
NY-16	Harlem[a]	Adam C. Powell, Jr.	1945–1967		
		Adam C. Powell, Jr.	1969–1970		
		Charles Rangel	1971–	49	35

Sources: Linda Williams, ed., *The JCPS Congressional District Fact Book*, 3rd ed. (Washington, D.C.: Joint Center for Political Studies, 1988), p. 20; *Congressional Quarterly Weekly Report*, November 10, 1990, pp. 3822–3823; "The 101st Congress, 1989–1990," Congressional Black Caucus Foundation, September 1990.

Note: BVAP = Black voting-age percentage of district population; HVAP = Hispanic voting-age percentage of district population.

a. During the 1960s, when it had a population that was 72 percent black and 10 percent Hispanic, Harlem was the eighteenth district; after the 1970 redistricting it became the sixteenth district and was 59 percent black and 17 percent Hispanic.

The Thirty-First District of California: Mervyn Dymally

Recent History

The thirty-first district of California is one of the most racially and culturally diverse in the nation. It is 33 percent white, 31 percent black, 18 percent Hispanic, and 8 percent Asian. Located in the southwestern corner of Los Angeles, the district encompasses several adjacent suburbs, including Inglewood, Hawthorne, and Compton. Connecting the cities is Harbor Gateway, a name given in 1984 to the eight-mile-long, four-block stretch of land that runs from the central part of the Los Angeles district to the harbor cities. As might be expected, the strip takes on the ethnic character of each town it passes through: to the north lies the city of Compton, whose population is heavily black; to the south is Gardenia, mostly Asian American; Lynwood and Paramount, mostly Mexican American; and Bellflower, mostly white.[3] The district has not always been so ethnically diverse. In 1960 only a fraction of the district's population was black (16 percent); ten years later blockbusting (realtors' concerted efforts to sell houses in white neighborhoods to blacks, an action that is designed to cause white flight) and other factors resulted in a district that was 41 percent black, with most of this population concentrated in Compton. By 1990 the overall black voting-age percentage of the population was 31 percent. Overwhelmingly Democratic, the district's predominantly working-class constituents find that unemployment, crime, and gang violence have become part of everyday life.

The Expansionist Stage: Dymally's Electoral Strategy

In 1980 Mervyn Dymally, a former California assemblyman and the state's first black state senator and lieutenant governor, was elected from the thirty-first district. A native of Trinidad, West Indies, Dymally came to the United States in 1946 and completed his bachelor's degree at California State University, Los Angeles, in 1954. He went on to earn his master's from California State University, Sacramento, in 1969, and in 1978 he received his Ph.D. from the United States International University in San Diego. Upon his election, he joined two other black representatives in the Los Angeles area, Augustus Hawkins (D-29th) and Julian Dixon (D-28th).

To win his seat in Congress, Dymally defeated Charles Wilson, a white Democratic incumbent of nine terms, and Mark Hannaford, a former representative of a neighboring district, in the primary election. Dymally was favored by the circumstances. Not only was he a former lieutenant governor with statewide name recognition, but Charles Wilson was enmeshed in a scandal and had been politically weakened by a House censure for converting campaign funds to personal use. There was a general perception among political observers that Wilson had lost touch with the racial and ethnic minorities in his district. He was spending too much of his time traveling abroad, and he was virtually unknown in the black community. "He seldom visited Compton, and he seemed totally unaware of changes in the district," Dymally remarked. "Sure, he had black surrogates, but he took the district for granted."[4]

Dymally's decision to challenge Wilson came after a member of the Compton city council suggested that he do so. At first he was not enthusiastic about the idea of challenging an incumbent, particularly because he had just been defeated in a statewide election and had made plans to spend time out of the country. He described to me how he had initially responded with much skepticism, largely because he had been the chairman of the Reapportionment Committee in 1971, when the district was 18 percent black, and he believed that a much higher percentage of blacks was needed to elect a black representative: he had written his Ph.D. thesis on the subject of economic and political factors influencing the electoral chances of black congressional candidates, and he was not encouraged by what he found in his research. "I went back to [the city councilman] and said: 'Why should I run?'" Dymally explained. "And he told me that other candidates were lining up and I should, too." Among these other candidates was Hannaford, who had moved into the district to run against the seriously weakened Wilson.

An experienced candidate himself, Dymally conducted his own "innovative type of research." He recounted the steps he took:

> We went and parked in front of high schools to see the population mix, and what we saw startled us. The white kids were not coming out of those high schools—they were Hispanics and blacks, and Asians; these were once all-white schools. Then we went to eat in the restaurants and they were black ones: restaurants which I had known to be all-white many years ago, and there was a different mix. Then we began looking at the white churches; some of them had pulled out, but others had congregations that were all black. Then we went to UCLA [University of California at Los Angeles] to look at the voting patterns in that district, and with the exception of Proposition 13, they had voted on the liberal side.[5]

Next he conducted a name identification survey and found that while over 75 percent of the registered voters had heard of him, only 45 percent had heard of the incumbent.[6] That voters were so familiar with Dymally's name gave him an important advantage over Wilson. Dymally followed this survey with a study of past elections. First, he analyzed the unsuccessful bid for attorney general by Yvonne Burke, a former member of Congress, and found that Burke had carried the thirty-first district. Next he studied the reelection bid of Chief Justice of the State Supreme Court Rose Byrd, a liberal white female, who had been reelected with 90 percent of the district vote. Last, he noted how Proposition 13—a proposal to reduce property taxes—had fared in the district: "I construed that their conservative vote [in favor of] Proposition 13 was a good omen, because it suggested they were all homeowners and they were protecting their turf. Clearly, the voters were sophisticated enough to respond to an issue-based campaign."

In the process of gathering these data, Dymally also noticed that in the lieutenant governor's race he had won the district over a white candidate. "That," he points out, "was another good omen. We then reasoned that for the challenger to defeat the incumbent, he had to attack him, so we let them fight it out in the white community and I just picked up the pieces in the black community."[7]

Dymally could select this strategy because he was the only black in a Democratic primary that included two popular white candidates (see Table 5.2). Using a strategy that was later to be imitated by other black politicians, he allowed the white candidates to attack each other while he concentrated on winning his ethnic base.

Raising campaign money was not a significant problem for Dymally. He proudly told me that his campaign had raised and spent more (over $500,000) than any other black congressional candidate had for a House seat. "Much of the money," said Dymally, "was raised from old sources. I had a statewide constituency. Of course labor did not support me the first time because they had already endorsed the incumbent."[8] The liberal political machine run first by U.S. Representative Henry Waxman (D-CA) and later by Assemblyman Howard L. Berman (D-CA) also helped.

Political endorsements were important, as well. Dymally's approach

Table 5.2. The election history of Mervyn Dymally

Year	Primary election opponents	Vote total (percentage)		General election opponents	Vote total (percentage)	
1980	Dymally	29,916	(49%)	Dymally	69,146	(64%)
	Hannaford	14,512	(24)	Grimshaw	38,203	(36)
	Wilson	9,320	(15)			
	two others	7,192	(12)			
1982	Dymally	43,498	(77)	Dymally	86,718	(72)
	Mitchell	7,146	(13)	Minturn	33,043	(28)
	O'Brien	5,631	(10)			
1984	Dymally	50,844	(84)	Dymally	100,658	(71)
	Smith	9,699	(16)	Minturn	41,691	(29)
1986	Dymally	40,339	(85)	Dymally	77,126	(70)
	Zondervan	7,394	(15)	McMurray	30,322	(28)
1988	Dymally	58,806	(85)	Dymally	100,919	(72)
	O'Brien	10,037	(15)	May	36,017	(26)

Sources: Michael Barone, Grant Ujifusa, and Douglas Matthews, *The Almanac of American Politics* (New York: E. P. Dutton, 1978, 1980); Barone and Ujifusa, *The Almanac of American Politics* (Washington, D.C.: National Journal, 1984–1990 biennial eds.).

was creative. Despite his reputation as a liberal, earned during his days in the state assembly and senate, he sought and won support from local and state police organizations:

> Police organizations used to regard me as a Black Muslim, Communist, radical because I was opposed to police brutality. But eventually I went to the police officers and said: "Look: there are two aspects of your advocacy here. One is guns and bullets and one is bread and butter." I said: "The liberals provide bread and butter for you, provide uniforms, overtime, scholarships. When you get shot and your wife is left with your kids, the conservatives are not around. The Democrats provide the basic support system." So, the police officers started changing their positions and looking at issues other than gun control, and they endorsed me.[9]

The strongest candidates are usually those who make politics a career,[10] and Dymally's status as a professional politician is evident in his carefully planned strategy. He never took his entrance into the race lightly, and he was at an advantage in the primary because there was more than one white candidate and there was no runoff primary. Once he had his party's nomination, it was a simple matter to win the House seat in the traditionally Democratic district that had in the past given its support to Democratic party presidential nominees Hubert Humphrey, George McGovern, Jimmy Carter, Walter Mondale, and Michael Dukakis. Dymally has not had any close elections since his initial win in 1980.

Interactions with Constituents: The Challenge of Representing a Multiracial Coalition

Dymally maintains a single district office in the city of Compton, one of the most crime-ridden areas in his district. The once predominantly white city began to change after the Watts riot of August 1965, when whites fled to areas such as Carson, Bellflower, and Hawthorne. Now violence permeates Compton. Near the congressman's office is a skyscraper, the tallest building in the city. Directing my attention to the new plates of glass, Dymally lamented: "Thugs take turns at shooting out the windows." One staffer commented that he and his colleagues feel they take their lives in their hands when they come to work each morning. He estimated that a murder a week was not uncommon for Compton. The city has no major industry, and about 60 percent of its population relies on some type of public assistance. In April 1992, in the rioting after the Rodney King verdict, Compton and surrounding areas suffered heavy property damage.

Prior to the passage of the Gramm-Rudman deficit reduction law, Dymally maintained two district offices—one of them in Hawthorne, a mostly white community. The two offices were consolidated as a budget-reducing move and as a way to improve communication, casework, and staff control. In addition to the budget constrictions, Dymally was also concerned that constituents might call one of the district offices and find it closed because of an overall shortage of staff or that the service would not be good enough because of poor communication between the two offices; he decided that a single office providing fast, efficient service would be superior to two uncoordinated ones. Given the sharp contrasts between the cities of Compton and Hawthorne, I asked Dymally how he decided which of the two offices to close. He replied that keeping open the Compton office fulfilled a campaign promise to have a presence in a black neighborhood. The biggest disadvantage associated with the current location, he stated, was a sharp reduction in casework from the district's white voters, many of whom are reluctant to enter Compton. Still, in the period when I observed him, more whites than blacks visited the Compton office and requested constituency service; Dymally termed this "an unusual flow of traffic."

Sometimes Dymally takes on casework from outside the district. "I'm not going to turn anyone away," he said. "By the time people reach my office, generally they have exhausted all other avenues." A champion of black businesses nationally, Dymally elaborated: "Who in this country is going to help a black firm in trouble? A white congressman from Louisiana? If a black member of Congress can't do it, who can?"[11] His belief that he has a mandate to represent a broader constituency has, for example, made him fight on behalf of congressional staffers who were often asked to work long hours without overtime compensation.[12]

Dymally's staff is one of the most racially diverse in Congress. It almost perfectly mirrors the racial makeup of his district. When I visited him in 1988, the district office employed one white, one Hispanic, one Asian, one Pacific Islander, and one American Indian. His Washington office had four African Americans, three whites, one Arab, one Hispanic, and one African. The racial makeup of his staff is a large source of pride for Dymally. "This," he said, "represents unbiased hiring." On the face of it, it appears to be the result of a more deliberate effort. A handout about a young scholars' program that Dymally's office sponsors reflects a concern with racial diversity. The brochure states that the program will select one Asian, one Samoan, one white female, two Hispanics, and four blacks for participation. The racial diversity among Dymally's employees is also related to the goal of hiring staffers who can speak the languages that are most common in the district. Having people of different racial backgrounds on hand to receive and relay information can lead to better representation of the district, and it shows a sensitivity to minority interests. Representative Mickey Leland, from Houston, Texas, had a similar staffing pattern in a district of similar racial diversity. His 1988 staff consisted of four whites, six blacks, and five members of other races. Leland's district office administrator commented that the racial diversity of the staff was intentional and paid off in the form of increased electoral support in the district.

Dymally's contact with his constituents follows a regular routine. He tries to send out some form of communication each month. During a typical year, newsletters are mailed at the beginning of each season. The mailings are followed by personal appearances in every city in the district, where, as Dymally puts it: "Rap sessions are held. They beat up on me and I beat up on them with conciliation." In addition breakfasts, lunches, gospel meetings, and conferences are regularly scheduled events. Dymally's annual fund raisers are gala affairs involving top media personalities.

To maintain his multiracial coalition, much of Dymally's efforts have centered on educating his district's significant minority population. When I asked him about his objectives for the district, he replied: "I'm trying to get the foreign ethnics to understand how this whole thing works [the American system]. I am concentrating on building coalitions with Asians, Koreans, Indians, Arabs, and other groups. Many are inactive because they have not yet been fully socialized to the political process."[13] Like many other black representatives, he therefore holds a number of educational forums.

As a consequence of his activities at home and abroad, Dymally has support that extends beyond his district's constituents. He was one of the early sponsors of the Japanese Reparations Bill. Arab Americans and East Indians in cities such as Detroit have held major fund-raising events for him. Hispanics in his district, however, have not been a prominent part of his coalition, largely because of their socioeconomic competition with blacks: they maintain that blacks are monopolizing jobs and political positions. But many undocumented aliens trust him enough to come to the district office and ask for help in obtaining legal status.

Jewish voters are also not a prominent part of Dymally's reelection constituency, because of his outspoken pro-Palestinian stance. The issue of Israel poses a major problem for black representatives, because they are closely watched by their black constituents whenever they make or seem to make concessions to Jewish constituents. Generally, Israel is a no-win situation. As Dymally said: "If I had a 30 percent Jewish district and the rest black, I would get support from the black community. Because by and large, [even though] the majority of blacks in the Black Caucus support Israel . . . their constituents don't. . . . If a black representative were in trouble, as evidenced by Gus Savage [D-Chicago], and Jewish people tried to make that an issue, the blacks in the district would come to the rescue."[14] He later qualified this statement by adding:

> . . . especially if you point out that your disagreement has nothing to do with Jewishness, it has to do with Israel. And that your record on Jewishness is a very good one, that you support Jews against desecration of their temples, you support them in the effort against discrimination, against anti-Semitism. That on your domestic record regarding American Jews you have a better record than some Jews in the Congress, but on Israel you disagree and you disagree because you think it is unfair to oppress the Palestinians and it is outrageous for the Israelis to be giving arms to South Africa to kill blacks. But if you had a majority of Jews [in the district], you would lose because most Jews do not see you as being anti-Shamir or anti-oppression or pro–Palestinian human rights, they see you as anti-Semitic and anti-Jewish, and anti-Israel, so it is difficult, if not impossible, to separate one from the other. [To Jewish voters,] you cannot be pro-Jewish and be anti-Israel.[15]

In spite of this perception, Dymally takes pains to explain that he is not anti-Israel, that he has supported foreign aid to the Israelis, and that he has often spoken out on their behalf. Nonetheless, his active support of black Jews who wish to emigrate to Israel is a source of friction, because the Israelis refuse to recognize the group.

Dymally is deeply involved in the international affairs that affect many of his constituents, and he is keenly aware of California's changing demography. He claims that soon his state will have a "Third World majority." One of his constituency mailings asked for monetary contributions for the following organizations: Americans Against Apartheid, African-American Political Action Committee (A-A PAC), Caribbean-American Political Action Committee (C-A PAC), and the Eighth District Coalition. On occasion he has negotiated with unpopular world leaders, such as President Mobutu Sese Seko of Zaire. This meeting, along with accusations that he gutted his own South African diamond sanctions bill, evoked criticism from groups such as the Rainbow Lobby and the New Alliance Party, which passed on damaging claims about him to the press.[16]

Dymally is incensed by the charges that he weakened his own legislation banning the import of South African diamonds after the diamond importer Maurice Templesman donated $34,500 to a young scholars' program in honor of the late Representative Mickey Leland.[17] Dymally says that when he met with Templesman the bill had already been amended in committee. According to him: "The story was a false plant. I never gutted any bill. The committee amended the bill because they did not have the votes. I was not a member of the committee at the time. This charge is too outrageous to be treated lightly. It is total bullshit from a white racist reporter."[18] In support of his contentions, Dymally cited a letter from Representative Howard Wolpe (D-MI), the former chairman of the Africa subcommittee, that confirmed his absence from the committee when the compromises were made.

Although this controversy has not caused him much trouble with his constituency, it has prompted him to sever his ties with numerous groups, including the African-American and Caribbean-American political action committees. He explained his decision: "It wasn't worth it. These things are mostly paper tigers. You take a beating for being part of a paper tiger. . . . These [newspaper] stories give the impression that I was wheeling and dealing, but here it is: a guy is a friend of yours and he gives you a campaign donation in 1980 and then comes in 1989 and asks for your help. What do you say?"[19]

In addition to his political activities, Dymally belongs to the American Political Science Association, and he has published numerous articles on black politics and has edited several books. He considers speaking with academicians an important part of his role as a congressman. Despite his sensitivity over the diamond issue, Dymally claims that he is not worried about reporters and says that he has nothing to hide from potential spies. He knows his own strengths and weaknesses, and he is confident and aware of the importance of the presentation of self.

Representation through Legislation: Making the Tough Decisions

Dymally is a member of the House committees on Foreign Affairs, the District of Columbia, and the Post Office and Civil Service—a sign of the variety of his interests. His voting record is similar to that of other black representatives. He scored 100 percent on both the COPE scale and the LCCR index, but his voting participation score of 87 percent was slightly below the congressional average of 92 percent (see Appendix C). He has supported bills advocating honesty in the car rental business, stronger enforcement of support payments, civil rights in Micronesia, and more fairness in awarding oil and gas leases on federal lands to minority firms. On the issue of defense he has not had a clear line: in a two-year span he voted for, present, and against continued funding for the MX missile, which was manufactured in his district. The "yes" vote placed him in the uncomfortable position of being the only liberal in his state to support continued funding for the missile, and this offended poor blacks, who felt excluded from jobs with defense contractors. Dymally has described the MX vote as the "toughest decision of my twenty years in politics."[20]

Dymally's constituency interactions and the maintenance of his coalition depend on his service record and the presence of liberal whites and of ethnic groups with Third World ties. The racial composition of his district continues to be very important in his political decisions, and it influences his choice of coalition partners. If the thirty-first district had had a higher white population, Dymally might not have run for Congress, and if Jewish voters had constituted a larger percentage of the population, he would have had to adopt a very different political style in order to be elected. He, like most black members of Congress, would have been forced to remain silent on the Palestinian issue; but because he is not dependent on Jewish voters for reelection, he has been more vocal. Overall Dymally's style is mild and nonconfrontational. The diversity in his district has given him more freedom than that enjoyed by black representatives of newly black districts.

The Sixth District of New York: Floyd Flake

Recent History

The sixth district of New York in southern Queens includes southern Jamaica, St. Albans, Howard Beach, and Rockaway. The district, once a purely middle-class white area, is now 47 percent black, 8 percent Hispanic, and 1 percent other, but continues to have a substantial white population (44 percent). Most of the poorer blacks live in south Jamaica; it is there that we find the poverty, crime, homelessness, and other serious problems that affect so many urban areas. White flight and racial tensions have characterized some parts of the district since the early 1980s. In 1981 white parents from the Rosedale area organized and protested against the busing of their children to achieve integration. Howard Beach, a predominantly white enclave in this racially mixed district, made national headlines in 1986 when three blacks entered a neighborhood pizza parlor and were chased and beaten by a gang of white teenagers; one of the black men died when he ran onto a freeway to escape the gang and was struck by a passing car. The district had always been represented by whites until 1986, when Reverend Floyd Flake was elected as its first full-term black congressman.

The Expansionist Stage: The Minister-Congressman at Work

The district's political life had been shaped by Joseph Addabbo, a liberal to moderate Democrat who had represented it for twenty-four years. His seat became open when he died in 1986, and a special election was held to fill the last few months of his unexpired term. Alton Waldon, Jr., a black assemblyman, won the seat in an election fraught with irregularities. Somehow the Reverend Floyd Flake's name was inadvertently left off the absentee ballots, and after winning the special election with 167 votes, he lost when the absentee ballots were counted.[21] Because a state court upheld the legality of the first contest, Waldon served until Flake defeated him several months later (see Table 5.3). Waldon lost despite his strategic use of his brief period of incumbency, during which he blanketed the district with literature showing him in his congressional role—standing in front of the Capitol, in conference with Senator Edward Kennedy, and with Governor Mario Cuomo. He was never able to achieve true legitimacy, however. Flake stressed the irregularities in the special election, and at the same time he promoted his own vision for transforming the district.

Flake, who had no prior political experience or ambitions, easily won the election. He recalls that he was recruited to run for the seat: "I became interested in running for Congress when the clergy and civic people asked me if I would run. At first I had no interest in politics other than just being involved to the degree of wanting good representation. I wanted us to have the kind of representation that would allow us to change this community."[22] Once in the race, he campaigned as a moderate who supported tuition tax credits but opposed Medicaid fund-

Table 5.3. The election history of Floyd Flake

Year	Primary election opponents	Vote total (percentage)		General election opponents	Vote total (percentage)	
1986 (special election)				Flake	12,378	(49%)
				Waldon, Jr.	12,674	(51)
1986	Flake	22,328	(46%)	Flake	58,317	(68)
	Waldon, Jr.	18,968	(39)	Dietl	27,773	(32)
	Golar	3,387	(7)			
	James	3,387	(7)			
1988	Flake	Unopposed		Flake	94,506	(86)
				Brandofino	15,547	(14)

Sources: Michael Barone, Grant Ujifusa, and Douglas Matthews, *The Almanac of American Politics* (New York: E. P. Dutton, 1978, 1980); Barone and Ujifusa, *The Almanac of American Politics* (Washington, D.C.: National Journal, 1984–1990 biennial eds.).

ing for abortions. Like most black politicians, he opposed both the death penalty and aid to the Contras in Nicaragua.

Flake's campaign style was clearly influenced by his status as senior minister of the Allen African Methodist Episcopal Church, which provided him with his political base. The church is run like a huge business enterprise. It includes a 300-unit senior citizens' home, a church school with 480 students (kindergarten to eighth grade), numerous small businesses, and social welfare agencies that provide clinical services, pregnancy counseling, and prenatal care. Most of the institutions, spanning several blocks, were built between 1980 and 1990. A former marketing analyst for Xerox and a Boston University official, Flake's ties to the district extend back for more than a decade. Under his leadership the church grew from an institution with 1,400 members and an annual budget of $250,000 to a concern with 5,000 members, 1,000 employees, and an annual budget of $12 million.

Crucial to Flake's success in defeating Waldon were the endorsement he received from the *New York Times* and strong support from Mayor Ed Koch. Since his first election Flake has not had any tough reelection bids and was easily reelected in 1990 despite his and his wife's criminal indictment in the summer of that year for embezzlement and tax evasion.[23] These charges were later dismissed after the judge decided that the prosecution had been overly zealous and that there was not enough evidence against the Flakes. It was Flake's close financial relationship with the church that had given rise to the suspicions.

Interactions with Constituents: Ministering to the District

Flake and his family live in the district, where he maintains two district offices. He compares the way he runs them with running a corporation. He explained to me: "I'm in politics and I'm in the ministry, but I've been with Xerox and I've been with Reynolds Tobacco, and I've been a college administrator, so this is a business to me. My chief of staff is a Harvard MBA, so we run [these offices] as a business that sets goals and objectives and measures productivity."[24] He said that when the Democratic National Campaign Committee conducted a study of congressional offices in 1986, it cited his offices as being especially well run because he understood the "business aspects of politics."

The church-affiliated institutions provide Flake with many opportunities to interact with his black constituents, and because he has initiated so many of the activities that have transformed the neighborhoods, it is difficult to discern where his constituency service ends and his ministry begins. "When I talk about an AIDS crisis or when I talk about a crisis of drugs, I'm actually involved in counseling families in those areas, so it's a whole different kind of matter. My contention was," he said, "that first of all, I had an obligation to get the church involved in the process of understanding its obligations. If it's going to worship in this community, it has an obligation to take care of it." According to Flake, before his revitalization efforts, the black neighborhoods in his district were in serious decline. Pointing up and down the street, he said: "This whole area was really run down. If you look on the corner of Linden and Merrick, which is just up the block, there's a $3.8 million school. On that block was an old, what they called Benson Burger restaurant that nobody could keep open. It was vacant with the windows out. Actually the winos slept over there, and the drug dealers used that corner . . . straight up the block here on Merrick going from the office there were just stores that were graffitied and some were boarded up and not well taken care of, so when we bought those eleven stores we rehabilitated them."[25]

Flake's constituents have accorded him celebrity status. One told me: "Before the Reverend was elected, our leaders would pass us by on the street without even speaking to us. Our so-called leaders that were supposed to speak *for* us would not even speak *to* us."[26] He is revered in much the same way that the late Adam Clayton Powell, Jr., another New York minister-congressman, was.

Flake's reforms have met with opposition from local drug dealers whom he tried to oust from the community. Several death threats have been made against him. He has encountered other problems as well: in 1988 a former church worker charged him with sexual harassment and tried to get him fired.[27] After this attempt failed, the woman was instrumental in spurring the criminal investigation for tax evasion and embezzlement already mentioned.

Like Atlanta's John Lewis, Flake finds that many of his black constituents have unrealistic expectations of a congressman's role: "Unfortunately black constituents demand very little of white elected officials when they are serving their communities, and they demand the world from black officials once they elect them. When a black official is elected by that same black constituency, they demand everything of them and the reality is you cannot deliver on all of the things that they demand and so there's an almost immediate turning on you, whereas they historically have had years and years and years of white leadership for which there was not a turning on."[28] Other black politicians have reached similar conclusions about their black constituents. Flake believes that their level of expectation is so high that it can never be met by a black representative trying to bring about substantive changes through the political process.

Perhaps because of his businesslike approach to matters, Flake is not shy about asking others for help. He credits former representative Joseph Addabbo with helping him with his building projects: "Addabbo helped me tremendously on the federally funded senior citizens project, even though the church had to put out some money. But the reality is that without his help, we would have built 100 units instead of 300. Addabbo called HUD together and called the U.S. senators—I think Javits was in at that point, and Moynihan—and we all met in his office, and he told them he wanted their support."[29] One more sign of Flake's nondoctrinaire approach was his ability to work with Ed Koch, who while serving as mayor of New York City was a highly controversial and much criticized figure in the black community.

> When we ran into problems like issues of the building department or getting a certificate of occupancy, and that kind of stuff, generally his people would respond because I had developed a relationship with the mayor's office beyond the personality and politics of the individual. When I needed to get things done, I could always call somebody in that office and know that it would get done. . . . I have also supported people like Senator Al D'Amato, who is a Republican, so that when I needed help from the Senate, especially since I have been in Congress . . . I've been able to lean on that

historical relationship and get the Senate Office to respond in a way that I don't think I could have done had I been partisan prior to becoming an elected official in a democratically controlled district.[30]

Balancing the various interests of his constituency consumes much of Flake's time. In his racially heterogeneous district, white support is crucial. Still, Flake claims that if he were given the opportunity, he would not exchange his district for one with a higher percentage of blacks, because he feels that the district's current racial composition allows him to be the most effective. He frequently finds himself relying on his Jewish constituents, who often have strong connections with influential people. Understanding the complexity and potential power of the black-Jewish relationship in America is crucial to his ability to represent the needs of his district:

> You take an issue like foreign affairs. You have a predominantly black district where the primary concern is about what's happening in South Africa. You have a Jewish constituency whose primary concern is about what's going to happen to Israel. You have an Irish constituency whose concern is about what's happening in Ireland, but also in terms of what's happening with Joe Doherty and so forth, so there is constantly a balancing act. The greatest balancing act, though, comes between the conflict of African-Americans and Jewish people simply because the Jewish people see their need for a response to Israel, which is more important than their demands for responses on immediate issues, whereas your African-American constituency is dealing with survival issues—housing, food, problems with food stamps, being on a waiting list for two years to get a place in public housing—which are not federal issues.[31]

As Flake described the competing interests and expectations of the various groups, it became clear that he believed his Jewish constituents were more informed than his other constituents about what to anticipate from a congressman. He has sought to educate his district's minority voters about the duties of a federal representative: "I probably have more town hall meetings than anybody because a part of the process is education. I do an article in one of the local newspapers, in which we discuss legislative matters, so that people will understand that the pruning of trees does not fall under my responsibility."[32]

His constituents were extremely loyal throughout his criminal trial, and he knew that he could count on their support. Flake knew that despite criticisms, bickering, or signs of jealousy, black constituents would be most supportive during a crisis involving one of their own leaders. Even if blacks criticize a black politician, it is rare for them to vote against that person in the next election. Black constituents will still vote for "one of their own." Flake comments: "I think we are an emotional people who are responsive to crises much more than we are to ongoing kinds of situations, so that if a crisis comes, blacks will galvanize and be responsive for that moment. But you cannot hold their attention span much beyond that. Once you get beyond that crisis, they go back to doing what they're doing. They may support you even more fervently during the moment of the crisis, but when that crisis is over, that's the end of that."[33] Thus, Flake seems to benefit from the freedom that African Americans give to their black politicians.

Representation through Legislation: Working on the Hill

Flake is a member of the Committee on Banking, Finance, and Urban Affairs, the Small Business Committee, and the Select Committee on Hunger. Except for the issues of abortion and his support for tuition tax credits for private schools, he is as liberal as other black representatives and northern Democrats, and has had comparable COPE and LCCR scores (see Table 3.3 and Appendix C). His voting participation score (88 percent), however, was below the congressional average (92 percent). He has been active in shaping new legislation. When he was on the banking committee, he attached an amendment to an omnibus housing bill to provide for the timely repair of equipment systems in public housing. He was also an active participant in the overhauling of minority set-aside programs for federal contracts. In addition, he was the primary sponsor of the Mickey Leland Peace Dividend Housing Act of 1990—legislation designed to provide assistance to people living in poverty who pay more than 50 percent of their income in rent. Explaining his support for the legislation, Flake said: "If we can spend over $160 billion to bail out the Savings and Loan industry, we can surely spend two cents of each federal dollar for housing."[34]

Flake's political style is similar to that of representatives who eventually move up into the higher echelons of the House power structure. He failed in his attempt to win a seat on the Budget Committee, however, possibly because of his then still pending criminal indictment. Also, although Flake has been diplomatic and skillful at building coalitions and is not afraid to cross party lines in search of support, he tends to be outspoken and frank on issues that are important to him, and this alienates some people. Floyd Flake is part of the new generation of black politicians who work within the system, but he is sometimes more assertive than the others.[35]

What Are the Constraints of Heterogeneous Districts?

We have seen that representatives of heterogeneous districts can have very different relationships with the racial and ethnic groups that sent them to Congress. Dymally, for example, understands, fights for, and depends more heavily on blacks and on his constituents with Third World ties. His empathy and personal concern for refugees, illegal aliens, and nonwhite immigrants has clearly affected his political style in his constituency and in Washington. His is a mission of education and advocacy. Because Jewish voters make up only a tiny percentage of his district, he has been able to take some controversial stances that many black representatives would seek to avoid, but Dymally still considers himself pro–Jewish American and laments the fact that one cannot be critical of Israel and supportive of Jewishness at the same time.

Flake, in contrast, is in a very different political situation and has a much better relationship with the greater number of Jewish constituents in his district. He has spent a considerable amount of time engaged in the delicate balancing act necessary to keep all groups, especially the black and Jewish populations, as content as possible. Flake believes he has a good record on the issues that concern his Jewish constituents, and he has asked them to help him whenever he thought he needed their clout.

Nevertheless, the legislative records of both representatives are not so different from those of other black members of Congress. Both were able to win the necessary support from their districts' key racial and ethnic groups. Dymally has enhanced his ability to maintain his winning coalition by convincing his constituents of his sincerity, by not trying to aggrandize himself through his office, and by having one of the most ethnically balanced staffs in the Congress. Flake, who also has a racially diverse staff, has enhanced his ability to get white support when needed by maintaining his friendships with Ed Koch and with Republican leaders in his state and in the House.

6 · Black Representatives of Majority-White Districts

There are no magical formulas for electing black representatives from majority-white districts. Black candidates can be elected in a wide variety of circumstances from a wide variety of backgrounds. If I can be elected in a majority-white district, so can a lot of other black candidates.

—INTERVIEW WITH REPRESENTATIVE ALAN WHEAT, *October 28, 1988*

Although over 90 percent of the nation's congressional districts with white majorities have white representatives, a few have elected black representatives at some point in their history (see Table 6.1). Generally, elections of black candidates from predominantly white districts are dismissed as flukes. Because any significant growth in the number of black representatives must come in majority-white districts, however, it is useful to consider how blacks get nominated in these areas and how they win (or fail to win) reelection. What type of representation do they provide their constituents? Are they more conservative on legislative issues than black representatives from historically black districts? What factors cause some of them to fail in their endeavors to forge biracial coalitions? By closely examining the styles, strategies, and elections of Alan Wheat (D-MO), Katie Hall (D-IN), and Ron Dellums (D-CA) we can begin to answer these questions.

The Fifth District of Missouri: Alan Wheat

Recent History

The mostly urban fifth district of Missouri has its heart in Kansas City. The city is important both as a manufacturing center and as a market

116

Table 6.1. Black representatives of majority-white districts

District	Principal city	Representative	Years served	BVAP	HVAP
CN-5	Waterbury	Gary Franks	1991–	4	3
MO-5	Kansas City	Alan Wheat	1983–	20	2
IN-1	Gary	Katie Hall	1982–1984	22	7
CA-8	Berkeley	Ronald Dellums	1971–	24	6
GA-5	Atlanta	Andrew Young[a]	1973–1977	40	1
IL-7	Chicago[b]	George Collins	1971–1973	44	3
TN-8	Memphis[c]	Harold E. Ford	1975–	47	1
MO-1	St. Louis[d]	William Clay	1969–	46	1

Sources: Compiled from data in Linda Williams, ed., *The JCPS Congressional District Fact Book,* 3rd ed. (Washington, D.C.: Joint Center for Political Studies, 1988); *Congressional Quarterly Weekly Report,* November 10, 1990, pp. 3822–3823; "The 101st Congress, 1989–1990," Congressional Black Caucus Foundation, September 1990; Michael Barone, Grant Ujifusa, Douglas Matthews, *The Almanac of American Politics* (Washington, D.C.: National Journal, 1984–1990 biennial eds.).

Note: BVAP = Black voting-age percentage of district population at the time the representative was in office; HVAP = Hispanic voting-age percentage of district population at the time the representative was in office.

a. Resigned his seat on January 29, 1977, to become U.S. ambassador to the United Nations.

b. Majority-black district since the redistricting of the 1980s.

c. Majority-black district since the redistricting of the 1980s, now the ninth district.

d. Historically black until the redistricting of the 1980s lowered the BVAP.

for farmers' cattle and winter wheat. IBM and Hallmark are among the major industries in the district, and in recent years the federal government has been a big employer. The heavily Democratic district includes part of the towns of Independence and Lee's Summit and was the home of President Harry S. Truman. Fittingly, it contains the Harry Truman Sports Complex and other institutions named after the former President.[1]

The population of the fifth congressional district is 20 percent black. The district does have pockets of poverty, but overall its socioeconomic characteristics vary significantly from those typically found in historically black districts. Over 60 percent of fifth district homes are owner occupied, compared with 52 and 41 percent, respectively, of homes in

Bill Gray's and George Crockett's historically black congressional districts.[2] Thirty-three percent of fifth district voters have college educations. (The comparable figure for Gray's district is 24 percent and for Crockett's, 26 percent.)[3] Racial strife has never been a major problem for Kansas City. Back in the early days of the Pendergast Democratic machine in the late nineteenth century, the black and white communities formed mutually beneficial alliances cemented by a patronage system that rewarded both groups.[4] Since 1962 Kansas City's black population has had its own political organization, Freedom Incorporated, a group that identifies and endorses candidates that are deemed supportive of African-American interests.

Between 1948 and 1982, Richard Bolling, an influential white liberal Democrat, represented the fifth district in Congress.[5] Bolling rose to become the chairman of the powerful Rules Committee. An author of important books on Congress and a close adviser to Speakers Carl Albert and Tip O'Neill, Bolling retired from his thirty-four-year congressional career in 1982. Because he did not endorse a candidate until after the Democratic primary, his open seat became a free-for-all, attracting eight contenders—seven whites and one black (see Table 6.2). Alan Wheat, the lone black candidate, won the Democratic primary by the slim margin of 1,004 votes.

The Expansionist Stage: Alan Wheat's Electoral Strategy

Alan Wheat, the fifth district's first black representative, is not a native of Kansas City or even of the Midwest. He was one of three children born to an Air Force colonel, and his family traveled extensively, living in a mostly white world and eventually settling in the Midwest. "Until I was about thirteen," Wheat once said, "the only other blacks that I knew were in my family."[6] Accustomed from childhood to being the only black in predominantly white settings, he attended Grinnell College, graduating in 1972 with a B.A. in economics. His background did not prevent him from advancing the interests of blacks. At one point, he led a campus protest to demand black studies courses.

Wheat's route into politics was indirect. He held a series of jobs before gradually drifting into the political arena. He worked first for the Kansas City Department of Housing and Urban Development (1972–1974). After a period of unemployment, he drove a taxicab for a time, during which he met a man who encouraged him to run for office. Wheat then worked as an aide to a local politician in 1974–1975. In 1977, at the age of

Table 6.2. The election history of Alan Wheat

Year	Primary election opponents	Vote total (percentage)		General election opponents	Vote total (percentage)	
1982	Wheat	21,279	(31%)	Wheat	96,059	(58%)
	Carnes	20,275	(30)	Sharp	66,664	(40)
	Campbell	16,197	(24)			
	five others	10,021	(15)			
1984	Wheat	53,141	(85)	Wheat	150,675	(66)
	Palermo	9,473	(15)	Kenworthy	72,477	(32)
1986	Wheat	51,333	(73)	Wheat	101,030	(71)
	Mitchell	7,146	(10)	Fisher	39,340	(28)
	O'Brien	5,631	(8)			
	four others	6,693	(9)			
1988	Wheat	Unopposed		Wheat	149,166	(70)
				Lobb	60,453	(28)
1990	Wheat	54,664	(80)	Wheat	71,890	(62)
	Dubbert	13,620	(20)	Gardner	43,897	(38)

Sources: Michael Barone and Grant Ujifusa, *The Almanac of American Politics*
(Washington, D.C.: National Journal, 1984–1990 biennial eds.).

twenty-six, he was elected to the state house from the predominantly black state legislative district that he represented until his congressional bid.

As Wheat contemplated whether or not to run for Bolling's seat, he initially failed to get support from anyone and received a great deal of bad advice. Convinced that the district was not ready for a black representative, Wheat's family, friends, and political advisers actively discouraged him from running. Early in his campaign, some Missouri Democrats thought that with seven white candidates and a single black, Wheat might win the primary and lose the general election, so they admonished him to withdraw from the race. Wheat, ignoring the advice of this experienced group of legislators, which included Senator Thomas Eagleton, stayed in the contest—a less secure person might have withdrawn. When it became clear that he was a serious candidate to the end, many people called him crazy, some to his face. (Most of these Democrats later became staunch Wheat supporters.)

Paid political consultants also gave him questionable advice. He was advised to run a dual strategy campaign, that is, to "press the flesh" among blacks and not to show his face on campaign literature designed for the white communities that constituted 80 percent of the district. Wheat spurned this advice on how to gain white support, arguing that "there are some districts where black candidates need to actively work for white support."[7] But his frustration and concern about the fear he saw in the eyes of some white voters caused him to turn to a psychologist for advice on how to deal with these fears. The psychologist advised Wheat to smile, look people in the eye, say their names, and touch them. After receiving similar counsel from a political consultant whose specialty was helping blacks get elected in white districts, Wheat made it his goal to shake hands daily with no fewer than 3,000 of the district's white voters, asking them personally for their support. He and his campaign workers entered predominantly white neighborhoods, restaurants, and stores, wherever large numbers of people congregated. Sometimes they would order meals—just to gain access to the patrons of the restaurants. Wheat would introduce himself, shake hands, and then move on to the next group he had targeted.

Tall, handsome, and extremely articulate, Wheat found that personal contact worked well for him. Throughout the campaign he never attempted to hide his liberal views on abortion, school prayer, and the Equal Rights Amendment (ERA). After one speech before a group of sixty white carpet installers, several men approached him. The first stretched out his hand and said: "I don't support you on abortion, I don't support you on school prayer or the ERA, but you've got my vote."[8] Wheat recalled: "Race came up all the time in the first election. In fact, if it didn't come up, I would bring it up because it was on people's minds. Most people wanted to know if a black person would represent their interests as well as the interests of the black constituents. I wanted them to know that not only was the answer yes, but I did not feel that there was a conflict between the two."[9]

During the course of his first campaign, Wheat went through five campaign managers, starting with a black male and ending with a white female, changing the title of the position after each turnover so as not to appear to be disorganized. Wheat was convinced that he must have the *right* individual in that role, one who believed that he could win and one who understood the dynamics of white-black relationships. He later said: "I won my white constituency over one at a time."[10] Not easily discouraged, Wheat says that he has found from his personal experience that whenever people tell him that "a city, a state, or a country is not ready for a black candidate, what they really mean is that *they* are not ready."

Wheat's success in the primary depended on three features of the context in which he was running. First, he was the only black in the race, so the white vote was spread over seven white candidates (Missouri does not have a runoff primary). Second, he benefited from the reluctance of his white opponents to criticize him. Most of his opponents did not take his bid seriously, and they did not want to appear racist by attacking a popular black leader. The other candidates wanted Wheat's good will to help deliver them the votes of Freedom Incorporated in the general election, so they concentrated on attacking each other. Third, the black vote was solidly behind him. Wheat won the primary with 31 percent of the vote, a third of which came from white voters with the remainder coming from the assistance of Freedom Incorporated. Once he had the nomination, Wheat encouraged Democratic party leaders to live up to the ideals of their party and support him.

Wheat won the general election with 58 percent of the vote. His victory was facilitated by endorsements from powerful white leaders. Procuring the good will of the retiring incumbent was critical to his strategy from the beginning: when other candidates in the primary criticized Bolling's record, Wheat promised voters a continuation of the good service that Bolling had provided their district for over thirty years. According to Wheat: "Other candidates attacked Bolling, saying that they could do a better job. To me the man's reelection for thirty-four years proved that he was doing something right."[11] The assurance that Wheat would continue in Bolling's tradition may have helped him combat white fears of what a black representative might do once elected. After the Democratic primary, Bolling endorsed Wheat and became a staunch supporter. Years later he would tell reporters and former colleagues: "Wheat was my choice from the very beginning."[12]

Wheat's background, style, and approach led others to compare him with Bolling. The *Kansas City Call*, a daily newspaper, endorsed him in an editorial: "When Bolling was first elected to Congress in 1948, he, too, was a young man and probably no better known in the Kansas City community than Wheat is today. [Bolling] was an intellectual, a serious young man, a hard worker, a man with vision and one devoted to worthwhile causes, civil rights being among them. Alan Wheat is much like the young Dick Bolling. He is our choice to succeed Congressman Bolling."[13] The editorial also argued that Wheat was the most qualified person in the race. Wheat had distinguished himself as a legislator during his several terms in the Missouri State House. During his first term he had been voted the best freshman legislator and in later years one of the ten best state legislators. He was responsible for the initiation and passage of key legislation involving the creation of urban enterprise zones, tax abatement for the poor, rehabilitation of substandard housing, aid for the elderly, and protection against domestic violence.

To raise money for his first congressional race, Wheat sold his car, courted possible donors, and convinced several political action committees to make major donations. The National Organization for Women, influenced by Wheat's views on abortion, donated $5,000 for the general election on top of the $3,000 that it gave for the primary. Jewish voters were more inclined to support his campaign fund after he pledged his support for Israel. The United Auto Workers and large business corporations in the area were also major contributors.[14]

Wheat spent over $100,000 during his first campaign for a series of television advertisements that helped him present himself. One television commercial pictured his father in full military uniform extolling the virtues of hard work to his son. In his reelection campaigns, advertisements featured person-on-the-street testimonials praising his outstanding constituency service. One advertisement mentioned the congressman's coming home every weekend and his reputation for hard work. Another boasted: "Alan Wheat: no one has worked harder for the people of Missouri."[15] Both television and newspaper endorsements mentioned Wheat's position on the Rules Committee and explained its importance. A disproportionate number of whites have appeared in the advertisements. His official emblem is his name flanked by two stalks of wheat, an appropriate and catchy symbol for a representative of a midwestern district.

Despite his successes, Wheat does not deceive himself about racism. He told a Kansas City magazine: "Kansas City is very little different than any place else in the country. It is a microcosm of the country in many ways, and racism cannot be dead here—just as sexism can't or elitism can't—if it's not dead everywhere in the country. But great strides have been made over the years. I won't tell you that there aren't people who view situations with an eye toward the race of the people who are involved, or that there aren't people who have prejudices and discriminate. That clearly just wouldn't be true."[16] He does not see his race as a handicap; otherwise he would not have run for Congress. He credits his life experience with giving him an opportunity to understand the concerns of white Americans. He believes that most white Americans are not racist.

When Wheat talks about his career and his ability to attract white support, he is always careful not to suggest that he is different from other black candidates. Not surprisingly, he has been in the forefront of encouraging black candidates to consider running for Congress in majority-white and barely majority-black districts. He believes that doing so does not require compromising the effective representation of African American interests. He tells black candidates to stress qualifications over race, a strategy that helped him win white support. In his first campaign he repeatedly told his district's voters, "I can promise you this: lots of candidates will spend more money than Alan Wheat to get your vote, but no one will work harder than Alan Wheat as a U.S. Congressman." Once elected, he took steps to fulfill his promise.

Interactions with Constituents: Forging and Maintaining a Biracial Coalition

In addition to having two district offices and a mobile unit, Wheat keeps his campaign office open year round. The campaign office mails hand-signed birthday and Christmas cards to numerous constituents. It is not unusual for the office manager to hand him a list of people to write condolence messages to. His Washington office stays in contact with constituents by mailing an average of six newsletters a year. The congressman writes a newspaper column, holds as many as fifty town meetings during a term, lectures to numerous school classes, and visits businesses and retirement homes. He initially spent an estimated 150 days in the district, but by 1988 this number was down to 120 days. Wheat seeks and wins the support of whites without alienating his core black constituency. Balancing his time between the two groups was once a major concern, but over the years his worries have dissipated: "When I was first elected I was concerned as to whether people would see me as spending more time in the white community or more time in the black community, and I was carefully trying to allocate my time fairly. But the fact is no one except my staff and my family and a few close observers know what I'm doing with my time . . . now I tend to respond to the groups that request my presence. I try to be fair, but I am not overly concerned about whether 62 percent of my time is in the white community and 38 percent of my time is in the black community."[17]

Wheat frequently participates in events sponsored by black groups as well as in the traditional holiday festivities honoring veterans and the founding of the nation. Among black representatives, he has hired the smallest number of black staffers (six out of sixteen in 1988). His hiring decisions are partly strategic and partly circumstantial. When he was first elected in 1982 at the age of thirty-three, he wisely kept on six of Bolling's experienced staffers. Five were still with him after his first term, and some remained even in 1992. When white constituents visit his district offices, they are usually greeted by white staffers. When he goes to speak before a predominantly white group, he is always accompanied by his highest-ranking staffer, who happens to be white. When he goes to speak before a mixed or predominantly black group, that person also goes with him, but depending on the subject matter other staffers may be brought along as well. Wheat hired a black personal secretary in 1990, and the presence of two black faces when one entered the office, instead of a lone black receptionist, changed the atmosphere of the office. He explains his predominantly white staff by arguing that congressional staff should mirror the racial composition of the district, which in his case is 80 percent white. Wheat takes issue with blacks who argue that black representatives should hire all-black staffs. "I don't believe in that philosophy," he says. "I believe that all members of Congress should be fair when they hire their staffs—white discrimination does not justify black discrimination."[18]

A strategic politician, Wheat has worked hard to discourage potential challengers.[19] In his first race he prematurely conceded the primary to his opponent. Since then, however, he has not had a close election. In his 1984 and 1986 reelection bids, he spent less than the funds his campaign raised.[20] In the 1988 Democratic primary he ran unopposed, and the Republicans have not been able to find strong challengers to oppose him. His reelection margins have steadily increased over the years (see Table 6.2).

As Fenno observes, representatives gain trust by convincing their constituents that they are qualified to hold office and are empathetic to constituency needs and concerns.[21] In Wheat's district, both whites and blacks consider Wheat to be "one of us." On one occasion, a black speaker introduced him at a church gathering by referring to their common racial group membership; on another occasion, a white speaker presented him to a group of railroad employees by referring to his past union membership—shared race was not necessary for him to be accepted.

Wheat's rapport with all groups is easy and relaxed. "Who do I work for?" he often asks young schoolchildren. The children give many answers before he tells them: "I work for you. Tell your parents that you have an employee." Senior citizens are sometimes told to keep their political donations because "Congressmen are well paid."

Fast on his feet, Wheat departs from prepared speeches when he senses a problem. Shortly after his vote against a proposed constitutional amendment that would have banned the burning of the American flag, for example, he attended an Independence Day celebration where he was dwarfed by a huge flag that hung from the ceiling behind the podium. Noting the flag, Wheat quickly switched from his planned statement blasting President Bush's switch on taxes to an explanation of his flag vote. "I'm very proud of the symbol of our nation," Wheat told the crowd of ninety men and women. "But I am also proud of our right to free speech and free dissent in this country. That is perhaps our most important right, the right to dissent." Citing the crushing of democracy in China's Tiananmen Square of the previous year, Wheat told the crowd that he had voted against the anti–flag burning amendment because it threatened Americans' right to dissent. The audience applauded.[22]

Representation through Legislation: Explaining the Tough Votes

Wheat has done well in Congress. With the help of Richard Bolling and the Black Caucus, he earned a seat as a freshman on the highly prestigious House Rules Committee, previously chaired by Bolling. *Politics in America, 1990* describes him as a "leadership lieutenant in the backroom world of Rules."[23] From that position he has secured passage of legislation beneficial to his district, including flood control projects for two major rivers in the district, funds for the Bruce Watkins Memorial Drive, and a ban on the foreign servicing of U.S. airplanes (a benefit to employees of Kansas City's large Eastern Airlines and TWA facilities). Wheat has also secured money to buy three buildings next to President Truman's home in order to expand the Truman Historical Site. Showing his support for broader political ideals, Wheat has spent several years working to secure passage of a rule that would allow congressional consideration of the regulation of firms transporting certain toxic chemicals.[24]

How well does Wheat represent blacks? To answer this question, we may turn to the COPE and LCCR indexes (see Table 3.3 and Appendix C). Wheat's record does not differ substantially from that of other black representatives. Wheat is an avowed, unapologetic liberal, earning high ratings from liberal interest groups for his progressive voting record. He also has a near perfect—98 percent—attendance score. Like Ron Dellums (D-CA), Wheat often scores 100 percent with both COPE and LCCR. His conservative coalition scores are similar to the low scores of other liberal Democrats and blacks.

Wheat's ability to get along with a broad spectrum of citizens and his service on the House Rules Committee in no way blunts his liberalism. Over the years, he has taken controversial positions. He opposed the death penalty for drug kingpins and opposed bans on dial-a-porn lines. In 1988, when other candidates were trying to back away from their pro-choice positions, Wheat stuck to his and widely advertised his stance. In addition to voting against the amendment banning the burning of the flag, he joined the Democratic majority in 1991 that opposed the use of force in the Persian Gulf.

Wheat uses his issue forums for educational purposes and to explain potentially controversial votes. It is not uncommon for 300 to 400 people to attend one of his issue forums on such subjects as women, the environment, South Africa, or veterans. Voters like him personally and appear to feel good about supporting him, even though (as his private polls show) a majority of them consider him too liberal for their tastes. In explaining his vote against the Catastrophic Health Care bill that was passed by Congress in 1989, he told an elderly lady: "Yes, the bill contained some very important new benefits to senior citizens and I will readily admit to that. However, I was one of nine Democrats to vote against the bill. . . . I voted against the bill because I thought that the financing mechanism was wrong, that the entire cost of the new benefits should not be imposed upon elderly citizens, and because the bill did not provide for long-term health care."[25] During that same forum, Wheat told a pro-choice supporter who was obviously concerned about a reversal of *Roe v. Wade:*

> Whether or not people are individually for or against abortion, most people in this country believe that it is every woman's individual right to make up her own mind about what she is going to do if she faces the question of whether or not she should have an abortion. And I think that it is perfectly appropriate for a woman to consult her mate, or her religious or spiritual adviser, but it is completely inappropriate for the federal government to inject itself—or for the state government to inject itself—into that situation.[26]

Not surprisingly, Wheat is in favor of stronger gun control legislation. He has said, "One of the things that I am going to do is introduce legislation in the near future that would raise the costs of a federal firearms license. Right now it is too easy to get one."[27]

Wheat has risen in the leadership structure of the Congressional Black Caucus. During the 100th and 101st Congress, he served as its vice chair. In addition, he chaired the Congressional Black Caucus Foundation, an independent, tax-exempt organization for public policy analysis, legislative education, and research. One of his major accomplishments as vice chairman of the CBC was the opening of the caucus to white associate members. In 1988 over thirty whites were listed. These members were accepted on the basis of their voting record and constituency characteristics. Their fees help subsidize the organization and give white representatives an opportunity to show publicly, especially to their black constituents, that they support black interests. Still, Wheat does not allow his role in the Black Caucus to compromise his independence. As he puts it, "I apply the same standard to the activities of the Black Caucus as to the activities of other groups. If I agree, I participate. If not, I don't."[28]

Wheat's role as a legislator extends beyond his district lines. In recent years he has been active on issues relating to South Africa and congressional reapportionment. He has stated: "My job is to do what's best for my country and district. What I do legislatively has ramifications for both."[29] Much of his low-key legislative style stems from a mixture of his personality, the advice that he has received from the retired Richard Bolling, and his own understanding of his responsibilities as a representative.

The rise of Alan Wheat demonstrates that it is possible for black candidates to be elected and reelected in majority-white districts without ignoring the concerns of their black constituents. There are no significant differences between Wheat's legislative record and that of other black and liberal Democrats. He has one of the highest voter participation records of blacks in Congress and has maintained that record since his first election. He does not engage in racially inflammatory speeches or call for black solidarity, and there is nothing in his background that would lead people to expect him to do so. He has shown that a black candidate can effectively represent blacks and whites at the same time.

The First District of Indiana: Katie Hall

Recent History

The first congressional district of Indiana, an enclave built around the steel industry, is 70 percent urban. Located on the shores of Lake Michigan, not far from Chicago, the district has a diverse ethnic population that includes Irish, Polish, Czechoslovakian, Ukrainian, and African Americans. Barone and Ujifusa note: "These groups live today in uneasy proximity, and much of the politics of the area has reflected ethnic and racial rivalries."[30]

Gary, the largest city in the district, was established in 1906 by J. P. Morgan's United States Steel Corporation. Its population grew rapidly until the mid-1960s, after which it dropped from a high of 188,000 residents in 1970 to 151,000 residents by 1980. During the latter half of the 1960s the city joined others in America in acquiring a black majority, and it elected its first black mayor, Richard Hatcher, in 1967.[31] Unlike Kansas City, the first district of Indiana has been plagued by racial tensions. These tensions culminated when Hatcher, a black political outsider, was elected. Largely a choice of the black working classes, Hatcher was never accepted by the white leaders of the local Democratic organization. Nor was he initially accepted by middle- and upper-class blacks.[32] Just as in Detroit after Coleman Young's election, white residents abandoned Gary after Hatcher's election and moved outside the city limits to form suburbs hostile to blacks.

Katie Hall's initial Democratic nomination took place after the death of the white incumbent, Adam Benjamin, in September 1982. After Benjamin died, Hatcher, along with two white council members (Robert Pastrick, the mayor of East Chicago, and Mary Cartwright, a Democratic party worker), formed a committee to nominate a replacement for Benjamin's unexpired term. Robert Catlin describes how Hall got the nomination without competing for it: "All members agreed initially that Benjamin's widow should be selected to serve out his remaining term provided that she would endorse the party's selectee [who would run in the general election] for the full term beginning January 1983. After hours of negotiation, Pastrick nominated himself for the full term while Hatcher and Cartwright cast their votes for Indiana State Senator Katie Hall. Upon the nomination of Hall, Mrs. Benjamin refused to lend her support; and Mayor Hatcher, who had the exclusive responsibility of selecting a replacement for the partial term, chose Mrs. Hall over Pastrick's opposition."[33]

In this traditionally Democratic district, Hall's nomination was equivalent to election. The November 1982 ballot included both the special election to cover Benjamin's term and the general election for the next term, beginning in January 1983 (the 98th Congress). Hall won 63.3 percent of the vote in the special election and 57 percent of the vote for the next term. The circumstances of her selection as a candidate did not help her with the white electorate. Many Democratic party leaders were upset by the manner in which she was selected—they felt Hatcher had dictated who would win the nomination, even though their first choice had been Benjamin's widow. Despite the controversial circumstances surrounding her first election, however, Katie Hall should have retained her seat in 1984, given the advantageous position all incumbents occupy. But as we shall see, she was defeated in the 1984 Democratic primary.

The Expansionist Stage: Factors That Led to Hall's Loss of Her Seat

Katie Hall was one of twelve children born to a Mississippi farmer. She grew up in an all-black Delta town, Mound Bayou, and graduated from an all-black college, the Mississippi Vocational School. Unlike Wheat, who had grown up constantly interacting with whites, Hall's childhood and young adulthood were spent in a mostly black world. This continued after she moved with her husband and infant daughter to Indiana. Shortly after arriving she became active in politics as a volunteer, working first for John Kennedy's presidential campaign and then for Richard Hatcher. Years later she attempted to launch her own political career, running unsuccessfully for the city council in 1970 and for the state legislature in 1974. She was elected to the state senate in 1976 and served there until Hatcher tapped her in 1982 for the unexpired congressional term.[34]

She had weak competition in the general election for the 1983–1984 term from the Republican candidate, Thomas Kreiger, an unemployed former teacher and computer programmer. Kreiger's campaign stances were out of tune with the traditionally Democratic district. Although the nation was confronting a recession and unemployment in the district stood at 18 percent, Kreiger argued that robots should be used in the steel industry that was the district's major employer. If this was not enough to defeat him, he advocated the replacement of the social security system with private insurance. He was not able to garner much support from the Republican National Committee. Ignoring her opponent, Hall ran against President Reagan's policies. She advocated the traditional Democratic remedies of more spending for social programs as a way to tackle unemployment and poverty. She opposed increased military spending, high interest rates, and tax benefits for the rich. She was pro-choice on abortion and favored affirmative action programs. Battered women, poor students, and unemployed breadwinners were the constituents she said she wanted to represent. Many people joined in her campaign. Hatcher helped her obtain the endorsements of important labor organizations. The National Organization for Women also endorsed her, and a group of white women introduced her to residents of suburban areas outside of Gary. This large support network helped her win a stunning victory on a rainy election day. As already noted, Hall took 63 percent of the vote in the special election to finish Benjamin's unexpired term, and 57 percent in the general election. She received 97 percent of the black vote and 51 percent of the white vote (see Table 6.3).[35]

Katie Hall's 1984 electoral performance was very different from her performance in 1982. In 1984 she was opposed in the Democratic primary by two white opponents, Jack Crawford, the Lake County prosecutor, and Peter Visclosky, a former aide to Benjamin. Hall literally handed her opponents ammunition to use against her. At the height of the recession, when unemployment in the district stood at 25 percent, she took a widely publicized trip through ten African nations to observe poverty and hunger. Upon her return she announced: "I'd seen a lot in my 45-year lifetime, but I'd never seen anything like this before. . . . While I have a lot of people in my district who are poor and suffering, they're still far better off than in many other parts of the world. People here who don't have food can turn to food stamps, surplus food . . .

Table 6.3. The election history of Katie Hall

Year	Primary election opponents	Vote total (percentage)	General election opponents	Vote total (percentage)
1982 (special election)	Hall	Appointed	Hall Kreiger	(63%) (37)
1982	Hall	Appointed	Hall Kreiger	87,369 (57) 66,921 (43)
1984	Hall Visclosky Crawford	43,345 (33%) 44,713 (34) 40,776 (31)		
1986	Hall Visclosky Smith Herbert	30,964 (35) 49,782 (57) 3,427 (4) 3,132 (4)		

Sources: Michael Barone and Grant Ujifusa, *The Almanac of American Politics* (Washington, D.C.: National Journal, 1984–1990 biennial eds.).

public welfare."[36] Her opponent Crawford took the most direct advantage of her travels; he criticized her for being overseas "at the same time [that the district] had 50,000 people on public assistance and people lined up blocks long in government cheese and milk lines." Crawford also pointed out that she had voted herself a 15 percent congressional pay raise "at a time when 40,000 constituents were unemployed."[37] Visclosky attacked her relationship with the mayor, charging that she "serves one constituent out of 550,000 in the district and that is Richard Gordon Hatcher."[38] He also stressed his own close relationship with Adam Benjamin. Neither opponent explicitly mentioned race, and Visclosky actually sought and won some black support.

In the face of these challengers, Hall changed her campaign strategy from the approach she used in 1982. She made only a few trips to white communities and mainly counted on a split white vote to give her the Democratic nomination. She also made mistakes in black communities: she scheduled her major fund-raising event on the same night that the *Gary Info,* the district's major black newspaper, was celebrating its anniversary. Not only did she fail to campaign in the white community as vigorously as she had in 1982, but she also brought Jesse Jackson into the district to mount a voter registration drive. This may have fueled a white backlash similar to the one that occurred in North Carolina's 1984 Spaulding-Valentine race. (In North Carolina white voters reacted to Jackson's presence by easily out-registering the blacks.)

Although some people attributed Hall's defeat in 1984 to racism, precinct data show that her greatest losses were in the black community, where the turnout had dropped drastically. She lost 4,800 votes in predominantly black precincts that had supported her in 1982. "One reason for the strong black turnout for Katie Hall in 1982," says Robert Catlin, "was the unprecedented opportunity to elect a black to Congress. When her ascent to Congress resulted in little, if any, change in the lives of Gary's black masses, enthusiasm waned and the turnout was lower."[39]

Although Hall kept her family in the district and commuted home on the weekends, she was unsuccessful in expanding her reelection constituency. Two black representatives, speaking anonymously, told me that her seat was one that need not have been lost. They described her as having "difficulty dealing with legislative issues." "She did not like to campaign or visit places where she would be questioned about legislative issues." This was a particular impediment for building a biracial coalition, because such questioning was more likely to occur when she spoke before white audiences.

Hall's position might have been strengthened by a system of regular constituency mailings. One of her former colleagues remembered: "One year into her congressional term she distributed one constituency mailing about something inconsequential." Another recalled: "I remember her angering labor leaders by failing to attend one of their meetings and telling them 'I have to go home to cook dinner for my children.'"[40] Labor had been one of her largest supporters in the 1982 campaign. Perhaps her most serious mistake, however, was not retaining Adam Benjamin's former staffers. Of the seven people who worked for Katie Hall during 1982 and 1983, only two were former staffers to Benjamin. By 1984 these two staffers were gone, as well.

Hall's approach to representing a majority-white district was strikingly different from Alan Wheat's. Both returned to their constituencies regularly. Wheat, however, established offices in the main parts of his district, offered jobs to all of his predecessor's staffers, mailed frequent newsletters and other communications, and kept his campaign office open all year. Most important, he never allowed his 1982 election organization to rust, he never spent his time registering black voters, and he never concentrated his efforts on the black community to the exclusion of the white. Wheat assiduously developed his white constituency; Hall registered and ministered mainly to the black community.

Representation through Legislation: Navigating through the House

Hall's voting record was indistinguishable from that of other black representatives. In 1984 she scored 100 percent with COPE, and her LCCR and voter participation rates were high. Her record resembles that of her white successor, Peter Visclosky, who scored 93 percent with COPE in 1986 and has gained significant black support since his election.

During her brief tenure in Congress, Hall chaired the subcommittee on Census and Population. She was one of the few freshmen who were able to get a subchairmanship, because she was serving the unexpired portion of a term. From that post she coauthored and helped with the passage of the Martin Luther King, Jr., Holiday bill, which was her most significant legislative achievement. Thus she concentrated much of her time on a symbolic issue likely to be of national interest to African Americans but of less interest to white constituents.[41] She almost totally ignored the white suburbs outside Gary, even though she was representing a constituency that was 71 percent white.

Although Hall's defeat is often cited as a case of white racism, the evidence suggests that other factors were at work. A consensus exists among blacks as well as whites that Hall did not work hard enough at doing the things politicians must do to be reelected. She did not mobilize blacks effectively, she had difficulty in dealing with issues important to her majority-white electorate, and she never quite mastered the institutional arrangements of Congress. White votes contributed to her initial victory; she needed only to retain their support while not losing that of blacks. She failed on both accounts.

The Eighth District of California: Ron Dellums

Recent History

The eighth district of California presents a picture far different from the fifth district of Missouri and the first district of Indiana. With a long history of radicalism, it is by no means typical of the rest of the country. The Free Speech Movement, the Symbionese Liberation Army, which kidnapped Patricia Hearst in the late seventies, and the Black Panthers all emerged from this district. The strongly Democratic district is 70 percent white and includes the University of California's Berkeley campus. It ranks eighth on the scale of the nation's best-educated districts (59.6 percent of the constituents are college educated) and fourth according to student numbers (16 percent).[42] But the district also contains Oakland, the sixth-largest city in the state and one of California's poorest metropolitan areas. The low-income blacks and Hispanics of Oakland have little in common with Berkeley's intellectuals, apart from being natural constituents for a liberal member of Congress.[43] The district, which has been described as "a mixture of poverty and intellectual ferment,"[44] has been consistently carried by liberal Democratic presidential candidates, including George McGovern, Walter Mondale, and Mike Dukakis.

Jeffrey Cohelan, a white liberal Democrat, represented the district in Congress for twelve years (1958–1970). He had a wide appeal with labor and traditional voters, but he also had what Ron Dellums calls his Achilles' heel—Lyndon Johnson and the Vietnam War.[45] Cohelan did not oppose the war strongly enough. In 1970, Dellums was able to defeat Cohelan by being more liberal and anti-establishment. Cohelan made mistakes in a district where, as Dellums put it, "you can't make political mistakes because people are very sensitive, very sophisticated politically. They can see a contradiction from a mile away. This is one district where you can't be wrong."[46]

The Expansionist Stage: Dellums's Emergence as a Leader

Ron Dellums was born and raised in the black ghettoes of Oakland. A former Marine, he holds degrees from Oakland Technical School, San Francisco City College, and the University of California at Berkeley, where he earned a master's degree in social work. Before entering politics, he was a psychiatric social worker, but in a sense he never had to "enter" politics. His uncle, C. L. Dellums, was a major leader in the nation's first black labor union, the Brotherhood of Sleeping Car Porters, and he was exposed to the militancy of his uncle from early childhood.

Dellums's own political career began in 1967, when he was elected to the Berkeley city council. There he established himself as an intellectual with oratorical skills. Articulate and troubled by the events of the 1960s and the lingering war in Vietnam, he was the perfect candidate for the Berkeley community. One observer described him as a product of the counterrevolution of the 1960s, who personified what Berkeley stood for. People in his district were said to want someone who would "horrify conservatives and appear as an unbending radical."[47] The tall, Afro-haired black man was ideal.

When Dellums decided to run for Cohelan's seat in 1969, his position on the city council helped him forge a coalition that transcended race. A broad coalition was necessary, because he could not win the election on the basis of the black vote alone. His core constituency is more ideological than racial, and it has always been true that many of his most committed supporters are white. He has said: "[I] entered the campaign for Congress with a fervent belief that beyond ethnicity, it would be possible to bring women, labor, seniors, youths, and the poor into a coalition of the 'powerless': those whom society . . . has traditionally excluded from its calculations of equity and justice."[48] Dellums's winning coalition was composed of blacks, whites, students, and left-leaning intellectuals as well as some traditional Democrats. His campaign succeeded in registering over 15,000 new voters. As he recalls, "When I first announced, the first response of the media was a racially oriented question: 'What makes you think that you can win in this district? You're black and the district is white.'" But on election day, "the black vote came out in extraordinary numbers, along with the intellectual community and the progressive community."[49]

Encountering the same kind of discouragement as that experienced by Wheat and other black representatives who have run in majority-white districts, Dellums (like Dymally) analyzed voting patterns in the district. He concluded that most people in the district did not think of their interests in racial terms; rather there were feminists, workers' advocates, peace advocates, consumer advocates, environmentalists, antiwar protesters, and black power advocates. His strategy was to pull together these different interests.

Although politically diverse, virtually all of this constituency expected its representative to challenge the political system, and he did so with vigor, becoming the "social conscience" of the liberal community in America. To accomplish this feat he needed more than good oratorical skills—hard work was required. Shortly after his election in 1970 Dellums said: "When I first came to the Congress I had a basic decision to make concerning the type of congressman I would be. This is not an unusual decision, as a congressman's personality is generally a combination of his previous professional style plus whatever modifications the politics of his getting elected to Congress brought about. My own situation was complicated by several factors: I was black, I was attacked as being a radical by Spiro T. Agnew, and I was from Berkeley."[50] Like all members of Congress, Dellums was influenced by the circumstances surrounding his election and by a constituency career that began during the radical sixties.

Bold statements have set him apart from other politicians, white and black. He is the only representative to risk insulting the country by calling it a "nation of niggers" in 1977—a variation of earlier statements made over the course of his career: "America is a nation of niggers. If you are black, you're a nigger. Blind people, the handicapped, radical environmentalists, poor whites, those too far to the left are all niggers."[51] In a similar speech Dellums said: "Black people no longer corner the nigger population in this country—there are brown niggers, white niggers, long-haired niggers, old niggers, women niggers—America's full of niggers."[52] Note that this list is comprehensive enough to include a majority of his constituents and is a call for unity among political rather than racial minorities. He refers to groups that are politically or economically disenfranchised, in some cases because of their different interests and values.

Dellums has been a militant and a gadfly, but never a *racial* militant. Intuitively, we would not expect a majority-white district to tolerate a racially militant black representative who attacked white institutions and people; and Dellums does not do this. Instead he is the "social conscience" who attacks traditional values and generates debate. In campaigning for Jesse Jackson in 1988, Dellums told white supporters in Berkeley: "This is not about Jesse Jackson. This is about putting a black man on the national ticket. I would vote for Jackson if he didn't stand a snowball's chance in Hell of winning." To a predominantly white group, he said: "Vote for Jesse Jackson, vote for the poor, for Martin Luther King, Jr., for the old, the dead, and the children unborn."[53]

Conservatives in the district receive little effective representation from Dellums. Over the years Republicans and conservative Democrats have regularly aligned and targeted him for defeat. His mean reelection margin between the years 1970 and 1990 was 59 percent. He has rarely received above 60 percent of the vote, but he has been able to survive redistricting that has increased the number of Republicans and conservative Democrats in his district (see Table 6.4).

One staffer noted that despite his lower than average reelection margins, Dellums had resisted efforts by state legislators to increase the number of blacks in his district. If the number of blacks were increased, Democratic votes would be taken away from white Democrats who needed them in adjacent districts, and therefore his office had argued for the number of blacks to stay constant. But in 1991 I was told by a high-ranking staffer that Dellums would fight for a district with a higher percentage of minorities in the next redistricting, because he was tired of having to work so hard to stay in office. His earlier decision to keep the number of minorities low can be contrasted with the situation in some newly black and historically black districts, where blacks may lobby for the creation of districts that are overwhelmingly black, resulting in wasted votes and reduced influence. In 1992, redistricters increased the black population in the eighth district, removing the outlying Republican leaning suburbs and thereby giving Dellums his safest seat yet.

Among the 435 members of Congress, Dellums is one of the biggest money raisers and spenders. In 1982 a Republican challenger was able to collect over $250,000 for his bid against him. In the same year Dellums raised $820,918, most of which came from outside of his district. In 1986 he raised and spent over a million dollars compared with the mere $74,000 his opponent was able to raise, and in 1988 Dellums raised $1,153,750 to his opponent's $7,071 (see Appendix B). One of his staffers commented: "Our ability to raise money lets potential challengers know that we have the capacity to defend ourselves." Essentially he is practicing what Edie Goldenberg and Michael Traugott had called "preemptive spending," that is, raising huge war chests to scare off potential challengers.[54]

Table 6.4. The election history of Ron Dellums

Year	Primary election opponents	Vote total (percentage)		General election opponents	Vote total (percentage)	
1970	Dellums	42,778	(55%)	Dellums	89,784	(55%)
	Cohelan	35,223	(45)	Healy	69,691	(42)
				Scahill	2,156	(1)
1972	Dellums	84,929	(73)	Dellums	126,913	(56)
	Sestanovich	31,188	(27)	Hannaford	86,587	(38)
1974	Dellums	58,340	(68)	Dellums	95,041	(57)
	Allen	18,381	(21)	Redden	66,386	(40)
	Murphy	9,139	(11)	Holland	6,385	(4)
1976	Dellums	Unopposed		Dellums	122,342	(64)
				Breck, Jr.	68,374	(36)
1978	Dellums	Unopposed		Dellums	94,824	(57)
				Hughes	70,481	(43)
1980	Dellums	Unopposed		Dellums	108,380	(56)
				Hughes	76,580	(39)
				Mikuriya	10,465	(5)
1982	Dellums	67,613	(76)	Dellums	121,537	(56)
	Vamis	21,193	(24)	Hutchinson	95,694	(44)
1984	Dellums	86,299	(79)	Dellums	144,316	(60)
	Vamis	18,122	(17)	Connor	94,907	(40)
1986	Dellums	67,696	(83)	Dellums	121,790	(60)
	Williams	14,378	(17)	Eigenberg	76,850	(38)
1988	Dellums	Unopposed		Dellums	161,221	(67)
				Cuddihy, Jr.	76,531	(31)
1990	Dellums	Unopposed		Dellums	119,645	(61)
				Galewski	75,544	(39)

Sources: Michael Barone, Grant Ujifusa, and Douglas Matthews, *The Almanac of American Politics* (New York: E. P. Dutton, 1978, 1980); Barone and Ujifusa, *The Almanac of American Politics* (Washington, D.C.: National Journal, 1984–1990 biennial eds.).

The key to this fund-raising success comes from Dellums's representation of a "national progressive agenda" as opposed to a district-wide geographical constituency. His mailing list includes the membership of the American Civil Liberties Union and the National Bar Association. The interests that fund his campaign are national. Although these involve constituencies that cannot vote for him directly, they make sure that he has all the money he needs. In 1988, for the first time since his initial election, he ran unopposed in the primary. His detractors had given up any immediate hopes of unseating him.

Interactions with Constituents: Maintaining a Biracial Coalition

Dellums has maintained a large district presence, with over 50 percent of his staffers located in his Berkeley, Oakland, and Lafayette offices. His district offices, like Wheat's, are located in key places, and Dellums employs a large number of white staffers. In 1988 six whites, eight blacks, and three members of other minority groups were on the staff.

Like Wheat, Dellums also mails a large number of newsletters. His constituency communications are highly detailed and appropriate for a district in which a majority of the voters are college-educated liberals. It is not uncommon for his letters to include updated information on human rights, defense spending and planning, veterans' affairs, social security, the environment, and immigration as well as news from South Africa and Central America. He also holds constituency meetings in the district's major cities and is regularly able to bring grants and projects to the area. Although he has been in Congress for over twenty years, he can still get a cadre of faithful volunteers to help with the constituency service.

Critics of Dellums can be found in both the white and the black communities. Bill Baker, a Republican state assemblyman, has described him as totally ineffective, and a local Democrat said: "He isn't interested in local issues. We don't contact him anymore, it's a waste of time."[55] Constituents sometimes say that Dellums doesn't do "a damn thing" for the district. Some Oakland activists accuse his office of using "walking around money" to buy the silence of otherwise vocal black activists.

Dellums may, in fact, provide white liberals with slightly more effective representation than he can give the poor blacks living in Oakland. First, his legislative agenda includes items that some blacks consider irrelevant to their immediate needs. Second, he has no district office located within the Oakland ghetto, although he had one there prior to the passage of the Gramm-Rudman deficit reduction law. From the black ghetto, trips to the Oakland office require a long bus ride to the downtown post office. His decision regarding which office to close prompted some black community leaders to say: "Dellums closed the [ghetto] office because he did not want the brothers and sisters coming in off the streets."[56]

Assessing the legitimacy of such charges sends the analyst back to the meaning of representation. If black representation means descriptive representation, then blacks are represented by Dellums, and if it means support for a progressive, liberal, redistributive social-welfare agenda, then he ranks among the top representatives of either race. If, however, black constituents want more service and a more convenient district office in Oakland, they may have legitimate complaints about the quality of their representation.

Representation through Legislation: Inside and Outside the System

Dellums has one of the more liberal voting records in Congress. He usually scores 100 percent with COPE and LCCR, and his voting participation record is consistently high (see Table 3.3 and Appendix C). He is chairman of the District of Columbia Committee and of the Armed Services subcommittee on Research and Development. During his first term he claimed credit for introducing over 227 pieces of legislation and getting action on 43 of them, helping over 5,000 people, and making 89 percent of his roll-call votes.[57] Among the legislation he sponsored were bills to impeach President Nixon, to remove all restraints on abortion and marijuana, to grant amnesty to all war resisters, and to impose sanctions against South Africa. He sponsored unofficial hearings on the Vietnam War, on racism in the military, and on government lawlessness. The South African sanctions bill, originally introduced in 1970, was passed in 1986.

Such legislative actions have helped him with liberals in his district and throughout America more than with the rest of the Congress where, until recently, he has been seen as a "wild card." Many black representatives have considered him too militant and too independent for their taste; as a consequence they regularly bypassed him for the chairmanship of the Congressional Black Caucus until the 101st Congress.

After Dellums's first term, some black leaders called for his resignation because of his "disservice to the nation's 26 million black citizens."[58] The black leaders cited his disregard of established congressional procedures as evidence of disservice. They seemed embarrassed by his actions. These complaints were apparently tied to their expectation that he serve as a role model for African Americans and their belief that an acceptable black role model should be less eager to challenge an institutional structure then almost two hundred years old.

A *Richmond News Leader* article points to the general dismay of some observers: "Dellums is coming on strong. . . . He has a lot to learn. He may be a hotshot freshman congressman from Berkeley, but he will be a freshman nobody. Tradition dictates that freshmen congressmen shall be seen and not heard, tolerated but not accepted. The experienced members of the House are old hands at squelching rude arrogant freshmen, and Dellums, with all his zeal for changing the world overnight, is riding for a fall."[59]

The legislative style Dellums employed was no accident. Given his highly educated, activist district, it was a reasoned choice. Dellums might have made himself less conspicuous by not pursuing the types of legislative issues he tackled, but such an approach would not have afforded him the opportunity to take stands on the issues that he and his supporters thought important. Staffers have described him as a shy, sensitive man, a personality not consistent with his early style. It is not uncommon for him to shed tears publicly over some societal calamity or injustice. Like Presidents Reagan and Bush, Dellums is allowed to cry on camera.

As chairman of the House District of Columbia Committee, Dellums further confused some local black leaders when in 1989 he introduced legislation that would have exempted spouses and children of members of Congress from paying District of Columbia taxes, a bill that would have cost the District millions of dollars in lost revenue.[60] Like many of his colleagues, Dellums is much criticized for his involvement in international issues and causes that are seen as irrelevant to ameliorating the condition of African Americans. A general criticism directed toward all black representatives was published in a major black newspaper: "The once 'black-focused' voting and the CBC's affinity to its black constituents has broadened; the group has made alliances and coalitions with individuals and organizations seen to be beyond its traditional base."[61] Some black representatives accuse the African-American press of declaring war on the Black Caucus. Criticisms of black politicians may increase as more and more blacks represent districts with white majorities.

The Potential for Electing More Black Representatives in White Districts

The election of black representatives from majority-white districts has increased black representation throughout America. Once elected, these politicians have represented the interests of both blacks and whites. If these black politicians had responded primarily to white policy preferences that were at odds with black interests, then black representation would not have been enhanced. But this is not what we find when we examine the voting record of these representatives; rather, they seem to represent progressives of all races. Moreover, the black Democrats from majority-white districts have not been more conservative than black representatives from historically black districts.

Nevertheless, as Katie Hall's defeat suggests, it may be impossible for black representatives of majority-white districts, or even of newly black or heterogeneous districts, to engage in purely "black-focused activities" and maintain their coalitions' support. To be successful, black representatives will have to do as Alan Wheat and Ron Dellums have done—find common ground between the races and emphasize that commonality. Such decisions need not hurt black representation. Wheat and Dellums have not moved to the center of the ideological spectrum. They are representing large numbers of people from both races.

It is also important to note that they were both discouraged by others from running for Congress in majority-white districts. Black representation in Congress will not increase substantially as long as blacks heed the conventional wisdom that they need districts with black majorities to win office. This belief results in weaker candidates, because black politicians averse to risk will not give up safe offices to run in unsafe districts. Naturally, if one does not run one cannot win.

A common set of characteristics and electoral circumstances have been associated with successful bids by black candidates in majority-white districts. The candidates tend to be well educated, articulate, and most have had political experience in an elective office. They vary in oratorical skill—Ron Dellums and Andrew Young, for example, are known as especially gifted speakers. Until the election of Gary Franks in 1991, Democratic partisanship seemed to be a requisite for winning.[62] Successful black representatives have actively sought white support, used white volunteers, and received white endorsements. A key factor motivating their bids has been their belief that their race was not an insurmountable handicap in gaining white support.[63] Rather than being flukes, the victories of these candidates are indicative of a pattern worth noting.

III · WHITE REPRESENTATIVES

7 · White Representatives of Minority-Black Districts

My choice was Jesse Jackson or Michael Dukakis. Of course, I'm going with Jesse Jackson from South Carolina over Michael Dukakis from Massachusetts. I mean it's pretty doggone obvious what I think any Democrat from South Carolina should do. . . . What would you do? Are you going to go with this fellow from Massachusetts that nobody can identify with or Jesse Jackson, a native son of South Carolina, he's down here, he's in my district—I don't agree with everything Jesse says, he doesn't agree with everything I say, but we can talk and get along. I can understand him and relate to him. I don't know what Michael Dukakis is talking about. . . . Look, I've got a South Carolinian whom I have known personally for years, a fellow from Massachusetts who is almost alien to me. There's no choice.

—REPRESENTATIVE ROBIN TALLON, *explaining his endorsement of Jesse Jackson to his district's white voters*

Do white representatives of minority- and majority-black districts represent the interests of the African Americans in their districts? How do they compare with black politicians? Do white politicians, for instance, manage their coalitions in the same way as black politicians? What do white politicians do when whites and blacks in their districts have different public policy preferences? In this chapter I examine two white representatives of districts in which blacks are in the minority but still form a significant proportion of the population (approximately 40 percent in 1988): Robin Tallon (D-SC) and Tim Valentine (D-NC).

As defined here, a minority-black district is a district that has a white representative and in which the percentage of black voters ranges from 35 to 49, with the remainder of the population being white. In 1990, all the districts that fit these criteria were located in the South, and all but one were represented by a Democrat. The white representatives of minority-black districts must balance the needs and concerns of a liberal black constituency with those of more conservative whites. How well a white representative balances what Merle Black calls "the new political algebra of biracial politics" will determine his or her electoral success.[1]

The growing responsiveness of southern white Democrats to their black constituents is documented in a substantial body of literature.[2] In districts throughout the South, white politicians are giving more meaningful representation to their black constituency, and they are increasingly likely to support legislation targeted by the Leadership Conference for Civil Rights and the Committee for Political Education.[3] The first sign of change came in the form of softened rhetoric; by 1975 most southern white politicians had abandoned the race-baiting that had characterized their earlier politics.[4] A striking example is former governor George Wallace, who in 1963 promised the people of Alabama: "I draw the line in the dust and toss the gauntlet before the feet of tyranny, and I say: Segregation now, segregation tomorrow, segregation forever."[5] The changes in Wallace's style were gradual but dramatic. Ten years after his pledge, he was courting black voters. In 1973 he "crowned a black home-coming queen at the University of Alabama and later told a biracial conference of mayors, 'We're all God's children. All God's children are equal.'"[6]

Without inquiring what sort of deeper conversion may be involved, we can trace the change in style of many southern white politicians to the politics of necessity and rationality. Once blacks became mobilized after the Voting Rights Act of 1965, serious white candidates for state-wide offices needed black support or at least had to be able to count on black indifference. Wallace was not the only white politician to make drastic changes in his behavior. On the congressional level, in both the Senate and the House, many white representatives changed their styles, retired, or suffered defeat. In 1982 Senator Strom Thurmond (R-SC), for example, whose opposition to civil rights led him to run for President against Harry Truman on the Dixiecrat ticket in 1948, cast votes in support of extending the Voting Rights Act and for the Martin Luther King, Jr., Holiday bill.[7] He also hired black staffers and increased his responsiveness to the state's black communities. One black South Carolinian told a researcher that whenever he wanted something done quickly, he preferred to contact Thurmond rather than Ernest (Fritz) Hollings, his Democratic senator, because Hollings took too long to respond.[8]

Robin Tallon, who has witnessed dramatic changes in his state, commented: "White politicians cannot write off the black vote any longer.

They cannot do it. The black vote in South Carolina may not elect by itself a United States senator, but that vote will decide who that United States senator will be. In other words, it will defeat a United States senator. If you ignore that 30 percent, or whatever it is, you can pack your bags and forget it."[9]

The Sixth District of South Carolina: Robin Tallon

Recent History

The sixth district has a mixture of social classes—poor blacks, rural working-class whites, and wealthy beachfront homeowners and merchants. Tobacco farming has long been the primary occupation of the constituents in the mostly rural district, with tourism around the prosperous Myrtle Beach area ranking second. Twenty-two percent of the district's population are college educated; 70 percent of the jobs are classified as blue collar.[10] Most of the state's poorest majority-black counties are in the sixth district. For decades, the preferences of sixth district black voters for civil rights and redistributive social welfare legislation were largely ignored by their conservative Democratic representative, John MacMillan. Eventually, however, the agitation of blacks for a more meaningful form of representation resulted in MacMillan's defeat.

MacMillan represented the district for thirty-four years, from 1938 to 1972. In 1948 he became the chairman of the District of Columbia Committee. In that capacity he earned his reputation for being insensitive to Washington's black majority. He routinely refused to report home rule bills and conducted meetings arbitrarily, often refusing to acknowledge his opponents. At home MacMillan neglected constituency service, particularly ignoring the African Americans in his district. He met defeat when a coalition of African Americans from the District of Columbia and his home district united to oust him. The movement to dump the incumbent was largely headed by Walter Fauntroy, Washington's nonvoting delegate, who wanted MacMillan replaced as chairman of the District of Columbia Committee.[11]

MacMillan's vulnerability first showed in 1970 when a black physician, Claude Stephen, ran against him and forced him into a runoff for the Democratic nomination. Stephen lost after whites united in the second primary. The closeness of the contest made MacMillan's precarious situation evident. If a black candidate could force the incumbent into a runoff, certainly a white opponent could do even better. By the time of the next election, black leaders had recruited a white liberal, John Jenrette, to run against the incumbent. Although Jenrette defeated MacMillan in the 1972 Democratic primary, he lost the general election when a majority of whites voted Republican for the first time in the century and elected Edward Young. Young's election was facilitated by Jenrette's violation of traditional southern mores, which forbade seeking black support.

The district suffered, though, because Young failed to provide poor and working-class whites with effective representation. These whites preferred the economic policies traditionally associated with the Democratic party. More meaningful representation for them did not come until 1974, when Jenrette was finally able to appeal to the mutual interests of both races and forge a winning biracial coalition. It is clear that it was the lack of representation of the rank-and-file white voters that had weakened Young's electoral base. Michael Barone and Grant Ujifusa write that for some whites, "MacMillan's condescending attitudes and Young's support from the country club set were more obnoxious than the fact that Jenrette was winning blacks' votes."[12]

Following his 1974 election to Congress Jenrette compiled a moderate to progressive voting record, but he was defeated in 1980 after a series of scandals. He had divorced his wife and married a younger woman who once posed nude in *Playboy* magazine, and he was one of the members of Congress ensnared in the Abscam scandal, in which FBI officers posed as wealthy Arab sheiks offering bribes for private immigration bills. Caught on videotape with a suitcase full of money, Jenrette said: "I've got larceny in my blood." Later Jenrette testified in his own defense that what he had actually said, or meant, was that he had alcohol in his blood and wanted to get out of the situation. He was convicted of bribery in October 1980, defeated in the November elections by John Napier, and in December he resigned rather than face expulsion from the House.[13]

Napier, who became only the second Republican in the twentieth century to represent the district, was extremely conservative and supportive of President Reagan's economic policies. In 1982 he earned a score of 27 (out of 100) on the LCCR rating scale and 25 on the COPE scale. In less than a decade, blacks in the sixth district went from little representation under MacMillan to meaningful representation with Jenrette, and then back to little representation under Napier. That this traditionally Democratic district elected the conservative Napier is understandable, given that the 59 percent white district also voted Republican in the presidential elections of 1972, 1984, and 1988, and that Jimmy Carter, a son of the South, barely carried it in 1980. Napier's failure to be attentive to the district's very substantial black minority led to his defeat. In 1982 blacks gained meaningful representation again when Robin Tallon was elected.

The Expansionist Stage: The Search for a Political Base

Born in the state and educated at the University of South Carolina, Robin Tallon owned and operated a chain of men's clothing stores that bore his family name before he decided to enter politics. By the time he was in his early thirties, he had reached the goals that he had set for himself in the business world: "I was looking for a new challenge." He had served two years as a member of President Carter's White House Council on small businesses, and this had whetted his appetite for a political career. At the same time, Tallon is very much a southern "good old boy," who prefers anonymity and might drink his beer from the bottle and swap stories with tobacco farmers, both white and black. He is unassuming in the extreme, and is easily embarrassed when his staffers or his wife call him "the congressman," but he took the initiative in running for office. One morning as he was casually reading the newspaper, he spied a vacancy in the state legislature, and without consulting anyone, he immediately filed papers to run for the seat. He won that election and served a single term before running for Congress.

Tallon's decision to run for Congress was predicated on his knowledge that African-American voters in the district were unhappy with Napier, and that they felt themselves to be without any representation:

> We had a situation in 1982 where a Republican had been elected in a traditionally Democratic district under some adverse conditions. It was the district that John Jenrette had represented before he got caught up in the Abscam scandal. And, although the Republican [Napier] was well thought of by virtue of having served for eight or ten years on Senator Thurmond's staff, and was a well-intentioned, bright, and capable person, he was in my mind out of touch with the needs, concerns, and challenges facing our people, the people with whom I had lived, so I decided I would run for Congress.[14]

Although the district was then close to 40 percent black, Napier had employed only one black staffer and had ignored the concerns of blacks and working-class whites. As Tallon put it, "Napier had wrapped himself in Reagan's coat-tails, and appeared oblivious to the recession and the suffering of his constituents."[15]

Because Tallon was virtually unknown outside his statehouse district, a tremendous grassroots effort was required to get him elected. Democratic party leaders advised him to go into the district's African-American communities to forge a base. After giving him the names of five prominent black leaders, they suggested that he ask them for their support and to provide more names. Walter Fauntroy and Claude Pepper (D-FL) campaigned for him because of the special link they had forged with the district during MacMillan's days.[16] Tallon himself sought a relationship with blacks similar to the one that Jenrette had had: "I immediately went to people who had been involved politically in the black community. . . . While the other Democratic candidates were out, I think, really working hard with the traditional rural white Democratic vote, I was in the black churches, as many as seven or eight some Sundays. I was talking to people who had been actively involved, blacks, leaders in their particular communities, the precincts or areas. And I won, I think, by going out immediately and securing that support."[17] Tallon's manner of approaching African Americans created excitement and the expectation among them that they would once again have strong representation in Congress. But that very expectation proved alienating to many of the district's white voters who favored Napier's stance.

Tallon knew why Napier had been so attractive to traditional white Democrats: "A lot of people didn't have any reasons to vote against my Republican opponent. He had sort of been the one to come riding in on a white horse when our district was going through a great deal of turmoil. He cleaned things up. He listened to people. He reached out, but it was obvious that he didn't understand the issues of the district. He sided with the President on most issues."[18] Tallon felt that the district's high unemployment and poverty levels meant that most constituents needed the types of redistributive programs normally associated with the Democratic party.

As he traveled around the district, Tallon found black communities much more politically aware than white communities about the issues of the campaign and about the ways in which Reaganomics affected them. "The black people," he said, "recognized the importance of their participation in the political process and that it could make a difference, whereas in the white community [the congressional race] was more of a personality contest."[19] He observed that his black supporters knew that the stakes were high, and they, therefore, worked hard to elect him. "Blacks don't contribute much money to campaigns," he noted, "but they are a small army when it comes to organization and field work."[20]

Tallon has had challengers in every Democratic primary since 1982 (see Table 7.1). And so sure was he in 1982 that he had lost his campaign against Napier that he had written his concession speech and determined Napier's whereabouts in order to deliver his congratulations. It turned out, however, that he beat Napier by a margin of 8 percent, winning 54 percent of the vote. His more recent congressional races have been much easier, and his winning margins have increased. Napier did not seek a rematch in 1984, and rumors that Jenrette might return to challenge Tallon in 1986 were quieted after Jenrette was arrested on a shoplifting charge. Tallon has won reelection despite the fact that a black minister, who charged that he was not liberal enough on foreign affairs, abortion, and school prayer, ran against him several times. Tallon has managed to retain most of his black support. In doing so, he has made

Table 7.1. The election history of Robin Tallon, Jr.

Year	Primary election opponents	Vote total (percentage)	General election opponents	Vote total (percentage)
1982	Tallon	35,806 (48%)		
	Brasington	12,679 (24)		
	Harwell	17,993 (17)		
	McGill	8,120 (11)		
Runoff	Tallon	40,836 (71)	Tallon	65,582 (54%)
	Harwell	17,017 (29)	Napier	56,653 (46)
1984	Tallon	51,929 (74)	Tallon	97,329 (60)
	Demetrious	14,974 (21)	Eargle	63,005 (39)
	Lightly, Jr.	3,668 (5)		
1986	Tallon	61,924 (90)	Tallon	92,398 (76)
	Lightly, Jr.	7,891 (10)	Cunningham	29,922 (24)
1988	Tallon	65,609 (89)	Tallon	120,719 (76)
	Lightly, Jr.	8,448 (11)	Cunningham	37,958 (24)
1990	Tallon	Unopposed	Tallon	Unopposed

Sources: Michael Barone, Grant Ujifusa, and Douglas Matthews, *The Almanac of American Politics* (New York: E. P. Dutton, 1978, 1980); Barone and Ujifusa, *The Almanac of American Politics* (Washington, D.C.: National Journal, 1984–1990 biennial eds.).

effective use of his black congressional colleagues. Bill Gray, Walter Fauntroy, Charles Rangel, and Edolphus Towns (D-NY) all traveled to the district to give their endorsements and campaign for him.

Tallon and Jenrette were both products of a political dynamic that would have been taboo in old-style southern white politics. Neither of them could have won office without the bulk of the black vote and some of the white. Once elected, they represented blacks in a way unprecedented in the district and the state. Both cases are good evidence for the theory of generational replacement, which posits that more liberal voting behavior on the part of southern white representatives is due to the supplantation of older politicians by younger, newly elected ones.[21]

Interactions with Constituents: Working to Build a Biracial Coalition

Since his election in 1982 Tallon has allocated much of his energy and resources to his district, where he maintains a home and where his family lives. Much of his time is devoted to district activities affecting both blacks and whites. During one of his three annual tours of tobacco markets, Tallon walked with a group of white tobacco farmers and manufacturers, listening intently to their complaints as he fingered dried tobacco leaves and boasted of how much he had learned about the product in a relatively short period of time. At an early morning meeting the farmers had complained mostly about the "laziness of their black workers," and how they were gradually replacing them with Mexican migrants. One farmer commented that perhaps "the blacks would work harder in the fields if the government would eliminate their welfare and food stamps." Another farmer added: "You can't blame them [blacks] for not working, since they can get more from the government than they can by working." Ignoring their racist comments, Tallon told the group that the current Congress had over 111 antitobacco bills to consider. After alluding to a conflict between Senator Jesse Helms (R-NC) and Representative Charlie Rose (D-NC), both members of the agricultural committees in their respective chambers, Tallon told the farmers: "We need to work hard to bring the tobacco family together. I'm on your side."[22]

Tallon has maintained two district offices, with 50 percent of his staff located in the district. He communicates with his constituents through quarterly newsletters, monthly targeted mailings, town meetings, and in person during tours of factories, businesses, and schools. His church visits are by invitation. Just as with the black representatives of majority-white districts, the racial makeup of Tallon's staff approximates the racial percentages in his district. He set up a procedure to ensure that hiring would be fair: "We formed a committee of people who had been involved in my campaign and that committee had more blacks on it than it did whites, because I had more blacks involved in my campaign. And gosh, we had 3,000 applications for sixteen jobs. The committee went through the applications, screened them, and interviewed people. That was the way that the staff evolved, and we ended up with a staff that was certainly representative of the district. It was probably 50–50."[23] "Out of the five top positions," Tallon said, "three or four went to blacks." Blacks were awarded the positions of administrative assistant, press and public relations manager, and economic development coordinator.[24]

Because of the so obviously mixed racial composition of his staff, I asked Tallon how he went about convincing white voters that he would represent them, too. After a long reflective pause, he replied: "Well, I can tell you, that it was difficult, real difficult. It was so difficult that I just backed away from it for a while, because people really resented [that I had defeated] this clean-cut incumbent [who had the support of white people]. A lot of people had never voted for Republicans before he came along. Over a period of time, I think two things helped. My outreach services and efforts to balance my political objectives."[25]

Real progress in forging a biracial coalition was extremely slow, and Tallon said that he did not try to change the minds of white voters immediately: "Eventually, I began to reach out, but it took more than any one term; it took four to five years for me to feel like I had turned the corner, and we were all working together, as color-blind as you can possibly be. But, I am not so naive to think that there's no racial polarization. There are problems, and unfortunately in my lifetime, I don't think we're ever going to see that completely diminished."[26] He credits his black staffers with working hard to represent the needs of everyone in the district. In this case, "everyone" means the white people.

Tallon puts special reliance on his black administrative assistant, Marva Smalls, who doubles as his campaign aide. He even sends his staffers to events where they are sometimes the only blacks:

> If I have a Chamber of Commerce event, there may not be a black face in that event, but if I can't be there, Marva goes, or my district field representative who is also black. The person who deals with minority and small business problems is black. We proved to voters that we were an important asset. We were a constituent service staff more than a policymaking one, because what in the world can a first-term or a second-term congressman

do when it comes to really making a difference in public policy . . . I mean we have a vote, and we have a voice. We can exercise that. Everybody knows our record. By golly, we rolled up our sleeves and we said we're going to serve the people, and proved we could deliver to both races.[27]

One of Smalls's contributions was to encourage Tallon to make changes in his campaign style. She advised him, for example, not to visit black churches without an invitation. "It is too demeaning," she explains, noting that white politicians do not "systematically visit white churches, so why visit black churches at election time?"[28] Marva Smalls is known on the Hill for her influence with her boss. As a member of the Black Caucus told me, "Whenever I want a favor from Robin, I ask Marva. She's the one who tells Robin what to do."[29]

As Tallon himself puts it, he has come a long way in his relations with blacks: "You have to look at where I came from. All my friends were Republicans, I came from a different community, I was a relatively successful small business person. I had credentials that played quite well in white communities. I first had to go prove myself in the black community, and I really think I did that in the General Assembly when I was up against things such as the reform of public utilities, and things that I think had a negative impact on blacks and poor people."[30]

Southern white representatives who seek to represent the blacks in their districts must ward off backlash on the part of white voters. Tallon remembers that "a lot of people didn't like what I was doing, but I developed a pretty thick skin through that whole process, and the notion that we're going to prove to the people that a majority of the voters made the right decision in choosing their congressional representation." As an afterthought, he added, "At first, we didn't know how to do all these things that we know how to do today, but we developed, learned, and worked together. I think somehow we've shown the white community, especially the business community which was totally against us, that we would represent their interests and we would take care of their programs, and that we were ready to bury the hatchet, no hard feelings, and that we could do this, and the end product would be in everybody's interests."[31]

How well Tallon has succeeded is evident from his recent reelection margins of almost 80 percent. As one political observer put it: "No one will ever accuse Tallon of being a brilliant legislative tactician, but he is smart enough to sense what his constituents want and learn how to use his seat in Congress to satisfy them."[32]

Representation through Legislation: Working with the Congressional Black Caucus

Tallon serves on the committees of Agriculture and Merchant Marine and Fisheries. Because tobacco and waterfront tourism are the district's main industries, these are particularly attractive assignments for him. In addition, he belongs to the Black Caucus and has publicized this membership in his congressional newsletters, an advertisement geared toward his black constituents. His decision to join the caucus met with some resistance from his white constituents. Tallon remembers that he had an especially difficult time at home after the first newsletter went out announcing his membership. He had town meetings scheduled all across the district, and he recalls that some white voters were very indignant because "I didn't just vote for the legislation, I was on the task force, and helped pass the King bill by lobbying Senate members." Despite this controversy, Tallon is not sure whether his actions have cost him any white supporters. "I knew there would be some problems," he said, "but I assumed those were the people that didn't support me anyway. . . . [Although] I don't think that I lost any votes, it took me, I think, four years for everybody to understand me."[33]

Tallon's support of black issues have led him to attempt an active role in the Black Caucus:

I didn't know that an associate member couldn't go into a regular Black Caucus meeting, that it was just for full members only. And so they had a Black Caucus meeting and I went to it, and I noticed everybody was real nice, but there was a lot of scratching their heads. And so when I came out of the meeting, Marva said: "What were you doing in that meeting? Didn't you know you weren't supposed to be there—white people aren't supposed to be in that meeting!" I said: "No, Marva, you're wrong. That fellow Gus Hawkins from California was in there." Marva said: "Congressman, he's black!" "No he's not!" I said. "Yes, he is!" Marva replied. I felt like a fool.[34]

But the stunned Black Caucus members said nothing to him about his inappropriate attendance at their closed-door meeting. In fact, Tallon said, "They've all helped me." He believes this to be the reason: "I didn't have sense enough not to walk into a meeting where [I] wasn't supposed to be, sit down and stay and say, 'Yes, I can go talk to Senator Thurmond [to get support for caucus initiatives], and I can do this, and I can do that.' I guess they thought, 'We better let him stay.'"[35]

Tallon's home style is based on his efforts to become the opposite of the Republican incumbent he defeated for the seat: "The other representative served the national interest and divided people. I am both parochial and inclusive."[36] By this he means that he has consciously chosen to focus on district concerns and on resolving racial group conflicts rather than on accentuating them. Bringing unity to the district, Tallon says, has been a major part of his role as congressman.

Tallon's voting record has changed over time, with increasing support for the congressional conservative coalition (see Table 7.2).[37] During the 98th Congress he supported it 63 percent of the time; by the 100th Congress he was giving it 82 percent support. What is more important for assessing black interests, however, are his COPE scores, which measure support for workers' and redistributive policies. His mean COPE score for the 98th Congress was 71 percent, for the 100th Congress 68 percent.

Tallon's mean scores are similar to those of Jenrette, while the scores of the defeated Republicans (Young and Napier) are similar to those of MacMillan, the defeated Democrat. Over a six-year period, Tallon's LCCR scores have dropped slightly, from 80 percent to 73 percent. The votes that lowered his LCCR score are primarily those he cast on certain economic issues and on legislation potentially beneficial to nonblack minorities. He opposed reparations to the Japanese, for example, and thus his score was brought down by an item that does not directly affect his constituents. (Japanese Americans constitute less than 1 percent of his district.) A more important measure for assessing his representation of blacks is his vote against job training for unemployed youth, an issue clearly affecting African Americans. In retrospect this vote seems puzzling, but it was cast soon after his election, in the early years of the Reagan Administration, when cuts in domestic programs were commonplace. Tallon now considers his overall voting record on economic issues excellent. He has worked hard for the causes he believes in. He says that he was the only member of his state delegation to vote for an increase in the minimum wage. "That absolutely floored me," he said. "I didn't just vote for it, I spoke on it, and I spoke out loud in the Chamber of Commerce. I can justify that, I can go into any predominantly white civic club in the state of South Carolina and tell them: 'If you can't understand that, then you can't understand me.'" And in explaining his consistent support for civil rights legislation affecting blacks, he said: "They're tough issues, but they're not as difficult as they used to be, because people know that I am going to support legislation that the black community is sensitive to. People [white businessmen] used to like to push us around a little bit with that, but no more, because they know that we've got a winning coalition. We won last time with almost 80 percent of the vote, but if we didn't get but 60 percent of that, we would have still won. So we're going to do those things that are important to the people we represent." "Now I can say to people," Tallon continued, "listen, if you've got a problem with the civil rights field, that's fine, but it's not my problem. It's your problem."[38]

The need to balance conservative whites and liberal blacks explains Tallon's trend toward moderation. Although he is not always a certain vote for the progressive agenda that is preferred by most African Americans, he is considerably more responsive to these issues than all his predecessors, with the exception of Jenrette. His conservative coalition scores are similar to those of Mike Espy, who has faced the same requirement of balancing the demands of black and white constituents. Occasional votes against redistributive issues do not hurt Tallon with his black supporters, because the manner in which he was elected gives him some latitude to vote as he pleases on a variety of issues. Not only does Tallon belong to the Black Caucus, but he was also (to the displeasure of many white constituents) one of the few whites to vote for Jesse Jackson at the 1988 Democratic Convention.[39] When Tallon votes against a redistributive measure that blacks support, such as job training for unemployed youth, it is usually an issue that the white majority in the district opposes with particular vehemence. His representation of a district that is 59 percent white dictates that white voters must win on some issues.

The saga of the sixth district suggests that when blacks who were traditionally shut out of political power in the old order succeed in electing a sympathetic representative, they are unlikely ever to be shut out again. Sixth district blacks reached their tolerance level for insensitive white representatives back in the early 1970s. Since 1974 the district has never allowed a conservative to represent it in Congress for long. After MacMillan, representatives of the sixth district have adopted a different style of representation.[40]

Fenno's work sheds light on the mental calculations representatives make when they attempt to defeat incumbents. One of the representatives he interviewed told him:

My predecessor paid no attention to his constituents and did not tend the district. His life was back there [in Washington] where he was a powerful figure because of his position and native ability. He was terribly important to the major interests here. He was powerful and feared here. But he

Table 7.2. Legislative records of white representatives by congress

	Tallon	Valentine	Boggs	Rodino
93rd (1973–1975)				
COPE rating			80	93
LCCR rating			70	100
CC score			35	5
VP score			90	95
94th (1975–1977)				
COPE rating			75	89
LCCR rating			88	100
CC score			42	7
VP score			83	88
95th (1977–1979)				
COPE rating			70	87
LCCR rating			92	83
CC score			41	3
VP score			89	63
96th (1979–1981)				
COPE rating			55	97
LCCR rating			86	86
CC score			42	6
VP score			86	68
97th (1981–1983)				
COPE rating			70	95
LCCR rating			73	100
CC score			59	5
VP score			91	97

couldn't abide coming back here. He hated to fly. When he did come, he did everyone a favor, so to speak. And he touched the elites—the Chamber of Commerce, the local establishment. He would attend ceremonies and cut ribbons. But he didn't care about mingling with the ordinary citizens. Everything I do is in contrast. He came home twice a year. I come home every month for a week, hold open houses all over the district, and talk to ordinary people. Out here, that makes news. It's nothing that lots of others don't do back East. But people see me as different because of the contrast with my predecessor.[41]

This statement could have been made by either Jenrette or Tallon. Both of them adopted home styles that allowed them to solidify a link between blacks and working-class white voters, two groups who had received little representation from Republicans. Tallon and Jenrette be-

Table 7.2 (continued).

	Tallon	Valentine	Boggs	Rodino
98th (1983–1985)				
COPE rating	71	37	72	94
LCCR rating	80	60	73	100
CC score	63	86	32	8
VP score	93	89	81	85
99th (1985–1987)				
COPE rating	62	38	73	95
LCCR rating	80	80	100	90
CC score	86	90	48	10
VP score	93	98	95	87
100th (1987–1989)				
COPE rating	68	44	76	100
LCCR rating	73	100	87	88
CC score	82	95	39	3
VP score	82	95	95	95

Sources: Michael Barone, Grant Ujifusa, and Douglas Matthews, *The Almanac of American Politics* (Boston, Mass.: Gambit, 1972, 1974); Barone, Ujifusa, and Matthews, *The Almanac of American Politics* (New York: E. P. Dutton, 1976, 1978, 1980); Barone and Ujifusa, *The Almanac of American Politics* (Washington, D.C.: National Journal, 1984–1990 biennial eds.); Leadership Conference on Civil Rights, *A Civil Rights Voting Record for the 93rd–101st Congress* (annual edition); *Congressional Quarterly Weekly Report* (Washington, D.C.: Congressional Quarterly, 1973–1991 weekly eds.).

Note: COPE = AFL-CIO Committee on Political Education (scores are not lowered by missed votes); LCCR = Leadership Conference on Civil Rights; CC = Conservative coalition score (percentage of votes cast in support of coalition between Republicans and Southern Democrats against other Democrats); VP = Voting participation score (percentage of roll-call votes cast).

fore him were able to make strategic use of the situation—to the advantage of otherwise poorly represented voters.

The Second District of North Carolina: Tim Valentine

Recent History

Located north of Raleigh and south of the Virginia border, the second district of North Carolina was the last remaining southern district to have a black congressman at the end of the Reconstruction era. George White represented the district from 1898 until his resignation in 1900, after which no southern district elected an African American to Congress until Andrew Young (D-GA) and Barbara Jordan (D-TX) were elected in 1972. Before the redistricting that followed the 1982 census and the court challenges to the initial plan, the district was predominantly rural and composed of small towns. It has always had the state's highest concentration of blacks. In the 1970s and 1980s the district was 40 percent black and the black population of voting age was 34 percent. From 1952 until 1982 the district was represented by L. H. Fountain, an old-style southern white politician described in the *Almanac of Politics* as "the kind of politician who wears white linen suits in the summertime and speaks with gentle southern courtliness year round."[42]

Fountain had a conservative voting record on civil rights and economic issues, often earning LCCR scores as low as zero or ten. His lack of responsiveness to black interests led to a strong challenge in 1972, after Chapel Hill, home of the University of North Carolina, was added to the district. The challenge came from Howard Lee, the black former mayor of Chapel Hill, who ran against him in a Democratic primary and won 41 percent of the vote. Although this represented a respectable showing, Lee declined to challenge Fountain in subsequent elections.

As a response to the times, Fountain made cosmetic changes in his method of operation, adding a black face to his staff, but he made no changes in his voting behavior. He retired in 1982 after his old rural district was merged with the city of Durham, which has a large black middle class, and Soul City, an all-black town located in Warren County. Durham's blacks are well known for their high level of political mobilization. Their political activity is chronicled in a well-known book by William Keech, *The Impact of Negro Voting*.[43] For decades blacks in the city have maintained a political organization now known as the Durham Committee on the Affairs of Black People. Rather than compete in a new political environment that would have virtually required him to reenter the expansionist stage of his constituency career, Fountain left Congress.[44]

The Expansionist Stage: Breaking Free of Fountain's Record

Fountain's retirement led to intense competition for the open seat. H. M. "Mickey" Michaux, a black former U.S. attorney and state legislator, and Tim Valentine, a white attorney from a rural town, were the strongest contenders. In a contest that made national headlines, Michaux won the 1982 Democratic primary with 44 percent of the vote but lost the runoff to Valentine after white voters, who were split during the first contest,

Table 7.3. The election history of Tim Valentine

Year	Primary election opponents	Vote total (percentage)	General election opponents	Vote total (percentage)
1982	Valentine	34,708 (33%)		
	Michaux, Jr.	47,132 (44)		
	Ramsey	24,179 (23)		
Runoff	Valentine	58,965 (54)	Valentine	59,745 (64%)
	Michaux, Jr.	50,949 (46)	Marin	34,282 (36)
1984	Valentine	65,893 (52)	Valentine	122,292 (68)
	Spaulding	60,535 (48)	Hill	58,312 (32)
1986	Valentine	Unopposed	Valentine	95,320 (75)
			McElhaney	32,515 (25)
1988	Valentine	Unopposed	Valentine	Unopposed
1990	Valentine	Unopposed	Valentine	130,979 (75)
			Sharpe	44,263 (25)

Sources: Michael Barone, Grant Ujifusa, and Douglas Matthews, *The Almanac of American Politics* (New York: E. P. Dutton, 1978, 1980); Barone and Ujifusa, *The Almanac of American Politics* (Washington, D.C.: National Journal, 1984–1990 biennial eds.).

united behind the single white candidate and voted along racial lines (Table 7.3). Michaux received nearly unanimous black support; Valentine received most of the white vote. Black dissatisfaction at the outcome manifested itself in general election write-in votes for Michaux.

Compared with some other southern campaigns, the one between Michaux and Valentine was relatively free of explicit racial appeals. Valentine campaigned as a fiscal conservative and labeled Michaux a liberal, but he made known that he was in favor of extending the Voting Rights Act, which Fountain had never supported. Racially polarizing elements were introduced into the campaign, however. Literature alluding to Michaux's "bloc votes" appeared, and Valentine embraced the theme that he would represent "all" of the district's voters, thereby implying that Michaux would not. Both candidates knew that race would be a determining factor in the election's outcome. Valentine explained his consideration: "The white people knew that I would make it my business to do what I said in the campaign, and that is to represent all the people of the district and they principally voted for me, while most of the blacks voted for my opponent. . . . And I came to believe that constituents, and some of my principal supporters, assumed I would be like L. H. Fountain."[45] As his comments suggest, Valentine has not viewed his promise to represent all of the district's voters as a racial innuendo. We can contrast the subtlety of his campaign appeals with the blatant tactics used by Mississippi's Webb Franklin (see Chapter 4).[46]

Valentine was again challenged by a black candidate in 1984, when state representative Kenneth Spaulding, an attorney and a member of a wealthy black family, took him on in the Democratic primary. Unlike Michaux, Spaulding campaigned as a fiscal conservative. He earned more white support than Michaux had, but he made the mistake of allowing Jesse Jackson to mount a voter registration drive in the district. Jackson's presence spurred a backlash among rural whites. Whites registered and turned out to vote in huge numbers, defeating Spaulding.[47]

Valentine's incumbency was the most important barrier to Spaulding's success. By 1984 Valentine had sought to mend his relationship with blacks, and he openly appealed to them for their support. He employed both white and black staff, nominated a black candidate for judge, and supported the Martin Luther King, Jr., Holiday bill. Valentine had also gained the endorsement of Howard Clements, a prominent black businessman. After winning the Democratic nomination with 52 percent of the vote in 1984, Valentine ran unopposed in the Democratic primaries in 1986 and 1988 and easily won the subsequent general elections.[48]

No sooner did Valentine seem to be free of competition within his own party than he was challenged in the 1990 general election by Hal Sharpe, a Republican who sought to undermine him with both his black and his white constituents. Sharpe told black voters that although the blacks who made up 40 percent of the district gave Valentine 100 percent of their vote, after the election Valentine gave "100 percent of his attention to the remaining 60 percent of the people." He also released a flier in the final days of the campaign quoting a 1956 statement by Valentine that he was "unalterably opposed to integrated schools." In addition he charged that Valentine was failing to campaign for Harvey Gantt, the black candidate who was opposing Jesse Helms in the Senate race. At the same time Sharpe took the opposite tack with white voters, declaring that Valentine "talks conservative but votes liberal."

Sharpe's approach backfired. To the surprise of many, Mickey Michaux rushed to Valentine's defense, declaring that "Tim is no flaming liberal, but neither has he ignored or done anything extremist." And he added that Valentine listened to black leaders, was receptive to their ideas, and had a good civil rights record. The Durham Committee on the Affairs of Black People came out for Valentine and issued mock ballots that included his name on the straight Democratic ticket.[49] Valentine won the election with 75 percent of the vote.

Interactions with Constituents: Balancing Conflicting Racial Interests

Valentine maintains two district offices located at opposite ends of the district. One is in downtown Durham, where most of the district's African Americans live, and the other is in a rural, mostly white area. His staff is biracial but has a lower percentage of blacks than the district does. Nevertheless, Valentine is emphatic about his commitment to employing a biracial staff:

> We have had an integrated staff from the beginning. It is not tokenism. At one time it was as high as four or five staff members, one of whom, Quentin Sumner, an attorney who worked for us part time, is now a superior court judge. . . . We did not involve ourselves in tokenism. Of the two staff positions in Durham, one has been black from day one. One of the blacks is no longer here because he left to become an administrative assistant for a member of Congress from New York. We had a black member of the staff who was a legislative assistant. We never had what some people refer to as a "director of minority affairs." We selected people for what we thought they could do. I was mindful of the need to fulfill that part of my responsibility, and we took great care, and still take great care, to be sure that our appointments to the service academies were without any considerations of race or sex or gender or anything like that.[50]

The number of blacks on Valentine's staff was down to two receptionists and an intern in 1991, but he was attempting to find additional black staffers.[51]

Valentine's efforts to gain black support increased significantly after his 1984 reelection. Immediately after the election he met with black leaders and asked what he could do to let black constituents know that they too had representation in Congress.[52] They came up with the idea of a "legislative day" for black constituents—an all-expenses-paid bus trip to the capital, where participants would meet with important national leaders. The black response to this legislative day was so positive that Valentine's office had to limit future invitations to the district's black elected officials.

Personal contact has been vital to Valentine's efforts to reach voters, and his campaigns have taken him into small towns all across the district. In 1988 his regular circuit of stops included country stores, banks, and homes. At one stop a white constituent told me: "No one ever paid attention to our town until Congressman Valentine was elected." A white woman in a bank exclaimed: "I know you, Congressman, you changed my tire one morning. I was stuck along the road with a flat tire and you stopped."[53]

On another occasion Valentine addressed a group of farmers, a constituency with whom he has a special rapport, in a country store. He talked about an issue in the coming presidential election, the refusal of the 1988 Democratic presidential nominee, Michael Dukakis, to sign a bill requiring teachers in Massachusetts to participate in the pledge of allegiance. Valentine, urging that the pledge not be considered a litmus test of patriotism, said that the issue had been "blown out of proportion" and "detracts from the real issues surrounding farms, the national budget, and defense." After he spoke, he thanked the store owner and presented him with an American flag. Reporters and local residents took pictures of the congressman presenting the flag to the patriotic audience.

It has not been an easy job to represent the second district. Valentine compared it to "walking through a briar patch," noting that, "by the time you walk out the other side . . . you get some scratches on you. To my chagrin and to my disappointment, I've lost the friendship of good close personal friends at home because of votes that I've cast."[54]

For a while there was speculation that Valentine's district would be redrawn to have a black majority, and this possibility may in part account for his responsiveness to blacks. Instead, redistricters decided in mid-1991 to form a black majority in the neighboring first district, a move that forced the retirement of Representative Walter Jones.[55] Valentine was initially given a sprawling district that took in several media markets. *Congressional Quarterly* described it as an "arachnid mass."[56] On December 18, 1991, however, the Justice Department ordered North Carolina to create a second majority-black district.[57] The additional majority-black district runs 190 miles along Interstate 85 and has a minimal impact on Valentine. Valentine's new district is 21.9 percent black, and it is relatively compact.

Valentine has been more responsive to African Americans than Fountain was, but he is less responsive than Tallon. In contrast to Tallon, Valentine was recruited exclusively by whites. (Friends urged him to run for office as a way of dealing with his grief after the death of his first wife in an accident.) The manner of his recruitment appears to have left white voters with the expectation that, like Fountain, he would be a conservative representative. His move to the left on economic and racial issues has therefore alienated some whites, while he has not been liberal enough to be strongly appealing to blacks. He may have trouble winning election in his new district, which, whatever its precise composition, is likely to be heavily white and rural. As Fenno reports, it is difficult for a representative to alter constituent expectations: "As a congressman's home style solidifies, so do the expectations of his supporters. Whether he imposes a style on them or they impose a style on him, constituents eventually come to expect the style they are accustomed to. And these constituent expectations in turn become a constraint on the congressman, keeping him in his mold whether he wishes it or not."[58]

The history of a district and the circumstances of a representative's election are important for understanding his or her behavior. Valentine campaigned in a conservative district in support of a conservative economic agenda. This conservatism has been important both in his voting in Congress and in his home style. He has had to fend off criticisms in local newspapers for taking "junkets outside of the country," although in his time in Congress he has traveled out of the country only twice since 1988, and on one of the trips, to Antarctica on a fact-finding mission, he flew in a cargo plane to save money.

One might expect a congressman who faces press opposition to respond vigorously, but in fact Valentine does not even take advantage of the six constituency mailings to which representatives are entitled. Explaining his practices in a 1988 newsletter, he declared: "The effort to maintain communication with second district citizens involves occasional newsletters such as this one. This is my first district-wide mailing in more than a year. . . . [Although] House of Representative rules permit members to use the franking privilege for up to six such mailings annually to every household in their districts, I have never sent more than two in a year. Nevertheless, my 1986 newsletter resulted in an editorial in a second district newspaper that advised me to . . . show more restraint in the use of the frank. . . . My current plans are to send two newsletters per year."[59] Whether Valentine's cautious, low-profile approach will win him continuing reelection in his new district remains to be seen.

Representation through Legislation: Casting the Tough Votes

Valentine, like Tallon, has chosen committees that relate directly to the interests of his constituents. He is a member of the Public Works and

Transportation Committee and of the Science, Space, and Technology Committee, which are appropriate choices given the presence of part of Research Triangle Park and two major universities within his district's lines. In 1991 he explained to me how he now allocates his time:

> I go into the district, but not as often as I did several years ago, because as you stay here [in Washington] and gather seniority you have more responsibilities. I'm now a subcommittee chairman, which takes a lot of time. I spent a good part of yesterday and today presiding over subcommittee meetings. There's only twenty-four hours in a day, but we still travel into the district. I accept invitations of black churches and other places where we might be expected to meet more blacks than whites, and we still have what we call citizens' meetings, where we go into every part of the district at least once a year.[60]

Because he is in Washington more than ever before, Valentine has had to defend himself against charges that he is no longer accessible to voters. Writing to his constituents in 1990, he said: "I have been home virtually every weekend and during periods when the House was not in session. I have maintained an active schedule of travel and public appearances in every part of the district, in addition to my regular and frequent office hours in both Durham and Rocky Mount."[61] Many of Valentine's white constituents have known him for most of their lives. As a product of rural North Carolina, he has personal relationships that allow him more freedom in the white community than he will ever have in the black community. Still, he is weakened by the belief of some whites in the district that he has made too many concessions to gain the support of blacks.

Valentine's legislative responsiveness to blacks is evident when his voting record is compared with Fountain's, who had a poor record on civil rights and had low COPE scores, averaging less than 30 percent. In contrast, Valentine's COPE scores have averaged in the 40 percent range, and he has had an excellent civil rights and domestic policy record (see Table 7.2). His LCCR scores increased from 60 percent in 1984 to 100 percent in 1988, but they dropped sharply during the 101st Congress from 100 to 43 percent. This may in part be a result of the particular bills that made up the LCCR scale for that congress, but it also was no doubt because he anticipated having to represent a more conservative district after the next redistricting. Nonetheless Valentine supported the 1990 and 1991 civil rights bills, which took considerable courage for a congressman from a state in which Senator Jesse Helms based his successful 1990 Senate race on opposition to affirmative action and quota programs. Valentine voices concern at what he sees as a tendency of the black community to focus on symbolic issues rather than bread-and-butter issues. He believes that blacks often set up litmus tests for white representatives and that they are on occasion "more concerned about South African sanctions than they are about public housing."[62]

Valentine may be right about the litmus test. In any event, he is not alone in his view. Charlie Rose, another white North Carolina Democrat, who serves a district in which the black percentage of the population is much lower, said: "When confronted with a new white boy, black voters will require that a white politician do all kinds of things to prove his loyalty. They will push him almost to the breaking point to prove that he's loyal. But if you are a white elected official and you have a solid track record of service when you're called on to serve, and if the black constituents know they can depend on you, then they look on you not as someone to test, but as someone to cherish and to protect and to hope you get reelected."[63]

Valentine has supported controversial legislature in which symbolism is central, including the Martin Luther King, Jr., Holiday bill and the Civil Rights Restoration bill as well as sanctions against South Africa and all of the more recent civil rights bills. It is not clear how much such votes gained him in black support, however. Although the Durham Committee has relented in its opposition (it now endorses him), it has never enthusiastically embraced him. He is between the proverbial rock and a hard place, knowing that he has lost support from the white voters who expected him to be another L. H. Fountain, while he has not gained the trust of as many blacks as he would like.[64]

In some respects, Valentine seems to be a classical delegate-style representative. As he puts it: "I represent people, and I'm supposed to reflect their sentiment. We try to find out how people feel about an issue. We read the mail. We take the telephone calls. I don't have any unlisted telephone numbers at home, in Arlington or Nashville. Someone called me recently and asked for the names of people whose phone calls I would return. I will return anyone's call. I don't ask who is calling. And so, you find out how your people feel about the flag amendment, Contra aid, the war in the Persian Gulf."[65] But he plays the part of a trustee, when that seems feasible: "When I don't receive an outpouring of advice from constituents, I use my own judgment, and confer with my staff, and do what I think is right. I make the decision, cast the vote, and take action. And I don't spend a lot of time worrying about it afterwards."[66]

Tallon's style is much more that of an out-and-out delegate, but both representatives have learned over the years which views can be safely discounted. Like many other southern white Democrats they have found that blacks rarely forgive white representatives who vote "wrong" on issues that they care about, but that in a minority-black district, they also have to take care not to lose their core white constituents.

A Delicate Balancing Act: Southern White Representation of African Americans

Given their constraints, southern white representatives of districts with substantial black minorities do a credible job of representing blacks. Robin Tallon and Tim Valentine are two white Democrats whose political survival in Congress has depended on their ability to balance the interests of conservative whites and liberal blacks. They replaced more conservative white representatives, and they have made important changes in order to represent the diversity of interests in their districts. Often forced to take controversial stances, they have told the whites in their districts of their duty to represent black voters, and they have reminded them that the world has changed, and with it the South.

As already mentioned, both Tallon and Valentine voted for the 1988 Civil Rights Restoration bill and the 1990 and 1991 Civil Rights acts. Their votes on these issues corresponded with the liberal position of the Black Caucus, the Leadership Conference on Civil Rights, and most members of their party. They managed to uphold their positions in spite of the vehement opposition in parts of the South to this legislation by fundamentalist groups, such as the Moral Majority, that have highly effective systems of communication. Southern white representatives have learned to discount the "word-processing capabilities" of such organizations; as one representative said: "It's all inspired [organization-instigated] mail, whether it comes from the civil rights community or the chamber of commerce. Most of the stuff we do just doesn't filter down to John Q. Citizen; he doesn't know what's in those bills."

When we compare Tallon and Valentine it must be said that Tallon has done a better job of forging and maintaining his biracial coalition. In order to win the confidence of the African Americans in his district, he has employed many of the same techniques that Mike Espy and Alan

Wheat used to gain white support. Starting with the racial composition of his staff, Tallon sought to demonstrate his concern for the welfare of African Americans, and his ingratiating "home folks" southern manner is also to his advantage. Valentine, in contrast, has allowed himself to be forced into a more defensive posture. Some African Americans have viewed him as antithetical to the representation of their interests. Having defeated two experienced black politicians in highly charged, racially polarized elections, and given the ideological split between blacks and whites in his district, it has not been easy for him to represent African-American interests.

From the examples of Tallon and Valentine, we can see that even in a relatively conservative Southern district, a white representative can effectively alter the style and content of his representation to include African-American interests and concerns. Although white representatives of minority-black districts may not provide as much substantive representation as African Americans would like, the degree to which white representatives have managed to balance white and black interests is significant.

8 · White Representatives of Majority-Black Districts

Everything I did was not unusual, except for the fact that the district was becoming more and more African American, and I sensed the fact that this was going to be a problem for me, and I sensed it because my district didn't have, at the beginning, many African Americans. And yet, I always supported whatever issues there were that related to civil rights when the Congress, itself, hardly responded.

—INTERVIEW WITH PETER RODINO, January 31, 1990

When Lindy (Corinne) Boggs (D-LA) announced her retirement from Congress in 1990, she gave African-American politicians their long-awaited opportunity to claim ownership of the last majority-black congressional district with a white representative. A black former state senator, William Jefferson, won her seat in the November elections. Two years earlier, New Jersey's Peter Rodino, another white representative of a majority-black congressional district, had retired from Congress after forty years of service, and he, too, had been replaced by a black representative. Boggs and Rodino, both well-known national figures, were the last white representatives of districts with a black majority. White politicians, regardless of how well they have represented their black constituents and no matter how long their tenure, have found themselves under increasing pressure to step aside whenever their political units have been redrawn to have black majorities or when demographic change has altered their district's racial majority.[1] Still, the po-

170

litical careers of Boggs and Rodino shed light on the representation of black interests in Washington, especially on the question of whether and how whites can be responsive to the blacks in their districts.

The Second District of Louisiana: Lindy (Corinne) Boggs

Recent History

Since the early 1980s, the area covered by the second district of Louisiana has roughly coincided with the boundaries of the city of New Orleans. This municipality is a tolerant one, with fewer of the racial problems that have characterized other parts of the South. New Orleans has the largest Honduran population of any U.S. city, a considerable number of Italian, Cuban, and Irish Americans, and African Americans make up 59 percent of the population. In its race relations the city follows Atlanta's tradition of liberalism rather than the more common southern conservatism. Nevertheless, a part of the district, Jefferson Parish, voted in 1968 for the segregationist presidential candidate, George Wallace; more recently, a town that was once a part of the district spawned David Duke, the former Klu Klux Klansman and Republican state senator, who made an impressive bid as an anti–affirmative action candidate. He won 44 percent of the vote in Louisiana's 1990 race for the U.S. Senate and in 1991 was a strong, though ultimately unsuccessful, candidate for the governorship.[2]

The second district suffers from some of the same economic problems that characterize other urban areas with black majorities. Long dependent on oil as its major industry, the city has seen a depressed oil market hurt its infrastructure, dry up state revenues, and cause property taxes to rise—all of which, together with deteriorating public schools, has made the area less attractive to business. Crime, unemployment, teenage pregnancy, and single parents on welfare have been a further burden on the city's resources. In 1989 New Orleans ranked fourth in homicides per capita in the country; of its murder victims, 87 percent were black and 75 percent were black males.[3]

For African Americans, the first sympathetic congressman to represent the district was Hale Boggs, an anti–Huey Long reformer, who was elected in 1940 at the age of twenty-six. To win his seat he had to defeat a "machine candidate," and in doing so he became the youngest member of the House. He was defeated after his first term but was reelected four years after that, settling into a long incumbency. Boggs supported liberal domestic legislation throughout his career, and was one of the few white southerners to cast votes in support of civil rights legislation. According to his daughter, Cokie Roberts, the congressional correspondent for National Public Radio, he was under some pressure from his family: "I remember the night before the debate on the 1965 Voting Rights Bill, and we were all giving daddy a hard time, and he said: 'I'm voting for it, leave me alone.' We said we don't want you to just vote for it, we want you to talk as well. He said we were asking too much from somebody from the deep South. But the next day we heard one of his colleagues saying there was no discrimination in Louisiana. He couldn't stand it, and he got up and gave the most phenomenal speech of his career."[4] In retaliation, Klu Klux Klansmen burned crosses on the family's front lawn. Hurt by his progressive stance on civil rights issues, Boggs was barely reelected in 1964 and 1968. His wife, Lindy, recalled that the vote was so close that she "would not allow Hale to go down and claim victory until all the precincts had reported."[5]

The situation improved after 1969, when the state legislature increased the number of blacks in his district to 37 percent and removed a large segment of Jefferson Parish, which was then, as today, hostile toward blacks and legislation perceived to benefit them.[6] The second district has had a black majority since 1983, when a redistricting plan created a new district as a result of the court case *Major v. Treen*. The case challenged a state plan jokingly called the "Gerryduck," because its boundaries resembled a duck's head. It diluted the district's black voting strength by splitting the black population of New Orleans in half, and was overturned after a three-judge panel ruled in favor of the black plaintiffs and ordered that the district's black population be increased from 40 to 59 percent (that is, a 54 percent black voting-age population).[7]

By 1983 Lindy Boggs was the district's representative. Her husband had been lost in a 1972 plane crash over Alaska. Altogether he had served twenty-seven years in Congress, and had risen in power. "In 1971 Hale was elected Majority Leader," Lindy Boggs said, "and it was widely assumed that he would become Speaker of the House, but then his plane disappeared." She continued: "Carl Albert, who was Speaker of the House, called to tell me the plane was eight hours late. . . . My first reaction was shock and disbelief. The search went on until Thanksgiving. There were fifty-five investigations of sightings during that time. I heard from a number of psychics all convinced that they were receiving information that needed to be investigated. The plane was never found."[8] Lindy Boggs finds that even today, people still contact her with sightings of Hale. "It is ironic," she said, "that Hale, who was a big advocate for statehood for Alaska, would be lost in that very state."[9]

The Expansionist Stage: Lindy Boggs, a Seasoned Politician

Unlike some congressional wives who have succeeded their deceased husbands, Lindy Boggs was no beginner. She was a congressional expert who had worked in her husband's office, run twelve of his campaigns, and earned the respect of his colleagues. She had also chaired the inaugural ball committees of John F. Kennedy and Lyndon B. Johnson. Her relationship with these two presidents and their families was so close that she said: "We raised each other's children."[10]

Boggs already had a strong organization and a constituency base: "When I ran for Congress and was successful, all of my people were in place. I had been the campaign manager for most of Hale's elections. I went into the office one day and all the staffers were arranged around my desk, and they said: 'Let's get this clear. You are the candidate, and we are the campaign staff; if you don't start behaving like a candidate, we will quit.'"[11] Nevertheless, she was not an eager candidate: "When I was finally persuaded to run for his seat, I'm not sure it was because I really accepted the fact that [Hale] was gone. I figured that if anybody was willing to give up the seat to him if he came back, it would be me."[12]

She won a special election to succeed her husband with 81 percent of the vote, and the Louisiana delegation supported her for the full term. Her election made her the first woman to serve in Congress from Louisiana. She did not have any trouble getting reelected (see Table 8.1), but many considerations went through her mind before she announced her candidacy: "I think one of my reluctances to be a congressman was that . . . I knew I had the delicious difference from Hale [when he was in Congress] that I didn't have to vote so that I could understand problems and be excited about challenges and work with everybody on every side and have the background information to discuss with him. . . . When you become a congressman you lose that privilege. You must vote and necessarily will vote on legislation that is never exactly what you wish it to be. You have to disappoint people."[13] Boggs once described disappointing people as her greatest fear, because she wanted them all to love her. She knew that pleasing everyone would be impossible once she became a politician.

Boggs won consecutive elections from 1973 on and had only token

Table 8.1. The election history of Lindy (Corinne) Boggs

Year	Primary election opponents	Vote total (percentage)		General election opponents[a]	Vote total (percentage)	
1973[b]	Boggs	41,526	(73%)	Boggs	43,255	(81%)
	Koppel	12,208	(21)	Lee	10,315	(19)
	Smith	1,345	(2)			
	Hillery	999	(2)			
	Fertel	781	(1)			
1974	Boggs	64,466	(87)	Boggs	53,802	(85)
	Clark	6,840	(7)	Morphos	9,632	(15)
	Fertel	2,428	(3)			
1976	Boggs	48,312	(83)	Boggs	85,923	(93)
	two others	9,770	(17)	Hillery	6,904	(7)
1978	Boggs	57,056	(87)			
	two others	8,411	(13)			
1980	Boggs	45,091	(61)			
	Couhig	25,521	(34)			
	one other	3,571	(5)			
1982	Boggs	44,968	(77)			
	Johnson	13,404	(23)			
1984	Boggs	76,272	(60)			
	Augustine	48,976	(39)			
1986	Boggs	105,661	(91)			
	Johnson	8,474	(7)			
1988	Boggs	63,762	(89)			
	Johnson	7,505	(11)			

Sources: Michael Barone, Grant Ujifusa, and Douglas Matthews, *The Almanac of American Politics* (New York: E. P. Dutton, 1978, 1980); Barone and Ujifusa, *The Almanac of American Politics* (Washington, D.C.: National Journal, 1984–1990 biennial eds.); Richard Scammon, ed., *America Votes 11* (Washington, D.C.: Elections Research Center, Congressional Quarterly Press, 1975), p. 145.

a. Louisiana has an open primary in which all candidates from all parties compete; if no candidate receives more than 50 percent of the vote, the top two compete in the general election.

b. Special election.

opposition until 1984, when her district was redrawn to create a black majority. Then she had her first strong challenger, a judge named Israel Augustine, who was a civil rights activist and one of the first blacks to win a citywide election. The only issue in the campaign was her race.

Relying on his color, Augustine attempted to mobilize black consciousness and get African Americans to vote for a black candidate. Careful never to criticize Boggs's performance, Augustine referred to her instead as a "nice lady." He explained to blacks that his campaign was part of a crusade to open doors for them.[14] His approach was only marginally effective. He received 39 percent of the vote to Boggs's 60 percent in an open primary in which it was estimated that black voters cast 64 percent of the vote.[15] Although he won a majority of the black vote, he was soundly defeated. To Boggs's advantage were her incumbency, her progressive voting record, and her strong roots in the district. In the end she won her toughest campaign with the support of a multiracial coalition.

Boggs was able to outspend the challenger heavily, spending $802,065 to his $81,866.[16] She was also able to get political endorsements from more than fifty black organizations, and they all printed mock ballots with her name on them. Thousands of dollars were allocated to local organizations devoted to getting out the vote. Using the strategy of preemptive spending, Boggs always allocated money to her campaigns, even in the years when her opposition was token. As she explained to me, this was necessary because party labels are not on the ballot in Louisiana. The lack of party labels causes a proliferation of small groups and organizations that operate much in the way a party does.

According to Marc Morial, the son of the former mayor of New Orleans, Dutch Morial: "No one could have beaten Lindy Boggs."[17] Her constituency service was exemplary, and she was well organized for her campaigns. During election years she had her executive assistant, Jean Chippell, who was black, move into the district to serve as a trouble shooter. A typical campaign week would have Boggs and Chippell attending rallies, forums, picnics, coffee mornings, cocktail parties, and worship services (mostly at black churches) where she might make monetary donations of $100 or more. In some churches the ministers would invite her to speak, openly endorsing her. Inside black churches she sometimes tapped her feet and swayed and rocked with the music, often joining in with black constituents to "amen" the rolling cadence of the minister.[18] She did not appear to be an outsider to the blacks in her district.

It was Chippell who made most of the decisions about which black organizations were to receive money. She also thought of ways to involve more blacks in Boggs's reelection efforts and was responsible for the creation of a local organization called "The One Hundred Ladies," a group composed of about 250 black female volunteers who worked in the reelection campaigns. It was not unusual for Boggs to hold lavish parties in her home to thank these ladies for their support.

The affection and high esteem with which she was generally regarded discouraged potential challengers, and not even Jesse Jackson, who traveled to New Jersey to campaign against Peter Rodino, ever urged the defeat of Boggs. She was simply too popular with her constituents. When I was in her district, it was not uncommon for black constituents—young and old—to approach me and warn me not to write "anything bad about Lindy." Indeed, Boggs left Congress when she was in her prime, and not because she had to. When she announced her retirement, her personal polls showed approval ratings of 70 percent, and she was 18 percentage points ahead of her closest challenger.[19] As she put it: "When I announced near the anniversary of Hale's first election, after fifty years in Congress [i.e., Hale's plus hers], it seemed so appropriate—most of the things that Hale and I had worked for had been accomplished. Many of the programs and projects that we had sought were in place, and all was right with my political world."[20]

It was well known that her retirement was in part motivated by a desire to spend more time with her terminally ill daughter, Barbara Sigmund, who was then the mayor of Princeton, New Jersey. Lindy Boggs was replaced in an open primary that included several black candidates and a single white male. State Senator William Jefferson and Marc Morial were the top two in a runoff primary in which Boggs endorsed no one. White voters were decisive in determining the outcome of the contest, in which Jefferson defeated Morial and became the state's first black representative since Reconstruction.

Interaction with Constituents: Satisfying the Poor

Boggs maintained one district office while in Congress, but her staffers held weekly rotating office hours in different public housing projects that were scattered throughout the district. Her decision to hold office hours in crime-ridden housing projects came after black staffers commented on the difficulty poor people had in reaching her downtown office.

Boggs's racially diverse staff never approximated the ratio of blacks to whites in the district. In 1988, she employed twelve whites and four blacks in total. As Boggs explained, she had few opportunities to hire her own staff. Most of her staffers had been hired by Hale Boggs before she was elected, in times when the district had a white majority: "I felt obligated to keep my husband's staff. They had all been wonderful and they loved the district. And they were all loyal to Hale and very proficient in their duties. But when changes occurred through attrition, I made a conscious effort to employ women and minorities on my staff. [In fact, at one point] a couple of male staffers began to petition me asking for equal representation."[21] In Lindy Boggs's district office, two whites and two blacks served the needs of the constituents. Black staffers held some of the highest-ranking positions: Chippell, for example, was an executive assistant who doubled as a campaign manager. Just as with Tallon's staff, there was a commanding black presence when one entered any of her offices—black faces were commonplace.

Boggs kept her family mansion, which is located in the historic French Quarter of New Orleans, on Bourbon Street. Some people were put off by what they described as her "sugary sweetness," but I found her to be approachable and accessible to those who sought her attention. During trips to various churches, when constituents would come to her with their requests, she listened, took notes, and was relaxed and cordial— even hugging people who appeared to be strangers. Sometimes Boggs personally worked out the details of bailing a constituent out of jail. From my observations, this was typical casework for her.

Jefferson, the black Democrat who replaced her, has taken a very different approach. He has increased the number of staffers that he keeps in the district office, and although he too emphasizes service, he prefers to work on legislative issues and delegate as much casework as possible to his staff. Perhaps as a result, there are some black constituents who still consider Boggs to be "their" representative, and she still gets requests for help.

Representation through Legislation: Advocate for the Downtrodden

When Boggs left Congress at the age of seventy-four, she had earned national recognition, and her departure signaled the close of a political dynasty started by her husband, Hale. She had been extremely energetic in the legislature. She ranked fourteenth of the thirty-five Democrats on the House Appropriations Committee, and she was active on the Select Children, Youth, and Families Committee that she helped establish. Because she devoted so much of her time to activities such as the American Revolution Bicentennial Administration and the Commission on the Bicentennial of the U.S. Constitution, and chaired the House

Bicentennial Commission for the 99th, 100th, and 101st Congresses and the Joint Committee on Congressional Bicentennial Arrangements for the 94th Congress, members asked her to play the role of George Washington at their re-enactment of the Constitutional Convention. To honor her retirement, her colleagues passed a bill naming a room in the Capitol the Lindy Claiborne Boggs Congressional Reading Room.

Boggs used her position in Congress to advance legislation in areas such as civil rights, credit access, and equity pay, which affect minorities, women, and poor people not only in her district but throughout the nation. Many of these advancements were achieved through her strategic use of the "markup" process, in which committee members examine the text of bills line by line, and the amendment process. She also authored some important legislation. Upon arriving in the House, she discovered that "congresswomen are really surrogate members of Congress for millions of women who feel they have no special voice in Washington, and in her legislative career she worked to rectify that situation."[22] She worked to make sure women would have fair access to credit and took the lead in amending a health professions bill giving loan deferments to individuals who work in health professions. She also introduced an amendment that "allowed a woman's income to be considered in a home mortgage": "Often times a woman's income was the only income in families where the husband had been in Vietnam or pursuing graduate work while the wife was paying for the education. . . . [When the bill came up in committee] I was a woman in the right place at the right time."[23] With characteristic generosity, she commented: "It was not a question of the people on the committee being prejudiced—obviously they weren't or they wouldn't have accepted [the bill at all]."[24]

Boggs used her committee position to shift financial resources from male-dominated jobs such as construction to positions that also included significant numbers of women. In addition she pressed for legislation that would help her district, working fervently in 1983 trying to gain passage of her Cargo Bill.[25] During the 98th Congress (1983–1985), she won approval for a $333 million navigation project to deepen the Mississippi River where it flowed through her district. During the 99th Congress (1985–1987), an amendment she made to a housing authorization bill relieved New Orleans of a $1.6 million debt that it owed the federal treasury under the old Model Cities program.[26]

Boggs's COPE scores inched steadily upward from the 67 percent support she scored in 1981 (see Table 7.2). Her scores were 100 percent in 1986 and 1988. From the 98th to the 100th Congress, she averaged 87 percent on the LCCR index and often reached 100 percent. The lower scores were never the result of her opposition to legislation benefiting blacks. Examples of votes that lowered her scores include those relating to abortion, to which she is strongly opposed.

Boggs was highly respected in the legislature, and she had good relations with colleagues of both parties. A fellow Louisianian, Jim McClery, a Republican, reported that when he had difficulty obtaining a committee assignment, Boggs tapped him on the shoulder one day and said: "Darlin', I understand you need a little help getting a committee seat." She helped him get a seat on the House Budget and Armed Services committees. Boggs also hosted two parties for George Bush in 1988 when the Republicans held their convention in New Orleans. According to William Nungesser, chairman of the Louisiana Republican Party: "She's a first class, generous lady. Unfortunately she was on the other side most of the time. On a national level she is a Democratic liberal, [but] most of what a congressman does is represent their constituency and she did a good job at that. . . . If you have to have an opponent, Lindy Boggs is as good as you're going to get."[27] House Speaker Thomas Foley (D-WA) said: "In twenty-five years, I've never regretted someone leaving more than Lindy Boggs. . . . There is no finer lady, no finer member in this body than Lindy Boggs."[28]

Like Robin Tallon, Boggs was a member of the Congressional Black Caucus, and she voted for Jesse Jackson at the 1988 Democratic Convention. Despite her exemplary record in black representation and strong support from most of her district's black voters, some national black leaders urged her to step aside and allow a black to represent the district.[29] It is clear, however, that her constituents would have allowed her to hold the seat for as long as she wanted it.

The Tenth District of New Jersey: Peter Rodino, Jr.

Recent History

The city of Newark constitutes over 60 percent of the tenth district of New Jersey. Once a thriving industrial city with middle-class neighborhoods, low crime rates, and some ethnic diversity, the area has changed significantly since the 1950s, when its population was 438,000. The city now has a population of about 275,000, and it has had a black majority since the early 1970s, when the percentage of African Americans was

54.7. In 1990 the city was 58.4 percent black, 28.6 percent white, and 12.9 percent other.[30] After several decades of economic hardship, there have been some positive changes in recent years in terms of the city's economic growth.[31]

In 1967 Newark was the site of an urban riot that hastened the flight of both its white and its black middle-class citizens. Left behind was a hull of a city that has been likened to "Berlin after the war." Not all whites left the city. Italian Americans remained behind in a section of the city known as the North Ward. After the riots its residents armed themselves, supposedly as protection against crimes from African Americans, and many supported Anthony Imperial, a former city councilman who organized a citizens' patrol to guard the streets in North Ward neighborhoods.[32]

The city elected Kenneth Gibson as its first black mayor in 1970.[33] Around this time black leaders decided to challenge the state legislature's redistricting plan that had divided Newark's black population among three different congressional districts: the tenth, eleventh, and twelfth. The plan was part of the Republican-controlled state legislature's effort to dilute the Democratic party's voting strength. In 1972 the fractured black vote led to a successful court challenge in the case of *David v. Cahill*, in which a federal judge ruled that a city cannot be divided three ways without a compelling reason.[34] The court also went a step further. The judge declared that there should be a black representative in Congress from New Jersey, and he ordered the boundaries changed so that instead of three congressional districts running through the city there would now be a single district with a majority-black population. Despite the creation of a black district, the white incumbent, Peter Rodino, Jr., held the seat until his voluntary retirement effective in January 1989.

The Expansionist Stage: Rodino's First Congressional Bid

Rodino, an Italian American, was elected to Congress in 1948 after the retirement of Fred Hartley, the district's long-term incumbent and the coauthor of the Taft-Hartley Labor Act. Prior to his congressional bid, Rodino served in the army from 1941 to 1946, where he achieved the rank of captain and was decorated as a war hero. In 1946 Rodino ran against Hartley, but lost by 4,500 votes in the heavily Republican district. Just one day after this narrow defeat, a Republican leader approached Rodino, saying that he thought it would make a great story and be a source of pride for Italian Americans if Rodino took Hartley's seat after his retirement. One small problem existed: Rodino was a Roosevelt Democrat who had cast his very first vote in 1928 for the Democratic presidential candidate Alfred Smith:

> I met the county chairman who addressed me as "captain" and we talked a bit and went over the fact that I came close to winning. And he said: "Well, do you want to go to Congress?" and I said: "Well, of course I do." And he came back to the point that he wanted to make, which was an offer of my becoming a Republican and getting the Republican nomination to run in the district. And I said: "Oh, I can't do that—I'm a Democrat." And he said: "Well, but you want to go to Congress, don't you?" And I said: "But not at that price."[35]

Rodino was not about to change his party allegiance, even though he understood why Italian Americans distrusted Democrats. He described how the relationship became strained during the 1940s: "President Roosevelt made a speech in which he said something or other about Italy having stabbed America in the back and Italians resented that . . . especially these Italians who had emigrated, and there were a lot of them and we were just growing up as a generation of Americans coming from an Italian background. . . . Italian Americans resented this terrible stigma by a Democratic president. So a good many of them became Republicans, and they used to vote that way, which was one of the reasons why I lost the first time."[36] In running against Hartley in 1946, Rodino used the same strategy of the African Americans who would later run against him—he appealed to his Italian-American voters' ethnic pride, urging them to "vote Italian": "I appealed to them in that way, because they were part of something that I understood. What they were saying went back to my roots. They could rely on me; they could be confident that I was part of them, that I was among them . . . because they were the people with whom I had lived, had grown up with, and our whole community was called Little Italy."[37] Rodino, of course, also sought votes from the Irish, Polish, and German Americans who lived in his district. He estimated that at that time the district's black population was only 7 or 8 percent and he therefore did not make a specific effort to appeal to African Americans. When he was finally elected to Congress in 1948, the election was of necessity decided by more than his appeal to ethnic group solidarity, because his Republican opponent, the former state assemblyman Anthony Giuliano, was also an Italian American.

The voters found their choices restricted: "As I campaigned against another Italo-American, I recognized that what those people in Glen Ridge were doing for the first time was inviting me, which they hadn't done the time before, because this time they didn't have much to choose from—two Italo-Americans!"[38] It was a debate in Glen Ridge between the two candidates that proved to be the turning point in the campaign. Rodino used the opportunity to give a presentation on the virtues of the Democratic party's platform: "I let them know that I felt strongly about the issues affecting the country. In fact, I told them that I was first an American, then I was a Democrat. And I said, that having gone through the war, and having seen what it was like to be able to fight for what I thought were all the great ideals—the promise of this country—that that's what I wanted, and that's what I wanted to represent in Congress."[39]

About his Republican opponent, he added:

> The man thought that all he had to do was just wave a magic wand, win and resolve everything. I knew we had great problems confronting the country, and it wasn't going to be that easy, and it was going to take dedication, devotion, understanding, commitment, and everything else . . . when it was all over they applauded me greatly, and then when they filed up after the debate, they would come by shake my hand and say: "You made a great statement here. You're a fine person. Too bad you're a Democrat." The next day the Glen Ridge paper had a headline, "Rodino, Democratic Candidate, Supporting Highly Unpopular Democratic Platform Wins Popular Support" or something of that sort.[40]

After his initial election Rodino was repeatedly reelected with only token opposition (see Table 8.2). This situation changed somewhat after his district was redrawn and acquired a black majority.

Although Rodino knew that his district had become more African American, he did not realize the extent of the hostility that his black constituents felt toward white elected officials. It was the riot of 1967 that opened his eyes: "I went through the riot area with the then-mayor of the city of Newark, Addonizio. And when I went through they didn't distinguish, I mean I recall going through and having rocks thrown at the car that I was in. I said, 'My God.' Then I could understand it, but it was tough, it was tough to accept."[41]

Rodino found himself plunged back into the expansionist stage of his constituency career. He had trouble even getting invitations before black audiences so that he could tell them of his long history of civil rights activism. Thrust into what was practically a new district through redistricting, Rodino began his outreach services almost immediately after

Table 8.2. The election history of Peter Rodino, Jr.

Year	Primary election opponents	Vote total (percentage)	General election opponents	Vote total (percentage)	
1968	Rodino	Unopposed	Rodino	89,109	(64%)
			Clemete	47,989	(34)
			Press	1,440	(1)
			Tyus	735	(1)
1970	Rodino	Unopposed	Rodino	71,003	(70)
			Jones	30,460	(30)
1972	Rodino	37,650 (57%)	Rodino	94,308	(80)
	Hart	24,118 (37)	Miller	23,949	(20)
	Richardson	3,086 (5)			
	Kurnegay, Jr.	718 (1)			
1974	Rodino	19,121 (89)	Rodino	53,094	(81)
	Giordano	2,330 (11)	Taliaferro	9,936	(15)
			Hill	2,508	(4)
1976	Rodino	Unopposed	Rodino	88,245	(84)
			Grandison	17,129	(16)
1978	Rodino	Unopposed	Rodino	55,074	(87)
			Pelt	8,066	(13)
1980	Rodino	26,943 (62)	Rodino	76,154	(85)
	Payne	9,825 (23)	Jennings	11,778	(13)
	Johnson	5,316 (12)			
	Fox	1,251 (3)			
1982	Rodino	Unopposed	Rodino	76,684	(83)
			Lee	14,551	(16)
1984	Rodino	42,109 (76)	Rodino	111,244	(84)
	Jones	10,294 (19)	Berkeley	27,712	(16)
	Tyree	2,779 (5)			
1986	Rodino	25,138 (60)	Rodino	46,666	(96)
	Payne	15,216 (36)	Brandlon	1,977	(4)

Sources: Michael Barone, Grant Ujifusa, and Douglas Matthews, *The Almanac of American Politics* (New York: E. P. Dutton, 1978, 1980); Barone and Ujifusa, *The Almanac of American Politics* (Washington, D.C.: National Journal, 1984–1990 biennial eds.).

his reelection in 1970. "I made sure that I developed the kinds of contacts and people who would then continue back home, back in my constituency, to carry the ball for me. I wasn't readily accepted at the very beginning," he said, "except that I had a few stalwarts, young African

Americans who believed in me, and notwithstanding the fact that my opponent was a black at the time."[42]

Rodino remained relatively safe from black opponents until the 1980s approached, when Donald Payne (Newark's current representative) and other blacks began to agitate for his seat. Payne had first thought of running for Congress in 1974, but decided not to challenge Rodino that year. By 1980, however, Payne was ready to make his move. He explained that with the decennial census under way, he was fearful that its results would not require the preservation of the district's black majority under the Voting Rights Act, and thus he felt it essential to run in 1980. But, he continued, "two other blacks jumped into the race, the Reverend Nelson Fox and Judge Golden Johnson. I defeated them handily, but with the three of us, Mr. Rodino won. Our total was not more than what his was either, but with the other two in the race, many people said that they were not going to vote for any of us."[43]

When Payne ran against Rodino again in 1986, he had considerable support from black leaders. Jesse Jackson came to the district to campaign for him and told voters that Rodino was on his list of white members who needed to be replaced, because majority-black districts should have black representatives. Rodino told me of his shock: "I was devastated by Jackson's actions. In my opinion it was just incredible that knowing the importance of having someone like me over there as head of the Judiciary Committee, knowing the assaults that were being made by the Reagan Administration that Jesse, a friend of mine, could do such a thing."[44] Rodino suffered another blow when a local newspaper published a list of black leaders who supposedly called for his resignation: "I went to Gus Hawkins, who was one of them; Hawkins knew me, he knew what I was made of. He wrote a letter to that newspaper and said you have no right to print this; it would be a tragic mistake to lose someone as important as Congressman Rodino."[45] Hawkins also had a tribute placed in the *Congressional Record*:

> The landmark 1964 civil rights bill passed because PETER RODINO took a leadership role and fought for what is decent and right in our Nation. Civil rights became a reality for millions of oppressed Americans because men like PETER RODINO were guided by the light of reason and strength of conviction. . . . And through the years his leadership on key national issues has remained steadfast. His advocacy for the Voting Rights Act extension; the Martin Luther King, Jr., Holiday bill; affirmative action; fair housing, jobs, and education; [these] are only a few of the many great programs he has stood for.[46]

Some black representatives came into the district and campaigned on Rodino's behalf, among them Mickey Leland (D-TX), Charlie Rangel (D-NY), Bill Clay (D-MO), and Louis Stokes (D-OH). Other Black Caucus members also inserted tributes in the *Congressional Record,* and the national and regional branches of the NAACP expressed their appreciation of Rodino's vigilance on civil rights.

The issue of Rodino's race did not affect blacks equally. Rodino fondly remembers a black woman's reaction to being told: "Well, you know, Donald Payne is a black, and he's running." The woman replied: "I don't care what color Rodino is, he's my man!"[47] In 1986 Rodino won his second race against Payne with 60 percent of the vote to Payne's 36 percent. Two other black candidates were in the primary (see Table 8.2).

Rodino's campaign literature advertised his many accomplishments. One brochure showed a clasped pair of hands, one white, the other black. Above the picture were the words "The Rodino Record, It's Here in Black and White." After a list of his many activities was the slogan: "Congressman Rodino is on the job in Washington working for all the people. Nobody has done more in the past. Nobody can do more in the future."

Under increasing pressure from black leaders and chastened by the heated 1986 campaign, Rodino made a promise to retire, words he later regretted: "It was during my victory statement that I said, and the people responded, 'I'm here until Reagan goes,'" he explained, "and I was determined that I would go after that. My only concern was that immediately following that statement bills were introduced in the Congress to repeal the 22nd Amendment and nominate Reagan for a third term."[48] After some hedging, much criticism, and strong encouragement from Democratic party leaders, Rodino reluctantly announced his retirement for spring 1988, but it was clear that given the opportunity he would have enjoyed serving longer.

Mayor Sharpe James, who had defeated the incumbent and Rodino supporter Kenneth Gibson in the election for mayor in 1986, said prior to Rodino's disclosure of his retirement: "Pete has earned a rightful place in history, and has been a most effective Congressman for the 10th District. But it's time for him to retire with dignity. The only issue is that the courts carved out the district more than a dozen years ago to elect a minority Congressman, and it's time to get that done."[49] It is apparent that Rodino did not have the type of support from blacks that Lindy Boggs had in her district. Black leaders were far more willing to criticize his performance and to demand that he step aside.

Interactions with Constituents: Traveling in Uncharted Waters

Over the years, Rodino maintained a single district office located in downtown Newark. Its staff was racially diverse, and he added more African-American staffers after the district was redrawn to have a black majority: "I recognized the importance of getting, first of all, staff that would not only be representative but would understand, have a feel for a constituency made up of a majority of African Americans." Whenever new hiring opportunities arose, Rodino tried to employ racial and political minorities. About his committee staff, Rodino said: "I brought a young man who was at the time a student at Rutgers University. He was a young African American, who today is the mayor of Orange, Bob Brown. . . . And I brought females on and different ethnics. Prior to my being the chairman, [the Judiciary committee] was pretty well dominated with Jewish ethnics, under Emmanuel Cellar as chairman."[50] He changed some of the functions of his congressional offices to place a greater emphasis on service, something African Americans value: "I recognized that I had a constituency with many needs. That they weren't provided with as many opportunities to be informed and literate. . . . So, we tried to make sure that we had people who would be caring and considerate."[51]

Rodino worked hard to be accepted and liked by his black constituents and tried to call them by the ethnic name that he thought they preferred. He remembered attending a club during the mid-1960s where the following incident took place: "I used the word 'black,' thinking that I was using the word that seemed to be more appealing than the others. You know, 'colored,' at that time was going out of style, and I used 'black'. . . . I could tell that I touched them [the audience], and they understood that I was genuine about what I was saying, and what I wanted to do. And after the speech someone came over to me and said, it was a great speech, except you shouldn't use the word 'black'. . . . And I was just dumbfounded, and I said, my God, have I offended anyone? Because I thought I was using what would be most appealing."[52] According to Rodino, the man who approached him was the one who was out of step with the times. "I remember going through those stages," he said, "and afterwards it was fine." Indeed, his efforts to find the proper manner of address continues in his retirement. When I interviewed Rodino in early 1990, he referred to blacks as African Americans.

*Representation through Legislation: The Chairman of the Judiciary
Committee*

Rodino had been in Congress for forty years and was essentially an
urban liberal Democrat representing an ethnically diverse constituency
until late 1973, when his performance as chairman of the House Judiciary Committee in the impeachment proceedings against President
Richard Nixon thrust him onto the national stage. The televised Water-
gate hearings helped to make him a hero across the country: the American people were impressed by his fairness, skill, and intellect.

Rodino's high seniority and committee chairmanship allowed him to
bring millions of federal dollars into his district. He helped liberal
Democrats in Congress by assisting in killing legislation such as proposed amendments to the Constitution involving school prayer, abortion, and busing. He often irritated the pro-gun lobby by not reporting
to the full House the legislation that they sought to promote. Major
criticisms of Rodino's legislative performance came in later years, when
he offended some of his colleagues by refusing to delegate to subcommittees, and when he was slow and cautious. His committee impeded
the progress of so much legislation that the conservatives in Congress
called it a "legislative mortuary."[53]

More important for African Americans, Rodino was literally out front
on civil rights. "When the whole of Congress was dominated by southern chairmen," he said, "I was concerned and, of course, I was tagged
as a nigger-lover."[54] He played a decisive role in almost all civil rights
legislation over three decades. He drafted part of the 1964 Civil Rights
Act, managed the 1966 Open Housing bill on the floor, and worked hard
for immigration reform. Moreover, he was instrumental in the passage
of the Civil Rights Restoration bill of 1988. As he put it to me: "It wasn't
by accident that we were able to write the Civil Rights Restoration Act
or the extension of the Voting Rights Act. I mean, that didn't happen
just because the administration was interested in writing stronger bills.
We had Bradford Reynolds who was there on the scene, and as most of
the people who kept up with legislation knew, they knew that Pete
Rodino was going to be vigilant, and was going to make sure that those
things didn't happen while he was there."[55] The 1990 and 1991 civil
rights bills were the first bills of this type to lack his experienced
guidance.

Given Rodino's legislative record on behalf of blacks, and the fact that at age seventy-nine his days in Congress were limited, it is ironic that Payne campaigned against Rodino with the argument that he was impeding black progress by staying in office. Payne, who was fifty-six in 1990, told me how he has differed from Rodino:

> I am much more accessible and I spend a tremendous amount of time out in the public. I go back every Thursday evening, and I don't come back to Washington until Tuesday morning. So I spend more time in the district than I do in Washington. I don't stay here any weekends. I just stay in Washington when I physically have to vote on the floor. So that's a big difference. If you're a committee chairperson, you have to study the issues and you have staff meetings with issues that are going to come before it. I don't have that responsibility, so it frees my time up. I give maybe a dozen speeches between the time I go home on Thursday until the time that I come back on Tuesday, and so that's one of the big differences.[56]

Payne notes other differences in his home style:

> I am a hands-on politician. I go out to where the people are. I'll go to the public housing projects or I'll be where the teenagers are in the evening to discuss their problems with them. I'll make a lot of time available in my office just to meet with constituents. I did it in city government. We used to have community forums where there were four or five hundred people, as an example. We just had a forum Monday night.[57]

Most of the differences between the two representatives do not hinge on race. Rather, they are based on Payne's status as a newly elected representative who is still very much in the expansionist stage of his constituency career. Although Payne has excellent committee assignments, Education and Labor, Government Operations, and Foreign Affairs, he lacks Rodino's seniority and influence. When he contrasts his style with Rodino's, he is comparing himself with a forty-year veteran who was long into the protectionist stage of his constituency career.

An Extinct Group

Peter Rodino and Lindy Boggs, the last white representatives from majority-black districts, used their seniority and committee positions to represent racial and political minorities. Their seniority allowed them to shape the national legislative agenda in ways that helped African Americans both in their districts and nationally. Both were considerably more liberal than the vocal white minorities in their districts, and both faced criticism for their active role on behalf of blacks. They persisted in their endeavors despite harassment of various kinds. After court decisions mandated majority-black districts, Rodino and Boggs held on to their seats because they had the trust of a majority of the district's voters. They maintained multiracial coalitions that withstood the assaults of black opponents who often sought to beat them using racially polarizing strategies.

No matter how well Boggs and Rodino represented the blacks in their districts, many black politicians from around the country argued privately and sometimes publicly that their two districts ought to have descriptive black representation. Whenever a black majority is not represented by a black politician, the argument that "only blacks can represent blacks" emerges. But the assumption that only blacks can represent black interests puts African Americans who want to maximize the descriptive and substantive representation of blacks in Congress in an untenable position. If the argument is carried to its logical conclusion, it follows that only whites can represent white interests. Promulgation of the view that shared race is a necessary and sufficient criterion for representation can harm blacks. It operates to hurt black politicians who need white support—those black politicians who seek to emphasize racial commonalities, those who seek to represent whites as well as blacks—the Alan Wheats, Gary Franks, and Douglas Wilders of this world. If the ethnocentric view were correct, the outlook for increasing African-American representation in Congress and elsewhere would indeed be gloomy.

IV · IMPLICATIONS

9 · Strategies for Increasing Black Representation of Blacks

Some time in the past it was necessary to have black faces in Congress to serve as role models for other young people who would aspire to be elected officials, to be at the table so that our voices would be heard, to insure that we were not overlooked. But at some point, we have to question the creation of districts in which the election of a black person is an end within itself. I believe that it is not an end in itself, it's a means to an end, and the end to be accomplished is to win. It takes a majority of the votes, 218, to win in Congress.

—INTERVIEW WITH REPRESENTATIVE CRAIG WASHINGTON, *October 22, 1991*

What will happen to black representation in Congress when courts and state legislatures can no longer draw new districts with black majorities? Do blacks have any other means of increasing their congressional representation? Can more blacks be elected from majority-white districts?

Factors Influencing Black Political Gains in Congress

African Americans have made unmistakable progress in Congress. In 1991, the 435 members of the House included 24 black Democratic representatives and 1 black Republican (see Table 9.1). Forty percent of the black representatives were elected from districts that were less than 50 percent black in their voting-age populations.

Increases in the number of black representatives have resulted from changes in the nature of political opportunities in the United States, particularly changes in the country's demography and in the electoral system. During the Reconstruction era, federally facilitated black voter registration and educational programs led to the election of black politicians at all levels of government. During the twentieth century black

Table 9.1. Congressional districts represented by blacks, 1991

Representative	District	Principal city	BVAP 1980s	HVAP 1980s	Total minority
Franks (R-CT)	5	Waterbury	4	3	7
Wheat (D-MO)	5	Kansas City	20	2	22
Dellums (D-CA)	8	Oakland	24	6	30
Dymally (D-CA)	31	Compton	31	21	52
Dixon (D-CA)	28	Los Angeles	37	24	61
Washington (D-TX)	18	Houston	39	27	66
Clay (D-MO)	1	St. Louis	46	1	47
Flake (D-NY)	6	Queens	47	8	55
Towns (D-NY)	11	New York	47	34	81
Rangel (D-NY)	16	New York	49	35	84
Ford (D-TN)	9	Memphis	51	1	52
Waters (D-CA)	29	Los Angeles	51	32	83
Jefferson (D-LA)	2	New Orleans	52	3	55
Espy (D-MS)	2	Greenville	53	1	54
Payne (D-NJ)	10	Newark	54	12	66
Stokes (D-OH)	21	Cleveland	58	1	59
Collins (D-IL)	7	Chicago	60	4	64
Lewis (D-GA)	5	Atlanta	60	1	61
Conyers (D-MI)	1	Detroit	66	2	68
Savage (D-IL)	2	Chicago	66	7	73
Collins (D-MI)	13	Detroit	67	3	70
Mfume (D-MD)	7	Baltimore	70	1	71
Gray (D-PA)	2	Philadelphia	76	1	77
Owens (D-NY)	12	Brooklyn	78	9	87
Hayes (D-IL)	1	Chicago	90	1	91

Sources: Linda Williams, ed., *The JCPS Congressional District Fact Book,* 3rd ed. (Washington, D.C.: Joint Center for Political Studies, 1988); *Congressional Quarterly,* November 10, 1990, vol. 48, n. 45, pp. 3822–3823.

Note: BVAP = Black voting-age percentage of district population; HVAP = Hispanic voting-age percentage of district population.

representation has been influenced by urban migration and by voting-rights legislation that led to competition for the black vote. In some areas African Americans were rewarded with congressional seats once the black population reached a certain percentage and the white incumbent left Congress. The Voting Rights Act of 1965 was one watershed for blacks; the decision of the Supreme Court to enter the "political thicket" of reapportionment and redistricting was another.

The history of congressional reapportionment in the twentieth century is well known.[1] The requirements for reapportionment and redistricting are based on Article 1, Section 2, of the U.S. Constitution. Reapportionment is the redistribution of the nation's 435 congressional seats among the fifty states, and this is done on the basis of successive decennial censuses.[2] Redistricting is the actual redrawing of district lines within the individual states. Officials of the states concerned draw the lines. The process is highly political, and the outcome is often based on which party controls the legislature in a state.[3]

Redistricting and changes in black representation in the twentieth century have been very much a function of key court decisions. After refusing to enter the apportionment arena in the case of *Colegrove v. Green* in 1946, the Supreme Court in 1961 decided to hear *Baker v. Carr,* which involved state legislative districts in Tennessee that had not been redistricted since 1901. By a vote of six to two the court declared the issue worthy of litigation but offered few guidelines about what would be a fair apportionment; political observers were left to grapple with the meaning of the decision. *Reynolds v. Sims* followed in 1964, resulting in more representation for urban areas and an increase in the number of African-American politicians in state legislatures—positions that have traditionally been stepping stones to Congress.[4] *Wesberry v. Sanders* (1964), a Georgia case, extended the principle of "one person, one vote" to the congressional arena.[5] Many of the subsequent cases have involved clarifications of what constitutes fair apportionment. *Kirkpatrick v. Preisler* (1969), *White v. Weiser* (1973), *Wells v. Rockefeller* (1969), and *Karcher v. Daggett* (1983) are cases in which a strict population standard was applied to congressional redistricting.[6]

Since the case of *Kirksey v. Board of Supervisors of Hinds County, Mississippi,* in 1977, courts have leaned toward a rule that directs mapmakers, wherever possible (that is, in areas with large minority populations), to create districts in which minorities make up at least 65 percent of the population.[7] The 65 percent rule takes into account lower voter turnout among racial minorities, and it assumes a racially polarized electorate in which white voters opt for white candidates and black voters for blacks, but it is not rigid.[8] Whether or not the 65 percent rule is adhered to may depend on factors such as the size of the minority population in a given area, its past turnout rate, party cohesion, and similar issues.[9] On court order, Georgia's fifth district was redrawn so that it became 65 percent black *after* it had already elected a black representative, Andrew Young, when it was majority-white. After the court had increased the size of the district's black population, the independent-minded electorate responded by electing Wyche Fowler, a

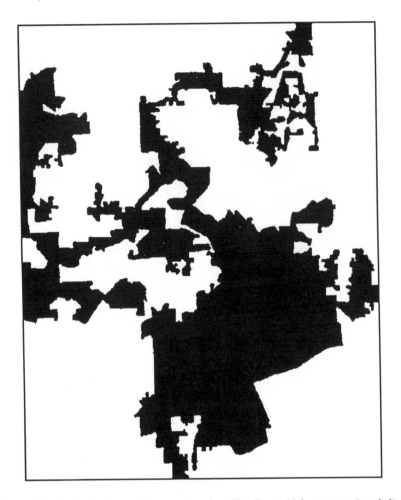

Figure 9.1. Portrait of a racial gerrymander: The Texas 30th congressional district. Redrawn with permission from a Texas state legislature map reprinted by the *Wall Street Journal,* October 18, 1991, and renamed the "Monster Map."

white representative (see Chapter 4). Georgia's fifth district did not need a 65 percent black population to elect a black politician with biracial appeal. What happened after the court's intervention illustrates that electorates do not always vote in a racially predictable and straightforward manner.

Much of the reasoning for drawing congressional districts to ensure the descriptive representation of minorities can be found in the case of

Thornburg v. Gingles (1986), which involved a challenge to North Carolina's multimember state legislative districts. The court devised a three-part test for discrimination that focuses on an analysis of the local political situation, its openness to minorities, and the ability of minority groups to elect the representatives of their choice. *Thornburg v. Gingles* mandates the creation of a maximum number of minority districts whenever a geographical area contains a large, politically cohesive minority group (that is, one that votes en bloc for minority candidates) whose choices of minority candidates have been defeated on a regular basis in the past by a bloc of white voters.[10] The decision in this case moved the nation one step closer to requiring proportional representation for racial and ethnic minorities.[11]

By 1992 compliance with the *Thornburg* decision had led to the creation of contorted computer-drawn districts that resembled spiders, masses of bacteria, pitchforks, and worse (see Figure 9.1). It is a major feat to determine where such a district begins and ends. One can only imagine the havoc that these twisted districts create for members of Congress as they campaign for election and reelection, and for voters as they seek constituency service.[12] If confusion is too great, all constituents in such districts may be ill served. Certain racial gerrymanders, however, are now sanctioned by law.

Racial Gerrymandering

Gerrymandering is the manipulation of district lines for political advantage. Racial gerrymandering occurs when district lines are drawn to enhance or reduce the representation of particular racial groups.[13] Its major forms are known as "cracking" (a significant minority population is dispersed across several districts to dilute its voting strength), "stacking" (large concentrations of minority voters are combined with white populations to create districts with white majorities), and "packing" (minority voters are put in districts that already have high minority populations).[14] Although it has ruled against cracking and stacking, the Supreme Court has not yet considered packing to be worthy of legal remedies (see *Wright v. Rockefeller*, 1964).[15]

Seven of the fifteen majority-black districts in Table 9.1 appear to be packed beyond what is needed to elect black politicians. The most egregious cases from the 1980 census were the first district in Illinois, which had a black voting-age population of 90 percent, and New York's twelfth district and Pennsylvania's second district, which both had black voting-age populations of 78 percent. Four remaining districts were also more than 65 percent black: Maryland's seventh (70 percent), Michigan's thirteenth (67 percent), and Illinois's second and Michigan's first district (both with 66 percent).

Black politicians consider packing less harmful than the other two forms of racial gerrymandering, because it adds to the safeness of their districts. At the Congressional Black Caucus legislative weekend in September 1990, Ronald Walters, chairman of Howard University's political science department, spoke of some of the dangers that redistricting might pose for John Conyers, representative of Michigan's first district: "[It is] an important national question because he chairs the Committee on Government Operations. . . . It's a black question in that the way he got his seniority is through black political power, black voters returning to him over and over."[16] Echoing his concerns was Bernard Anderson, a representative of Philadelphia's Urban Affairs Partnership, who said that although decreased black population density did not necessarily mean that black congressmen would not be reelected, "it does mean the congressman then has to deal with a wider variety of issues, and perhaps become . . . less directly [involved] with racial interests. It's likely we'll see more black elected officials like [Virginia Governor L. Douglas] Wilder than the CBC members of the past."[17] Many blacks would consider this a negative outcome, and many minority leaders would prefer to be dependent only on the votes of members of their own racial group.[18]

Only a minority of black politicians oppose the packing of black voters. Representative Craig Washington, a Texas Democrat, is among them, and he is outspoken in his views: "If you take 20 percent of those blacks who are in a 90 percent district and put them in an adjoining district that is probably 75 or 80 percent white, you'd get the white percentage down to where the impact of the black community is a lot greater. Instead of one district with black influence, you can have two."[19] Representative Washington argues that isolating black voters in overwhelmingly black districts places them in a situation where their policy preferences can be more easily ignored. "We shouldn't warehouse black people in districts," Washington declares. "You don't need a threshold of 90 percent in order to allow blacks to elect someone black. My district is 30 percent black. I would like to hope that it keeps the same ethnic breakdown after the 1991 redistricting."[20]

Washington is not alone in questioning the wisdom behind drawing overwhelmingly black districts. The legislative expert Phil Duncan points to the irony of the existing remedy: "Let's just suppose someone suggested that the United States adopt a policy of segregating blacks for the purpose of providing them congressional representation. . . . A shocking suggestion? In fact, just such a separatist approach to congressional redistricting is widely and favorably discussed by many politicians and legal scholars who regard themselves as vigorous advocates of minority rights."[21] Similarly, Mississippi's Mike Espy told me: "Although nothing's guaranteed, I think that the need for a 65 percent black population has been disproved. Look at Doug Wilder [Governor of Virginia], look at David Dinkins [Mayor of New York], look at Norm Rice [Mayor of Seattle]—black men and women all over the nation are running and winning in areas that are not predominantly black. And, in the deep South, we've got a lot of successful examples, too."[22] As redistricting approached after the 1990 census, Espy argued for keeping his biracial coalition intact; black leaders in the district fought for a 60 percent black population so that any black candidate could win with black support only.[23]

Among the examples of blacks who have been elected to Congress from districts that fell short of being 50 percent black are: Ron Dellums (1970, Berkeley, California), Andrew Young (1972, Atlanta, Georgia), Harold Ford (1974, Memphis, Tennessee), Alan Wheat (1982, Kansas City, Missouri), Katie Hall (1982, Gary, Indiana), and Gary Franks (1990, Waterbury, Connecticut). This list is remarkable in that it goes far beyond the traditionally liberal constituencies in Massachusetts that elected Senator Edward Brooke and those in California that we might expect to be liberal. Since the early 1970s, a much larger group of black representatives, including Barbara Jordan (1972, Houston, Texas), Julian Dixon (1978, Los Angeles, California), Mervyn Dymally (1980, Los Angeles, California), Mickey Leland (1978, Houston, Texas), Floyd Flake (1986, Queens, New York), and Craig Washington (1990, Houston, Texas), have been elected from districts in which no racial group constitutes a majority. Others, such as William Clay (1968, St. Louis, Missouri) and Charles Rangel (1970, Harlem, New York), have been able to hold on to their seats as their once majority-black constituencies have become either majority-white or majority-other.

That districts with black majorities are clearly not the black politician's only route to Congress refutes the logic behind the belief that a minority must constitute at least 65 percent of the population to guarantee descriptive representation.[24] Each election of a black candidate from a non-black-majority district, such as Gary Franks's 1990 election from a 4 percent black district, further weakens this argument.

Thus far the Supreme Court has not been sympathetic to the pleas of white voters who complain about racial gerrymanders that crack and stack their populations in order to make way for minority districts. The case of *United Jewish Organizations v. Carey* in 1977, for example, involved white voters who complained about a redistricting plan that split two Hasidic Jewish communities in order to create a district with a black majority. Undeterred by their arguments, Justice White, writing for the majority, argued that a group can be represented by legislators elected outside its district lines. He declared that "the white voter who as a result of the 1974 plan is in a district likely to return a nonwhite representative will be represented, to the extent that voting continues to follow racial lines, by legislators elected from majority white districts."[25]

Why Question the Strategy?

When African Americans question the common strategy of drawing legislative districts with large black majorities, they are sometimes viewed by other blacks with suspicion and regarded as "enemies of the group." Yet the electoral demography of the United States favors such a policy. The statistics on the distribution and concentration of blacks in the population reveal a need to look beyond the creation of majority-black political units as a way to increase political representation of African Americans. Blacks have already made the most of their opportunities to elect black politicians in congressional districts with black majorities. In 1991 the only states providing real prospects for new minority-majority districts were Alabama, Florida, Georgia, Louisiana, Maryland, Mississippi, North Carolina, South Carolina, Texas, and Virginia.[26] The creation of a new district in Alabama would require combining the city of Birmingham with the city of Tuscaloosa and several rural areas, and this would result in another odd-shaped district. Some experts suggest that African Americans and Hispanics might be able to find twelve to fifteen new districts for themselves after the 1990s redistricting. Beyond that, and in years to come, we can expect severe limitations on what can be achieved by relying on the creation of black districts to ensure the election of black politicians.[27]

Consider the problem of gaining adequate congressional representation for blacks from the South, who account for 60 percent of the nation's African-American population and who will account for an even greater percentage if a recent trend toward reverse migration continues. Although 67 percent of the nation's black elected officials are from the South, the region contributes only 20 percent of the black representation on Capitol Hill.[28] Bernard Grofman and Lisa Handley have shown that the underrepresentation of southern blacks in Congress appears to result not from the factors that might be first suspected, such as white racism, lack of campaign funds, or low black turnout, but from the geographical dispersion of southern blacks. Most black representatives are elected from large cities in which the black population is 300,000 or more (the setting in which it is most feasible to create black districts), but there are few southern cities that match this criterion.[29]

Not only is the strategy of carving out predominantly black districts from urban areas with dense concentrations of blacks unlikely to encourage adequate black representation in the South, but it is also likely to become ineffective in the future in the Northeast and Midwest, which are presently the largest "producers" of black members of Congress. Of the seventeen black-represented districts that lost population in 1980, 29 percent lost more than a fifth of their population (see Table 9.2). Seventy percent lost more than a tenth. Although the overall population losses were smaller between 1980 and 1990, districts with significant black populations were usually the most seriously affected. Some of the greatest losses occurred in northeastern and midwestern districts.[30] Illinois, Michigan, New York, Ohio, and Pennsylvania have continued to lose congressional representation.[31] In states losing seats, courts and state legislators have promised to preserve the black districts; it may not be possible to do this, however, while at the same time complying with the equal-size guidelines established by the Supreme Court.

The experiences of George Crockett (D-MI) and his successor Barbara Rose Collins point to some of the specific problems of seeking to expand black congressional representation by creating predominantly black districts. Crockett, who had already seen his black-majority district diluted with the addition of conservative white suburbs, told me that he expected the 1990 redistricting to reduce further the ratio of whites to blacks in the district. He commented: "They're going to have to redraw my district lines, because I have lost almost 100,000 residents. I am told that my congressional district has lost more people than any other congressional district in the country."[32] He was correct; the district lost

Table 9.2. Population change for black-represented congressional districts

District	1970–1980 Percentage change	1980–1990 Percentage change
Michigan–13	–37.3%	–23.2%
New York–12	–31.4	+10.6
Ohio–21	–24.7	–10.9
Missouri–1	–23.9	–10.0
Illinois–1	–20.0	–20.4
Illinois–7	–19.8	–14.2
Michigan–1	–15.9	–12.3
Pennsylvania–1	–15.3	–8.3
Missouri–5	–14.2	–4.7
Maryland–7	–13.8	–5.9
New Jersey–10	–10.8	–11.5
Tennessee–9	–9.4	–8.7
Georgia–5	–8.7	–1.8
Texas–18	–8.4	–14.7
California–8	–5.1	+6.8
New York–6	–4.3	+1.9
New York–11	–3.5	+4.8
California–31	0.0	+13.9
Illinois–2	+.02	–11.9
California–28	+.09	+14.1
Louisiana–2	+1.7	–11.1
Mississippi–2	+4.6	–6.2
California–29	+5.2	+3.5
Connecticut–5	+7.3	+7.8
New York–17	+13.2	+22.2

Sources: "Urban Districts Suffer Big Population Losses," *Congressional Quarterly Weekly Report*, April 25, 1981, pp. 646–649; "Official 1990 Count by District," *Congressional Quarterly Weekly Report*, May 18, 1991, pp. 1309–1312.

185,000 residents. It will be preserved, however, by a further expansion into the white-dominated suburbs. This effort to preserve the seats of black members occurs at a time when the state is losing two congressional seats.

Other black representatives, such as Mike Espy (D-MS) and William Clay (D-MO), are convinced that census data showing their districts to have black majorities are flawed.[33] Espy believes that his district is really majority-white. Clay, whose district is majority-white in voting-age population, considers himself the beneficiary of a black undercount that works in his favor because it misleads the potential opposition.[34] According to one of Clay's staffers, white opponents who take Clay on quickly learn that the district is really majority-black. At any rate, confusion about the size of black districts and the decline in their black populations further signal the limitations of electoral strategies based solely on the creation and preservation of districts with black majorities.

Even when it is feasible to create or maintain heavily black districts, it may be undesirable. Large concentrations of poor black voters, who normally elect black politicians, are often plagued by high crime rates, drug abuse, and other ghetto problems. This makes areas less attractive to all inhabitants, leading to both black and white flight. Research has shown that attitudes on racial segregation in housing are such that most whites are willing to live in neighborhoods with some integration.[35] As the percentage of black residents increases, however, so does the percentage of whites who leave the area or decide not to move into the neighborhood. Even black residents indicate a preference for more integrated neighborhoods, with two-thirds to three-quarters preferring mixed neighborhoods to those composed mostly of blacks.[36] A more heterogeneous population might elect a more racially diverse group of politicians, and this can lead to broad coalition building across racial groups and therefore to improvements in the district, including a higher tax base, which might stem the tide of out-migration.

There are other ways in which less overwhelmingly black districts could have a positive effect on black representation of blacks. Black representatives would have to work harder at increasing voter turnout in their districts. Voter turnout in historically black districts is now abysmally low. Turnout, for example, was 13 percent in Major Owens's (D-NY) 78 percent black district in 1986. Lowered black population in such districts might mean that black representatives would have to compete actively for white as well as black voters and would therefore become more responsive to all of their constituents. Race relations suffer when "electoral remedies" favor one racial group over another or in environments where candidates can engage in racially polarizing tactics without fear of defeat.[37]

At present, few black representatives have any incentive to tackle the problems that lead to high population losses in their districts. They know that they are protected by a legacy of court decisions. *Beer v. United States* (1974 and 1976) led to the establishment of a "no retrogression rule," mandating that a redistricting or electoral change cannot leave minority voters worse off. Black federal and state legislators know that the district lines are likely to be drawn to capture the voters who have fled into outlying suburbs.[38] Regardless of high population losses, black representatives can rest assured that their states will maintain the districts of black members. They are not, however, necessarily guaranteed a district with a black majority. In 1991 officials at the Justice Department began to question what enforcement of the no retrogression standard actually entails. According to John Dunne, the head of the department's Civil Rights Office: "The law doesn't endow anyone with a right to office. . . . It may be appropriate to reduce the percentage of the non-white population in a majority-black or Hispanic district without violating the [retrogression standard that prohibits the dilution of minority votes]."[39] Violating the no retrogression standard might entail lowering the black population percentage in certain historically black congressional districts.

As we have seen, building a biracial coalition does not mean that black politicians have to "sell out" the interests of their group to gain the white support needed. Some black representatives from historically black districts have done an excellent job of representing whites without neglecting the interests of blacks. Representative Louis Stokes (D-OH), for example, expects a population that will be 45 percent white after the 1990s redistricting. He has already made changes in his outreach services. After the 1980s redistricting, he added another district office in a newly annexed white suburb. He described to me how these changes affect what he does:

> There's been a shift in what we have to do congressionally. I don't know that we work any harder. That is, we work hard as it is, but in the suburban part of my district the problems are different. In the central city I've got all these problems related to crime, inadequate health facilities, housing problems related to public housings, things of that sort. But suburban problems are different. I deal more with people who have personal problems related to immigration and trade—things of that nature. We address all the problems of anybody in our district without any reference to their race, ethnicity, or color. We realize that the problems in the predominantly white community are different from, and not as magnified as, the problems related to the inner city. But we address them all, whether it is the person who calls up and says, "Hey, we're having trouble getting a visa or a passport," or a person who calls up and says, "They've shut the gas off at my house because I haven't been able to pay." It means a transfer of application of time to a totally different series of problems.[40]

Stokes has effectively combined outreach to whites with mobilization efforts in the black community. His observations about the different nature of the constituency requests are similar to those made by Floyd

Flake and others. He does not seem afraid of redistricting, because he knows that he has biracial appeal.

Black Representation and the Republican Party

The quest to increase minority representation took a new twist during the early 1990s when the Republican National Committee combined redistricting with its outreach program to minorities. Republican leaders have zealously urged the creation of the maximum number of "safe" black and Hispanic districts. In doing so they have encouraged unrealistic goals. Benjamin Ginsberg, chief counsel for the National Committee, for example, declared: "If I were a member of the Congressional Black Caucus, it wouldn't be unreasonable to think that my membership ought to be doubled after the 1992 elections if I got a fair shake in the redistricting process."[41] The Republican position on minority districts may seem surprising, given that Republicans have gained so much political mileage by opposing affirmative action quotas. Why would Republicans want more minority-elected officials, if most are likely to be Democrats? Why do Republicans care about the number and size of black districts?

The answers would appear to be simple. It is in the Republican interest to want large black districts. To the extent that the black Democrats are concentrated in legislative districts, it is easier for Republican candidates to win more seats overall. The creation of a newly black district is likely to drain black voters from other districts, many of them represented by white Democrats. The more "lily-white" the districts so drained become, the easier it is for Republicans to win them.[42] In short, by adopting such a redistricting strategy, Republicans give African Americans the opportunity to increase their descriptive representation but, quite possibly, at the expense of their substantive representation.

Representative Craig Washington described such a process and explained how blacks could lose ground: "If you have four districts in a state like Alabama, for example, with a sufficiently large black population to neutralize Republicans on some issues, and if you can create one black district by gathering up all the blacks in such a fashion that they could elect a black person to Congress, and in the process you lose the leverage that you had in the three other districts, then that's foolish to me. Every time the one person votes for the things that I'm for, and that the black community is for, the other three from the state will probably vote against them."[43]

In Washington's view, Republican efforts to encourage predominantly black districts are part of the larger question of how Republican policies relate to the interests of blacks:

> Ninety percent of the Republicans vote against things that are centrally important to blacks, like the Civil Rights Bill, Family Medical Leave Act, the Child Care Act, things that by and large will benefit the broad cross-section of American people, including large segments of the black community, not because Republicans are targeting for or against them, but because blacks happen to be in the lowest socioeconomic groups. Republicans are against most of the programs that are designed to help people who happen to fit the strata in which 90 percent of black people fall. . . . It doesn't take a fool twenty years to be able to figure out that [Republicans] are against what I stand for.[44]

Many white liberal Democrats have a big stake in how redistricting is done. Representative Martin Frost (D-TX), for example, who stood to lose many of his minority voters, questioned what he was hearing from voting rights advocates: "There are some in the civil rights community who say they don't care; let the chips fall where they may. I do not believe that represents the majority view. Their larger agenda cannot be enacted unless there are both [minorities and supportive whites in Congress]."[45] A sympathetic Alan Wheat (D-MO) noted the difficulties of achieving the goals of both white incumbents and civil rights activists without causing some "individual tragedies" that most representatives would prefer to avoid.[46]

The Republicans are not united with regard to their position on minority districts. The inconsistency of the party's opposition to affirmative action quotas on the one hand and its eagerness to extend such quotas to minorities for reasons relating to electoral politics on the other has been pointed out by a number of prominent Republicans, most notably the former Reagan Administration drug czar William Bennett.[47] The eagerness of Republicans to help blacks on redistricting issues, but not on other equally important issues, makes them especially vulnerable to charges by Democrats that they are wolves in sheep's clothing. Fortunately for those who seek to increase African-American representation, there is no need to rely on the growth of black Republicanism and the ostensibly benign intervention of the party. Other possibilities abound.

10 · The Future of Black Congressional Representation

I would rather have three white representatives who vote with me and one who votes against me, than one black who votes with me and three whites who vote against me. It's real simple; it's mathematics.
—INTERVIEW WITH REPRESENTATIVE CRAIG WASHINGTON, *October 22, 1991*

What are the preconditions for increased representation of black interests in Congress? Do black members of Congress have distinctive characteristics? What can be expected from the future?

Preconditions of Increased Black Representation

1. Creating newly black districts will not significantly increase black representation.

The most common strategy for electing black representatives has centered on claiming and creating districts with black majorities. At one time this was the surest means of electing blacks to Congress, but in the 1990s its potential as a strategy has been exhausted. Black politicians are already representing all of the country's majority-black congressional districts, and after the 1992 elections relatively few areas remain where blacks are sufficiently concentrated for courts and state legislatures to create new districts. Future significant growth in the number of blacks in Congress cannot come from creating newly black districts.

2. Increased black representation from majority-white districts is possible.

A more promising strategy is to elect blacks in districts without black majorities. Only 1 percent of majority-white districts have African-

American representatives, but they offer blacks the greatest potential for growth. Over 90 percent of the nation's 435 congressional districts have white majorities. Black politicians are already elected from districts of widely varying racial composition (see Figure 10.1). From 1970 to 1990 eight black representatives were elected in majority-white districts that ranged from 4 to 46 percent black in their voting-age populations; an additional nine black representatives were elected from heterogeneous districts, and still another seven were elected from districts that fell short of being 65 percent black. We can assume that each of the majority-white

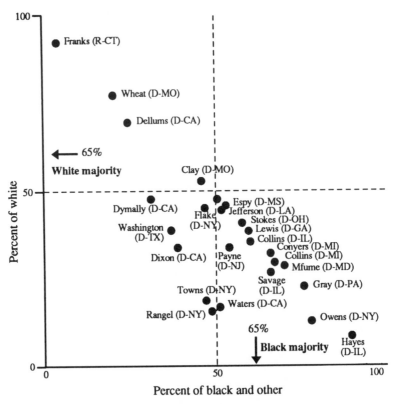

Figure 10.1. Black voting-age percentage of population in congressional districts represented by blacks in 1991. Data compiled from Linda Williams, ed., *The JCPS Congressional Fact Book* (Washington, D.C.: Joint Center for Political Studies, 1988).

districts that elected black representatives had actual black voter registration and turnout rates somewhat lower than the population percentages listed in the election history tables.

There have been black victories in white districts despite the fact that black candidates are often discouraged from running for office in majority-white geographical areas. According to the conventional wisdom, black candidates will lose in such areas because of the racism of white voters. At present, knowledge of why voters sometimes vote along racial lines and sometimes cross over to support a candidate from a different racial group is deficient. What we know is based on a handful of comparative studies of local governmental elections and case studies of the statewide races of Tom Bradley, Douglas Wilder, and Edward Brooke.[1] Broader studies on the electability of black candidates running in white constituencies tend to focus on the attitudes white Americans hold toward blacks as a group.[2] From the negative stereotypes that many whites use to label blacks, these studies reach pessimistic conclusions about the prospect of electing more blacks in majority-white constituencies. They fail to take account of a key electoral fact: candidates run as individuals and not as categorical groups. This is a crucial distinction. It is possible for someone to dislike a group, but to make exceptions for individual group members.

Voters do usually favor candidates from their own racial or ethnic group.[3] Indeed, a candidate's race is an important cue for predicting his or her position on a host of issues. Henry Brady and Paul Sniderman have demonstrated that voters use their likes and dislikes of "politically strategic groups" to calculate their policy positions on major issues. Similarly, Edward Carmines and James Stimson have found that whites and blacks have a striking ability to estimate each other's positions on issues such as busing, guaranteed jobs, minority aid, and rights of the accused.[4] Because blacks tend to be more liberal than whites on many issues, in the absence of further information whites will tend to assume that black candidates are liberal. It follows that conservative white voters who know no more about a candidate than that he or she is black may vote against that candidate. In effect, the racially polarized voting of such individuals is a rational response to a lack of information. By the same token white voters who learn that a black candidate shares their views and values may well vote for that candidate on the issues. It is instructive that the black candidates who have been most successful in winning white support typically have provided the voters with plenty of information about themselves.

3. *"Packing" black voters diminishes the overall representation of blacks.*

In 1991 seven congressional districts ranged from 66 to 90 percent black. The result was wasted black votes and influence. Less concentrated black populations in these districts might have made it possible to elect more black politicians overall. Let us consider what might happen if policymakers abandoned the practice of drawing "safe" black districts with an aggregate majority of at least 65 percent. Assuming, of course, that the black electorate is politically active, or that it can be mobilized when necessary, the dispersion of a large black population across different congressional districts could have positive results. There could be better representation for blacks overall.[5] Instead of one black politician representing a congressional district that is 70 or 80 percent black, one black representative might have a 50 to 55 percent black district, and other (possibly white) representatives would be influenced by the remaining black voters in adjacent districts.

To accept reduced black populations in existing and future black-majority districts, African Americans would need to think beyond their desire for black faces and black solidarity. Black faces in political office do not guarantee the substantive representation of the policy preferences of the majority of African Americans. President Reagan responded to minority demands for such representation by appointing a conservative Hispanic (Linda Chavez) and a black (Clarence Pendleton) to the Civil Rights Commission. Neither of them reflected the policy preferences of large numbers of the members of their respective groups.

Black districts with smaller percentages of black voters would give more African-American candidates an incentive to build multiracial coalitions. Lowering the threshold of black voters has other implications: blacks dispersed over more districts might encourage greater responsiveness from white elected officials. No politician can afford to concentrate on one racial or ethnic group to the exclusion of others. Most representatives know that ignoring a significant minority population can be political suicide, because an opponent can build a coalition of disaffected groups.[6] Less overwhelmingly black districts would also undoubtedly make their own representatives feel less secure. Many of the representatives would become more attentive and vigilant, and therefore their constituents would profit.

Much of the future growth of black substantive and descriptive representation will depend on coalition building with other racial and ethnic groups. The issue of biracial coalitions between whites and blacks has been intensely debated since the 1960s, when Stokely Carmichael and Charles V. Hamilton wrote their classic book on black power.[7] Carmichael and Hamilton warned against coalitions with whites until blacks had had the opportunity to develop independent bases of power that would allow them to be more than junior partners. Now, in the 1990s, it can be argued that the time has come.

4. Whites can represent the interests of blacks.

White representatives who support the goals of blacks, however these goals are defined, are a further source of black representation. As we saw in Chapter 8, Peter Rodino and Lindy Boggs (and before her, Hale Boggs) took seriously their mandate to represent black interests even when their districts were still majority-white. They supported and helped push civil rights legislation and Great Society programs through a reluctant Congress at a time when the few blacks in Congress lacked the seniority, clout, experience, and other resources to take on leadership roles.[8] Rodino and Boggs, nevertheless, found themselves assailed by the argument that "only blacks can represent black interests." African Americans who advance such arguments may not recognize that they are placing such a high value on descriptive representation that they are ignoring other characteristics of representatives that may be in the group's interests, such as age, seniority in Congress, and history of responsiveness. Whenever a black majority, regardless of whether it is in a newly created district or not, is not represented by a black politician, the argument that only blacks can represent blacks is made. Yet descriptive representation of blacks guarantees only black faces and is, at best, an intangible good; substantive representation is by definition real and color blind. Substantive representation can be measured by a politician's performance on indicators such as voting and casework.

Many white members of Congress perform as well or better on the indicators used in this book than some black representatives. Many of the white associate members of the Black Caucus have already shown that they are prepared to and can serve the interests of blacks by actively working to frame legislation that will benefit disadvantaged groups and by supporting causes that the majority of African Americans consider in their interest (see Table 10.1). Some of them, moreover, are high in seniority and hold congressional leadership positions that enable them to act effectively on advancing their legislative agendas. Although associate members are not allowed to participate in the CBC's closed-door

Table 10.1. Legislative records of selected Congressional Black Caucus associate members, 101st Congress

District	Representative	Year elected	BVAP 1980s	HVAP 1980s	COPE rating	LCCR rating
NY-7	Gary Ackerman	1983	11	17	99	100
AK-1	Bill Alexander	1968	16	1	70	100
WI-1	Les Aspin	1970	3	2	86	87
CA-44	Jim Bates	1982	13	22	83	93
CA-26	Howard Berman	1982	4	20	87	93
LA-2	Lindy Boggs	1973	52	3	77	87
CA-36	George Brown, Jr.	1972	7	20	90	93
CA-10	Don Edwards	1962	5	24	94	100
PA-1	Thomas Foglietta	1980	29	7	96	93
MA-4	Barney Frank	1980	1	1	91	100
TX-24	Martin Frost	1978	29	11	79	93
CT-2	Sam Gejdenson	1980	3	1	95	80
MO-3	Richard Gephardt	1976	1	1	82	89
NJ-14	Frank Guarini	1978	11	24	92	80
MD-5	Steny Hoyer	1981	31	2	94	100
MA-8	Joseph Kennedy II	1986	4	3	93	100
NC-3	Martin Lancaster	1986	25	2	73	87
CA-11	Tom Lantos	1980	6	12	94	87
CA-18	Richard Lehman	1982	6	21	93	100
MI-17	Sander Levin	1982	10	1	95	100
OH-1	Thomas A. Luken	1976	14	1	78	100

meetings, some would if they were given the opportunity, as Robin Tallon's attendance and participation at a Black Caucus meeting suggested (see Chapter 7). Furthermore, the white associate members of the Black Caucus are not the only whites on Capitol Hill who are willing to help blacks.

What difference does the race of the representative make for the representation of black policy preferences? If the mean interest-group scores of white and black Democrats on two of the indicators of black interests are contrasted, there is only a shade of difference between white and black Democrats (see Figure 10.2). Similarly, in a multivariate regression analysis that includes the race of the representative as one of the independent variables, race is statistically insignificant (see Table 10.2).[9] It is evident that partisanship and region are far more important than race in predicting whether representatives will pursue black interests as here defined. The black Republican representative Gary Franks confirms this pattern by following party lines. Franks was the only black

Table 10.1 (continued).

District	Representative	Year elected	BVAP 1980s	HVAP 1980s	COPE rating	LCCR rating
WA-7	James McDermott	1988	8	2	—	—
MD-4	C. Thomas McMillen	1986	19	1	100	100
CA-13	Norman Mineta	1974	2	10	89	87
MD-8	Constance Morella	1986	8	4	63	93
NC-5	Stephen Neal	1974	15	1	54	80
OH-20	Mary Oakar	1976	2	2	94	87
CA-5	Nancy Pelosi	1987	9	12	96	86
FL-18	Claude Pepper	1962	13	50	94	100
VA-2	Owen Pickett	1986	21	2	83	80
WV-4	Nick Rahill II	1976	6	1	88	100
NJ-8	Robert Roe	1969	12	10	91	87
NC-7	Charlie Rose	1972	25	2	64	87
CO-1	Patricia Schroeder	1972	11	15	75	87
SC-6	Robin Tallon	1982	37	1	69	73
PA-18	Doug Walgren	1976	2	—	85	93
OR-3	Ron Wyden	1980	5	2	31	100
Mean scores, white CBC members			12.9	8.6	83.8	91.7
Mean scores, black CBC members					98.4	93.0

Source: "The 101st Congress, 1989–1990," Congressional Black Caucus Foundation, September 1990.

Note: BVAP = Black voting-age percentage of district population; HVAP = Hispanic voting-age percentage of district population; COPE = AFL-CIO Committee on Political Education; LCCR = Leadership Conference on Civil Rights. This table excludes senators and members of the Congressional Hispanic Caucus who are also Black Caucus members.

House member to vote in support of the war in the Gulf, against civil rights legislation, and against family leave.

The staffs of the white Democrats that I interviewed were racially diverse, and staffers can be said to provide a surrogate form of representation for racial subgroups. The black representatives of heterogeneous, newly black, and majority-white districts also had racially diverse staffs. Such staffs enable representatives to avoid being perceived as representatives of only their own racial group. One way they do this is by placing aides from other racial groups in strategic locations. As one high-ranking white staffer of a black representative explained to me, a key part of his job is to "just hang out" and mingle with prominent whites in the district, watching for any dissatisfaction with the congressman.

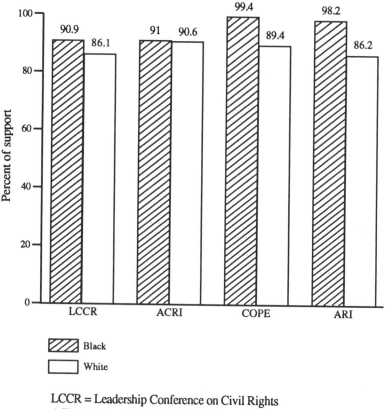

LCCR = Leadership Conference on Civil Rights
ACRI = Alternative Civil Rights Index calculated by author
COPE = AFL-CIO Committee on Political Education
ARI = Alternative Redistributive Index calculated by author

Figure 10.2. Racial comparison of Democrats' voting behavior on the four indicators of black interest, 100th Congress. Data compiled from U.S. Census, roll-call votes, and published reports of the Leadership Conference on Civil Rights and the AFL-CIO Committee on Political Education.

Many white Democrats appear to be fully at ease in interacting with their black constituents, just as black representatives like Alan Wheat are with their white voters. A black aide to the white North Carolina congressman Charlie Rose, who represents a district that is 27 percent black, told me that "black folks make my boss feel right at home." Rose

Table 10.2. Multivariate analysis of influences on representatives' support of black interests

Variables	Indicators measuring support			
	LCCR	COPE	ACRI	ARI
Party	48**	55**	48**	59**
	(2.2)	(2.0)	(2.4)	(2.0)
Region	–17**	–16**	–16**	–12**
	(2.6)	(2.3)	(2.8)	(2.4)
Interactive term[a]	6	15	8	12
	(9.7)	(9.0)	(10.7)	(9.1)
Race of representative	2	3	–3	6
	(4.8)	(4.6)	(5.4)	(4.6)
R^2	.58	.67	.52	.70

*p ≤ .05.   **p ≤ .01.

Note: The regression coefficients are unstandardized. The numbers in parentheses are standard errors.

LCCR = Leadership Conference on Civil Rights rating; ACRI = Alternative Civil Rights Index; COPE = AFL-CIO Committee on Political Education rating; ARI = Alternative Redistributive Index.

attends many family reunions, weddings, and similar functions in his district. As his aide put it: "[Rose] loves to sit down and chew the fat with blacks. He loves going into their homes. When we ride through the district, he'll just stop by people's homes. He doesn't wait for events or invitations. If he knows that someone is having a homecoming or something like that, he'll stop by the church. That's just the way he is."[10]

A white representative who makes an effort to get along with blacks may find it possible to get valuable campaign support from black representatives. In Rose's case a tradition of such support began when the District of Columbia's nonvoting delegate, Walter Fauntroy, showed him a notebook listing prominent blacks in the district:

He thumbed through his notebook and said to me, "Charlie, do you know these people?" I said: "Do I know them! That's the people that sent me here." "Well," he said, "all of these people want you to vote for home rule for the District of Columbia." I said: "I'll be very happy to do that, but I need something from you first." I got Andy Young and Fauntroy together and told them both: "I'm going to vote and work to help you pass home rule for the District of Columbia, but I want you to come down to my district and speak for me, when I'm running for reelection." They both agreed, and for fifteen years or more, it has been sort of a tradition that I invite a black congressman to come into my district to make a speech.[11]

White representatives have other ways of gaining black support. They may, for example, donate large sums of money to black churches and other black organizations, or purchase seats for the Black Caucus's annual legislative weekend dinner, perhaps giving tickets to black leaders in their districts. Perhaps the most controversial strategy is the use of election day "walking around money," which can be viewed as vote buying. Indeed, some local black leaders are known to take advantage of white politicians' need for black support and collect money from both the Democrats and the Republicans.

Unfortunately, white liberal Democrats who view themselves as the allies of African Americans cannot always count on black support. Many white liberal representatives are threatened by redistricting plans that ignore their records of responsiveness to blacks and their interests. Some reverse discrimination suits may come from the former allies of blacks when white liberals find themselves redistricted out of seats to make way for black descriptive representation.[12] Black politicians argue that a person's race should not be used against him or her, but many also argue that only blacks can represent black interests. They are, in effect, using a double standard and leaving themselves open to attack. When the argument is advanced that only blacks can represent blacks, this implies that blacks and whites are separated by an unbridgeable gap. White Americans are noticing that some black politicians use blatant racial appeals such as "vote black" to galvanize their supporters. Yet white politicians who dare hint at racial solidarity will find themselves forever branded as racist.[13] Black leaders must reflect on how white politicians fit into their overall plan to increase black political power. An abandonment of double standards would facilitate cooperation between whites and blacks.

5. Blacks can represent the interests of whites.

As we have seen in Chapters 4, 5, and 6, black representatives can represent the needs and desires of white voters without compromising their ability to support the type of public policy agendas favored by the majority of African Americans. The election of blacks in heterogeneous and majority-white districts is particularly fruitful because it can increase black representation descriptively *and* substantively. Mike Espy,

Alan Wheat, and Ron Dellums are among the black representatives whose support among whites increased during their time in Congress. These members have gained the trust of white voters while representing the legislative agenda that most blacks seem to prefer.

6. Descriptive representation has its own value.

Although a white representative can "think, act, and talk black," he or she can never *be* black. White representation of blacks will never replace black representation. Like the members of other ethnic groups, African Americans are proud of the achievements of their group. Blacks are especially pleased when there is a black "first"—the first black to do or achieve something, to break a real or perceived barrier. The presence of black representatives in Congress, regardless of their political party, fulfills a host of psychological needs that are no less important for being intangible. One need only attend an annual Black Caucus legislative weekend to see the pride that the hundreds of blacks who attend the affair have in the group of congressional black representatives. Black representatives are celebrities—icons for their group. Michael Preston writes: "Symbolic representation is not only desirable but necessary for black Americans. Blacks need role models in government; they need representatives that they believe will represent their interests; they need to know that good leadership (or bad) is not dominated by one race or group."[14]

Although black Republicans do not represent the substantive interests of the majority of African Americans, they have something valuable to contribute to both whites and blacks. Their counterintuitive positions help to remind people that blacks are not monolithic. Confronted with this information, as Americans were in the case of the Clarence Thomas confirmation hearings, when impressive blacks testified for both sides, white Americans may be more likely to treat blacks as individuals and less likely to succumb to racial polarization.

The Special Characteristics of Black Representatives

From George Crockett, the old-style radical, to Mervyn Dymally, the former lieutenant governor of California with a Ph.D., we have seen that black representatives are marvelously varied. Nonetheless, they tend to have numerous qualities in common. Many, if not all of them, for example, have a broader view of what makes up their constituency than do most white representatives. Richard Fenno, Jr., has observed that representatives' perceptions of their constituencies resemble nests of concentric circles, consisting of their personal, primary, reelection, and geographical constituencies: that is, their circles of friends and intimates, voters they can count on in a primary election, those they can count on in a general election, and all the people who reside within their districts.[15] Most black representatives have a still wider sense of their constituencies that extends to national and even international concerns.[16] The national constituency includes all blacks and disadvantaged people within the United States; the international constituency extends to people of color throughout the world.

A sign of this broader view of constituency was evident in my interview with Dymally, who complained that too much of his time was taken up by people not technically his constituents, but added that he would never send anyone away. Representatives George Crockett and William Gray expressed their eagerness to help non-Caucasians from Africa, the Pacific, and the Caribbean nations. Dymally summed up the feelings of many when he told me that "if the Jews can advance the interests of Israel, surely a black congressman can do something for his people."[17] The Texas Democrat Mickey Leland provided poignant evidence of the breadth of identifications of many black representatives in his tragic death while in Africa on a mission of famine relief. He once told constituents and colleagues: "I am now an activist on behalf of humanity everywhere in any part of the world where people are desperate and hungry for the freedoms and rights they deserve as human beings."[18] Before Leland's death, his district administrator told me: "What people don't understand is that Mickey Leland must be the Congressman for the entire Southwest. There isn't another black congressman in this general vicinity, unless you go to the deep South or the Midwest."[19]

The efforts of black representatives to represent international interests can be a source of tension in most American black communities, as constituents struggle to overcome the ravages of drugs, AIDS, homelessness, and unemployment at home. To some black constituents, black representatives appear more concerned with conditions in South Africa and the Middle East than they are with the crises in their own constituencies. Some black representatives make themselves vulnerable to such criticisms by turning to foreign policy issues that appear to be easier for them to tackle than domestic issues.

Whenever a black representative is elected, he or she is likely to be contacted by blacks throughout the region for assistance. This might be expected, in view of Sidney Verba and Norman Nie's finding that African Americans tend to be reluctant to contact white public officials.[20] Representative Donald Payne has observed some of these tendencies. He comments: "Black constituents feel comfortable with me, and see that I feel comfortable with them. I always have, because I have always been a minority in this majority. They don't take me as a threat. They know that I'm very concerned about issues that affect them. If you don't care about your own number one, there's something wrong with you."[21] Because so many African Americans share his view, black representatives are confronted with an above-average number of requests. Serving needs beyond district lines can, of course, be a significant burden on the resources of any black representative. A similar phenomenon occurs when there is only one Democrat within easy reach in an area: often people who are Democratic party members are reluctant to request casework from a Republican representative.

Not surprisingly, black representatives generally come from districts that have many problems, and their constituents generate many requests for service. Nevertheless, black representatives vary enormously when it comes to their actual approach to casework. Some black members (and a few whites) run their offices like social welfare agencies. Some become actively involved in legal matters and will even write to parole boards; others steer clear of such matters. Representatives set the tone for the type of constituency service that their office will render. They do this by either seeking or discouraging cases, by making themselves accessible to their constituents, or by closely monitoring and responding to complaints. In rare cases they adopt a hands-off approach, leaving everything to the staffers. Several black representatives and staffers have complained to me: "Black constituents are difficult to help because they wait until the eleventh hour. They appear at the office shortly before an eviction or job loss." "Black constituents are so demanding. They want us to turn over the world in a minute, and then they wonder what took us so long." "Our policy is for all of our staffers to stop what they are doing when someone enters the office. That individual gets our attention."[22]

Often black representatives' emphasis on casework is evident in their allocation of staff. Most of the black representatives I interviewed placed more of their staffers in their district office than did white members. Such a decision is reasonable, given the findings of Bruce Cain, John Ferejohn, and Morris Fiorina, who conducted a comparative study of British and American legislative-constituency relations and found that blacks consider policymaking the least important of a representative's activities; in their view, it lags behind helping constituents and protecting the district.[23]

Another characteristic marks many black representatives, especially those in historically and newly black districts (although it does not distinguish them from all members of Congress). They are relatively immune from an incentive that Mayhew and others view as central to congressional behavior—preoccupation with reelection.[24] Black representatives from historically black districts are essentially guaranteed reelection if they survive their primaries. They have reelection rates exceeding even the high rates of House incumbents in general. This presumably helps to explain the fact that in 1989, in spite of intense public uproar about a proposed 51 percent congressional pay raise, 56 percent of the blacks in the House (13 of 23) voted for the increase in contrast with 8 percent (35 of 412) of the non-African-American House members.

Issues of self-esteem, real or alleged wrongdoing, and unfair treatment or even persecution present other special problems for black representatives and contribute to the uniqueness of their concerns. For most black representatives a measure of respect and status in the world outside of politics comes with the job. This may not transfer to their dealings with colleagues inside the chamber, where everyone is supposed to be equal. Individuals who have been accorded high prestige in their communities may find they have to fight hard for the respect of their white colleagues.

This may help explain why many black representatives feel that a white establishment is seeking to discredit them through charges of misconduct related to the use of their official positions for financial gain. Charges against black representatives are often unsubstantiated and have to be dismissed after the accused has spent thousands of dollars in legal fees.[25] Although there are also white representatives who find themselves in similar situations, most blacks see a double standard in the accusations and in the manner these cases are resolved. The harassment of black elected officials has been the subject of several reports by human rights groups.[26] Some black representatives have reacted to what they see as their vulnerability by being exceptionally cautious.[27] Even so, many of them complain about being victimized by white journalists who they believe are rewarded for writing negative stories about black politicians. The weight that black representatives attach to maintaining a respectable public image makes the charges of misconduct a particularly crippling part of their political lives.

Another distinctive aspect of the legislative experience of African Americans in Congress is the financial security provided by holding office. In contrast with whites, many of whom take salary cuts to serve in Congress, blacks often enter Congress from low-paying jobs—as low as $15,000 per year, according to some members' accounts. Moreover, positions beyond the congressional level have traditionally always been available to whites, but only more recently have changes in the political environment made it possible for blacks to aspire to higher office. Jesse Jackson's presidential bids and the election of African Americans to statewide offices raise new possibilities for all blacks—positions that were once considered unobtainable are now well within reach. As strategic politicians, representatives know what is needed for winning such offices, and some are quietly amassing financial war chests. The Black Caucus has for a long time pursued statehood for the District of Columbia, and this goal is related to the pursuit of higher office by blacks. If the District is granted its statehood, blacks will have a chance to attain . several very powerful positions: a governorship and two senatorial seats as well as one representative seat. In anticipation, several black representatives have positioned themselves so that they could easily declare residency and run for office. Presently the cost of running for higher office is great, and blacks have so far had only limited success in winning statewide races (though the number of successful candidacies is increasing). One representative commented: "I would love to be a senator, but if I run and lose I have no place to go." Black representatives are usually rational enough not to give up seats to run for higher office. Two who did, Yvonne Burke (D-CA) and Parren Mitchell (D-MD), were defeated—thus serving as powerful reminders to other blacks.

If financial incentives keep some black representatives from contesting statewide offices, they may lead others—particularly those whose congressional service makes them marketable in the private or not-for-profit sphere—to leave Congress for better positions. William Gray, for example, substantially increased his salary when he resigned from Congress in 1991 to head the United Negro College Fund.

To the extent that black members of Congress aspire to leadership positions within the House of Representatives, they may exhibit still other characteristics. One of these may be a muting of any militant impulses or radical views that they may have held. Recognizing the truth of Sam Rayburn's aphorism that getting along requires going along, they are likely to try to fit in rather than rail against the political system.

It should not be surprising that black representatives have a number of distinctive qualities. Overall, however, blacks who have served in Congress in the twentieth century have fit into the system well and have succeeded in adapting it to their purposes and to those of their constituents.

What Lies Ahead?

What is on the horizon for black congressional representation? The picture for the future is complex and not wholly consistent, but a number of trends are evident. One is that the advantage of incumbents in reelection will allow more black members to gain seniority. These gains will result in additional African-American influence in committees and on the Hill. But blacks in institutional power may become less willing to support controversial issues that are in the interests of the disadvantaged majority of American blacks. To the extent that black members of Congress turn into traditional legislative brokers, there will be a further weakening of the Black Caucus. Similarly, a loss of Black Caucus influence is likely to occur as its senior members retire—as has already occurred in the departure of Augustus Hawkins, chairman of the Education and Labor Committee, who left in 1990 after twenty-eight years of service, and in the resignation of Bill Gray as Majority Whip in 1991.

Another, different trend may result from the Republican party's strategy of providing voting rights activists with the technology to draw black-majority and Hispanic-majority districts in the next round of redistricting. If blacks and other minorities are packed in homogeneous districts, it will be less possible for minority voters to increase their descriptive and substantive representation.

In addition, a variety of developments are possible as a result of the close ties between black representation and the fortunes of the Democratic party.[28] To begin with, black influence would drop precipitously if the Democrats were to lose control of the House. Were this to happen, most African American legislators would automatically become minority members of the minority party. Gone would be the committee chairmanships, the leadership posts, and other key assignments.

The dependence of African Americans on Democrats for representation of their interests has other important implications for the future. Through 1988, the Democratic party had lost five of the last six presidential elections. As Merle and Earl Black show, a majority of white southerners have economic priorities that are different from those of blacks. Moreover, there is much evidence that increasing numbers of young people in the South are identifying themselves as Republicans.[29] This trend is also apparent in older age groups.

To the extent that the Democratic party finds it difficult to win presidential elections or to be in a position to promise all Americans a piece of the fading American dream, it must devise new public relations strategies to improve its image with members of all races. As Carmines and Stimson have shown in their fifty-year longitudinal analysis of issue evolution, race has transformed American politics in ways that are now harmful to the Democrats.[30] They cannot allow their party to be seen as the party of blacks any more than the Republicans can allow theirs to be the white man's party. Black leaders must, therefore, cooperate and allow the Democrats to pursue legislation that will benefit both races. Charles Hamilton explored an alternative strategy in 1976 when he addressed the National Democratic Party Convention and advocated a "de-racializing" strategy for the party. He suggested that blacks concentrate on the attainment of full employment, national health insurance, and income maintenance programs that would cut across racial lines.[31] Several social scientists have conducted research that suggests that legislation geared to help particular social classes, and not racially based remedies that alienate whites, will go furthest in helping blacks to achieve their public policy objectives.[32]

The current unrest among white Americans suggests that it is more important than ever before that blacks recognize white interests and be aware of the implications of pursuing racially polarizing issues.[33] African Americans cannot expect to win on all fronts. Their failure to get a particular policy enacted or supported by a white representative, moreover, does not mean that they are completely unrepresented. Rather, representation of blacks cannot be viewed in isolation from representation of whites. On some issues blacks should expect to lose. In past battles, southern white conservatives have regularly lost on civil rights. Only in racially and socially homogeneous districts can we expect stable representation of constituency opinion.[34]

The rise of black Republicans such as Gary Franks will reduce the dependency of blacks on the Democratic party for their congressional influence.[35] Prior to Franks's election, black Republicans ran almost exclusively in no-win situations with limited financial support from their party. In fact, they were routinely promoted in races in which they stood no chance of winning. Examples of the latter include Virginia's senatorial race in 1988, when Maurice Dawkins, a black, ran against former Governor Chuck Robb, an extremely popular opponent, and Alan Keyes, who in 1988 took on incumbent Paul Sarbanes in Maryland, a state in which Democrats outnumber Republicans two to one. Both senatorial candidates complained of financial problems and a lack of party support.

The election of a black Republican has the result of increasing black descriptive representation, but ironically it does nothing to enhance black substantive representation as defined by groups such as the NAACP and the LCCR. Still, one cannot say dogmatically that the election of black Republicans will necessarily diminish the substantive representation of all African Americans. Not all blacks are poor or liberal. The existence of a growing black middle and professional class, often geographically and socially separate from poorer blacks, makes it difficult, if not impossible, to generalize about the "black interest."

Other changes can be envisaged. In addition to the election of black Republicans, we can expect black representation to be enhanced by the presence of black Democrats in the Senate. This has never occurred in the history of the institution (the only three black senators, so far, have been Republicans), but there are indications that it will. In North Carolina's senatorial race in 1990, for example, Harvey Gantt, a black Democrat, beat several white primary opponents, won the runoff election against a single white opponent, and came within several points of defeating Jesse Helms, the arch-conservative incumbent in a state that is 20 percent black. Despite speculation that racism was a major factor in the final outcome, Gantt's vote percentage (47 percent) was consistent with that of Helms's previous white opponents. He was able to hold Helms to his usual margin of victory.[36] Gantt's gains, along with the increasing number of blacks elected to statewide offices elsewhere in the nation, illustrate the potential for electing blacks to the Senate. The time may be coming when the U.S. Congress will be a truly racially diverse body. The defeat of two-term senator Alan Dixon (D-IL) in the 1992 Illinois Democratic primary by Carol Moseley Braun, a black woman, points in that direction.[37]

Nevertheless, it is not clear what the future holds for representation of black interests in the broader sense. Black communities are beset with problems. The needs of these communities cannot be adequately addressed by black representatives in Congress alone, even if we include the representatives from districts without large black populations. Not only must blacks in Congress make alliances with like-minded representatives from other races and ethnic backgrounds, but they must also rethink their own priorities and the relationship of those priorities to African-American needs. Twentieth-century black representation has been more substantive than ever before, but further progress requires new alliances and new strategies—and that in turn calls for recognizing the substantive representation of blacks coming from white members. As African Americans become more diverse and more politically sophisticated, we can expect further expansion in what constitutes "black interests," but there will be no reduction in the urgency of finding better and more effective ways to represent African Americans.

Appendix A · Research Methods

To research the representation of black interests in Congress, I have used a multifaceted approach involving several different methods of data collection and analysis: participant observation, roll-call data, historical analysis, and interviews of representatives and staffers. What results is a study that mixes descriptive data and explanatory generalizations with normative policy prescriptions. It may be useful to discuss the specific methods and limitations of the study.

Participant Observation

Participant observation involves field research on subjects in their natural habitats. Lewis Dexter, Alexander Heard, and James Robinson were among the pioneers of this methodology, but the "soaking and poking" approach of Richard Fenno, Jr., provided the model for this study.[1] I traveled with, observed, and talked to several representatives as they worked in their districts. The black representatives served districts with aggregate populations that ranged from 20 to 90 percent black; the white representatives had districts that were at least 40 percent black in aggregate population.[2] Few of the subjects represented a truly "safe" district. Ron Dellums (D-CA), Lindy Boggs (D-LA), and Alan Wheat (D-MO), for example, represented districts in which the majority of voters were from a racial group different from their own. Mervyn Dymally (D-CA) and Mickey Leland (D-TX) served districts with three or more large minority groups. Mike Espy (D-MS), John Lewis (D-GA), Robin Tallon (D-SC), and Tim Valentine (D-NC) served districts in which biracial coalitions were essential to their election and reelection.

Field research enabled me to gather individual perspectives on the ways politicians represent blacks. When I arranged my trips, I first mailed a letter to each black member of Congress and requested permission to travel with him or her. Next, for those representatives who responded positively, I made appointments with the staffers responsible for coordinating district trips. If my initial travel request was denied, I made an appointment directly with the representative. Usually I was able to persuade the representative to grant me a district visit. I followed a similar process with white members of Congress who represented districts with significant aggregate minority populations. Only two black members declined to participate at all, each giving a different reason for refusing the request. As it turned out, these were members from historically black congressional districts, and as such their participation was not crucial to the analysis. We know more about these districts than any other type of black-represented district, and I was also able to focus on other historically black districts in the case studies.

Participant observation proved crucial for understanding typical constituent-member relationships: it allowed me to question and interview representatives personally about their views, policies, and tactical approach while they were actually "at work." In this practical aspect of my research I discovered links and connections that cannot easily be seen in statistics. I asked representatives and staffers very specific questions about how they decided on office locations and staff selection, and how they allocated time for their district and for work on the Hill. I tried to get them to talk about their supporting and opposing coalitions. I asked them how they saw their roles as representatives, and I asked them to describe how they spent their time. Field questions included: How did you decide on your office location(s)? How often do you visit the district? How do you select your staff? What changes have you made over time in your views, campaign style, or voting behavior? Why? Who are your strongest supporters? Not every representative was asked every question; representatives varied, of course, in their enthusiasm for my project, and I had a greater rapport with some interviewees than with others. In the case of Mickey Leland, I interviewed his district administrator, several months before Leland's death. William Gray was never able to find time for an interview.

Interviews

To supplement the field data, I conducted interviews with twenty-seven present and former members of Congress (twenty blacks and seven whites) and many of their staffers. Prior to the participant observations, I interviewed a retired black congressman (Parren Mitchell) and several former and present employees of the Black Caucus Foundation. I used these preliminary interviews to gain insight into the concerns and constraints of black representatives, to make valuable contacts, and to generate ideas on how best to approach specific individuals. The types of questions asked of interviewees varied, depending on their districts, interests, and backgrounds.

Natural circumstances eradicated racial bias between the black members and myself. Shirley Hatchett and Howard Shuman discovered in their study of the mass public that the race of the interviewer can influence responses to interview questions.[3] They found the race of the interviewer to be an important determinant of certain black racial and nonracial attitudes. These findings can be extended to elite interviews. In my case, several black representatives commented that my race was a factor in their decision to participate in the study; they said that they would have refused access to a white researcher. One black representative would not even speak openly in front of his white staffers. In their absence, he "talked black talk."

During my interviews in 1988, I only took notes, but most of the later interviews (1989–1991) were tape-recorded conversations. I gave the recorder to the subject and encouraged him or her to switch the machine off at will, although only two representatives chose to do so during the course of their interviews. Some interviewees asked to be anonymous, and a few requested permission to read the sections in which they were quoted. I gave this option to all representatives who are subjects of chapters or are quoted a great deal.

Historical Analysis

The interviews and participant observations were supplemented with historical and background information gathered from newspaper clippings, constituency mailings, published interviews, and position papers. For each black member, I examined files maintained by the Joint Center for Political Studies (JCPS) in Washington, D.C. Data from the JCPS files provided an opportunity to examine public statements and accounts of district activities. Articles, letters, and campaign documents portrayed evidence of representatives engaged in what David Mayhew refers to as credit-claiming, advertising, and position-taking. In some instances, the newspaper clippings provided evidence of whom black representatives blamed for the socioeconomic status of blacks.[4]

Multivariate Model

Variations of the multivariate model listed below were run for members of the 100th Congress. The dependent variables were a representative's support scores on four indexes: LCCR (indicator for civil rights support), COPE (indicator for redistributive issues and workers' support), ACRI (alternative civil rights index), and ARI (alternative redistributive index).

$$Y = A + B_1X_1 + B_2X_2 + B_3X_3 + B_4X_4 + B_5X_5 + E,$$

where Y = interest group score (LCCR, COPE, ACRI, ARI),
A = constant,
X_1 = representative's party identification (1 Democrat, 0 Republican),
X_2 = district's region (1 = South, 0 = non-South),
X_3 = district's percentage urban (0 to 100 percent),
X_4 = the race of the representative (1 = black, 0 = white),
X_5 = district's percentage black (0 to 100 percent),
E = error term.

I ran several models that examined demographic data on blue-collar workers and education, as well as some that included an interactive term for race and urbanization. Most of the models were uninteresting. The coefficients for the interactive term (race and urbanization) added little to the fit of the model.

Limitations

Some limitations are apparent in the research design. First, because this was primarily a qualitative study, focusing on a particular subset of the 100th (and 101st) Congress, it is not certain whether these findings can be generalized. The ease with which we can generalize depends, in part, on the content of the theory underlying the analysis. As yet, there is very little theoretical grounding for studies of this type, primarily because the pretheoretical "inductive" style of background data gathering has not been completed by researchers. This research is a step in that direction.

Second, the participant observation component included few black representatives from overwhelmingly black districts (65 percent or more); this means that much of the data on these politicians' attitudes and behavior were drawn from interviews with their staffers and from secondary sources. I did visit several such districts, but usually with only the rather limited cooperation of their representatives. Third, the study has a partisan bias. At the time I started this study, no Republican members of Congress qualified (based on their race and the racial compositions of their districts) for participant observation. It would be worthwhile to travel with Republicans who have districts that are more than 20 percent black to observe the type of representation made available to the constituents.

Fourth, the time span for data collection could conceivably have resulted in a distorted view of member activity. I collected much of the field data between 1988 and 1991. The spring of 1988 saw Jesse Jackson winning several primaries, and this made it an atypical year for African Americans. Unlike 1984, when there was bickering among black elected officials, by April 1988 black representatives were united in their support for Jackson.[5] For a brief time he was the Democratic party's front-runner, and many black representatives spent the year campaigning for him. Jackson's early successes may have changed their approach and their goals. Some white representatives were certainly under pressure to endorse Jackson, too. Ernest Hollings (D-SC), a white Democratic senator, surprised observers by endorsing Jackson after he won South Carolina's delegates. Obviously, Jesse Jackson's presidential bid was a contextual variable that cannot be ignored. Nor, however, should it be given undue emphasis. In my opinion, that 1988 and 1990 were both election years had a minimal impact on the data. I defend the use of election years for such research because they are the best time to find members in their districts. Many of Fenno's trips were conducted during fall sessions and in election years.[6] Moreover, several representatives told me that election years caused them to make relatively minor adjustments in their schedules.

Appendix B · Campaign Finance, 1980–1990

Representative	Years	Total receipts	Receipts from PACs	PAC %[a]	Expenditures	Unspent balance
Boggs (LA-2)	1988	$266,033	$144,300	54%	$252,835	$13,198
	1986	318,411	157,150	49	261,984	56,427
	1984	796,527	298,784	38	807,062	−10,535
	1982	476,779	63,924	13	464,594	12,185
	1980	264,612	60,875	23	280,198	−15,586
Crockett (MI-13)	1988	97,827	63,822	65	84,024	13,803
	1986	71,784	38,370	53	56,271	15,513
	1984	66,897	29,168	44	54,375	12,522
	1982	74,199	17,747	24	56,039	18,160
	1980	44,592	9,050	20	43,619	973
Dellums (CA-8)	1990	790,386	71,935	9	840,029	−49,643
	1988	1,153,750	87,299	8	1,174,676	−20,926
	1986	1,370,820	93,123	7	1,223,490	147,330
	1984	951,097	77,002	8	981,171	−30,074
	1982	820,918	45,960	6	798,419	22,499
	1980	356,661	32,605	9	312,378	44,283
Dymally (CA-31)	1990	434,143	173,316	40	418,232	15,911
	1988	488,149	156,449	32	481,799	6,350
	1986	386,427	71,358	18	385,063	1,364
	1984	339,424	88,858	26	338,118	1,306
	1982	290,366	54,936	19	294,434	−4,068
	1980	494,254	82,230	17	540,807	−46,553
Espy (MS-2)	1990	448,212	219,225	49	365,825	82,387
	1988	880,227	480,490	55	886,540	−6,313
	1986	600,375	307,865	51	591,002	9,373

Representative	Years	Total receipts	Receipts from PACs	PAC %[a]	Expenditures	Unspent balance
Flake (NY-6)	1990	$240,869	$122,440	51	$205,031	$35,838
	1988	344,391	150,681	44	370,236	−25,845
	1986	401,263	23,350	6	359,382	41,881
Gray (PA-2)	1990	725,717	516,953	71	814,125	−88,408
	1988	656,859	377,752	58	660,456	−3,597
	1986	663,653	460,861	69	551,836	111,817
	1984	201,902	127,668	63	165,085	36,817
	1982	250,408	117,062	47	251,494	−1,086
	1980	178,850	42,040	24	182,192	−3,342
Hall (IN-1)	1982	43,446	30,675	71	38,306	5,140
Lewis (GA-5)	1990	271,450	175,510	65	108,118	163,332
	1988	193,584	142,915	74	101,540	92,044
	1986	381,754	157,994	41	380,314	1,440
Rodino (NJ-10)	1986	394,739	232,525	59	407,220	−12,481
	1984	203,445	167,829	82	206,054	−2,609
	1982	125,006	83,237	67	93,379	31,627
	1980	201,550	93,266	46	212,925	−11,375
Tallon (SC-6)	1990	231,293	145,550	63	95,350	135,943
	1988	381,464	203,958	53	243,559	137,905
	1986	344,115	126,650	37	269,708	74,407
	1984	420,202	222,197	53	422,252	−2,050
	1982	416,746	93,371	22	412,669	4,077
Valentine (NC-2)	1990	261,712	159,202	61	286,351	24,639
	1988	78,527	58,650	75	84,671	−6,144
	1986	178,317	109,755	62	164,680	13,637
	1984	383,619	166,236	43	349,038	34,581
	1982	371,618	103,413	28	368,732	2,886
Wheat (MO-5)	1990	311,266	224,435	72	245,132	66,134
	1988	303,515	205,500	68	240,623	62,892
	1986	268,786	188,627	70	192,612	76,174
	1984	466,774	284,989	61	407,069	59,705
	1982	316,791	117,374	37	314,735	2,056

Source: Politics in America (Washington, D.C.: Congressional Quarterly, biennial vols., 1982–1990).

a. Political action committee receipts as percentage of total receipts.

Appendix C · Legislative Records of All Black Representatives, 100th Congress

Representative	COPE rating	LCCR rating	Conservative coalition	Voting participation
Historically black districts				
Collins (IL-7)	100	80	1.5	90
Conyers (MI-1)	100	100	4.0	86
Crockett (MI-13)	97	100	6.0	86
Ford (TN-9)	100	53	7.0	70
Gray (PA-2)	100	87	11.5	84
Hawkins (CA-29)	100	100	7.5	84
Hayes (IL-1)	100	73	2.5	92
Mfume (MD-7)	100	100	15.0	98
Owens (NY-12)	100	93	5.0	85
Savage (IL-2)	100	93	5.0	92
Stokes (OH-21)	100	100	4.5	84
Mean score	*99.7*	*89.0*	*6.3*	*86.4*
Newly black districts				
Espy (MS-2)	90.5	93.0	41.0	86
Lewis (GA-5)	100.0	100.0	8.5	96
Mean score	*95.3*	*96.5*	*24.8*	*91*
Heterogeneous districts				
Dixon (CA-28)	100	73	5.0	87
Dymally (CA-31)	100	100	3.5	87
Flake (NY-6)	100	100	8.5	88
Leland (TX-18)	100	80	5.0	83
Rangel (NY-16)	100	93	3.5	87
Towns (NY-11)	100	87	1.5	81
Mean score	*100*	*88.8*	*4.5*	*85.5*

Representative	COPE rating	LCCR rating	Conservative coalition	Voting participation
Majority-white districts				
Clay (MO-1)[a]	100	100	1.0	79
Dellums (CA-8)	100	93	2.5	94
Wheat (MO-5)	96.6	100	5.0	98
Mean score	*98.9*	*97.7*	*2.8*	*90.3*

Sources: Phil Duncan, ed., *Politics in America: 1990, 101st Congress* (Washington, D.C.: Congressional Quarterly Press, 1989); *Congressional Quarterly Weekly Report*, November 19, 1988, pp. 3321–3376; Leadership Conference on Civil Rights, "A Civil Rights Voting Record for the 100th Congress," January 1989.

Note: COPE = AFL-CIO Committee on Political Education (scores are not lowered by missed votes); LCCR = Leadership Conference on Civil Rights; Conservative coalition = Percentage of votes cast in support of coalition between Republicans and Southern Democrats against other Democrats; Voting participation = Percentage of roll-call votes cast.

a. Majority-black district that became majority white in voting-age population.

Notes

1. The Representation of Black Interests in Congress

1. I am using the terms "black" and "African American" interchangeably to refer to people of African descent.
2. Hannah F. Pitkin, *The Concept of Representation* (Berkeley: University of California Press, 1967); J. Roland Pennock and John W. Chapman, eds., *NOMOS X: Representation* (New York: Atherton Press, 1968); Ronald Rogowski, "Representation in Political Theory and in Law," *Ethics*, 91 (April 1981), 395–430; Robert Weissberg, "Collective vs. Dyadic Representation in Congress," *American Political Science Review*, 72 (1978), 535–548.
3. Bernard Grofman, "Should Representatives Be Typical of Their Constituents?" in Bernard Grofman, Arend Lijphart, Robert McKay, and Howard Scarrow, eds., *Representation and Redistricting Issues* (Lexington, Mass.: Lexington Books, 1982), p. 99.
4. Their usage differs from Pitkin's use of "symbolic representation" as a phenomenon that occurs when constituents believe in the legitimacy of the representative because of what he or she is perceived to be, rather than what he or she actually achieves in office. Unlike descriptive representation, which can be discerned by the presence of shared demographic characteristics, or substantive representation, which can be identified through activities, symbolic representation is more ambiguous and less useful for characterizing black members of Congress. See Robert C. Smith, "Recent Elections and Black Politics: The Maturation or Death of Black Politics," *PS*, 22 (June 1990), 160–162; Dianne Pinderhughes, *Race and Ethnicity in Chicago Politics* (Chicago: University of Illinois Press, 1987), p. xix; Mack H. Jones, "Black Office-Holding and Political Development in the Rural South," *Review of Black Political Economy* (Summer 1976).
5. W. B. Gallie, "Essentially Contested Concepts," in Max Black, ed., *The Importance of Language* (Englewood Cliffs, N.J.: Prentice Hall, 1962).
6. William E. Connolly, *The Terms of Political Discourse*, 2nd ed. (Princeton: Princeton University Press, 1983); Isaac D. Balbus, "The Concept of Interest in Pluralist and Marxian Analysis," *Politics and Society*, 1, no. 2 (February

1971), 151–177; Brian Barry, *Political Argument* (London: Routledge & Kegan Paul, 1965), chap. 3; Andrew Reeve and Alan Ware, "Interests in Political Theory," *British Journal of Political Science*, 13 (October 1983), 379–400.

7. William Julius Wilson, *The Truly Disadvantaged: The Inner City, the Underclass, and Public Policy* (Chicago: University of Chicago Press, 1987), table 2.4, p. 31; Carol M. Swain and William R. Keech, "Race and Decision Rules in Economic Voting," paper presented at the meetings of the American Political Science Association, Chicago, September 1987.

8. *Brown v. Board of Education of Topeka*, 349 U.S. 294 (1954).

9. Gerald D. Jaynes and Robin M. Williams, Jr., eds., *A Common Destiny: Blacks and American Society* (Washington, D.C.: National Academy Press, 1989), pp. 331–379.

10. National Urban League, *The State of Black America, 1989* (New York: National Urban League, 1989), p. 189.

11. U.S. Department of Commerce, *Statistical Abstracts of the United States: 1989*, 109th ed. (Washington, D.C.: U.S. Government Printing Office, 1990), p. 74.

12. National Urban League, *State of Black America*, pp. 55–56.

13. Jaynes and Williams, *A Common Destiny*, p. 439.

14. U.S. Dept. of Commerce, *Statistical Abstracts*, p. 158.

15. Wilson, *The Truly Disadvantaged*, p. 22; Jaynes and Williams, *A Common Destiny*, p. 419.

16. Jaynes and Williams, *A Common Destiny*, pp. 28–29.

17. *The Gallup Report*, no. 273 (July 1988), 4–15; *The Gallup Report*, no. 280 (January 1989), 25–29.

18. Louis Harris and Associates poll of 1,650 white adults and 531 blacks conducted January 20–26, 1988, *Business Week*, March 14, 1988; Wilson, *Truly Disadvantaged*, table 2.4, p. 31; Swain and Keech, "Race and Decision Rules."

19. Jaynes and Williams, *A Common Destiny*, pp. 211–212.

20. Robert Erikson and Norman Luttbeg, *American Public Opinion* (New York: John Wiley & Sons, 1973), pp. 186–188.

21. Jaynes and Williams, *A Common Destiny*, pp. 214–215.

22. A *New York Times* poll based on telephone interviews conducted June 17–29 with 1,047 New Yorkers. The poll included 484 whites and 408 blacks. Persons with no opinion were excluded from the analysis. *New York Times*, October 29, 1990.

23. Amelia Parker, "History and Background," *101st Congress*, booklet distributed by the Congressional Black Caucus, Washington, D.C., January 1989.

24. Linda S. Lichter, "Who Speaks for Black America," *Public Opinion* (August/September 1985), 43. In a Gallup survey conducted by the *Times Mirror*, 37 percent of the black electorate were characterized as "partisan poor" Democrats who favored the death penalty. See also Congressional Black Caucus Foundation, "Victim's Race Is Factor in Death Penalty Cases," *Point of View*, Summer 1984, 20–21.

25. Glenn Loury, "The Moral Quandary of the Black Community," *Public Interest*, 79 (1985), 9–21.

26. "Some people say that to make up for past discrimination, members of

minority groups should be given preferential treatment in getting jobs and places in college. Others say that ability, as determined by test scores, should be the main consideration. Which point of view comes closest to how you feel on this matter?" in Lichter, "Who Speaks," p. 43.

27. Ibid., pp. 42–43.
28. It is worthwhile to note that a more recent public opinion poll showed a majority of blacks (82 percent) and whites (55 percent) in favor of affirmative action programs in business for blacks and other minority groups. Only 51 percent of blacks and 12 percent of whites, however, were supportive of preferential treatment to make up for past discrimination. The poll indicates that there has been some movement in public opinion on this matter. Survey by Peter Hart and Robert Teeter for NBC News/*The Wall Street Journal,* June 22–25, 1991, in "Public Opinion and Demographic Report," *American Enterprise,* September/October 1991, 82.
29. Louis Harris poll of 500 black adults conducted in the week of August 29 to September 2, 1991, in "How Blacks View Thomas and Their Leaders," *Business Week,* September 16, 1991.
30. Richard T. Carson and Joe Oppenheimer, "A Method of Establishing the Personal Ideology of Political Representatives," *American Political Science Review,* 78 (1984), 168–188.
31. Kenny Whitby, "Measuring Congressional Responsiveness to the Policy Interests of Black Constituents," *Social Science Quarterly,* 68 (1987), 367–377.
32. Table 1.3 reports the results of a regression on four independent variables—party, region, urbanization, and the district's percentage of black population. Multiple regression allows us to evaluate the impact of each of the independent variables on the rating scales, while holding the others constant. The R^2 measures the proportion of the variance in support of black interests calculated by the independent variables working together. The ARI and COPE indicators account for 67 and 70 percent of the variance, respectively.
33. In the case studies I will focus only on the black and Hispanic voting-age population percentages in the various districts, because I believe that these exert more influence on representatives than do aggregate population percentages.
34. Following the lead of Kenny Whitby, I also tested a model that included an interactive term for the percentage of blacks and urbanization. Again the coefficients were insignificant for the interactive term. See Whitby, "Effects of the Interaction between Race and Urbanization on Votes of Southern Congressmen," *Legislative Studies Quarterly* (November 1985), 505–517.
35. These Democrats were Lindy Boggs from Louisiana, Robin Tallon from South Carolina, and Tim Valentine from North Carolina.
36. John E. Jackson and David King, "Public Goods, Private Interests, and Representation," *American Political Science Review,* 83, no. 4 (December 1989), 1143–1164.
37. See V. O. Key, Jr., *Southern Politics in State and Nation* (New York: Knopf, 1949); Donald R. Matthews and James W. Prothro, *Negroes and the New Southern Politics* (New York: Harcourt, Brace & World, 1966); William R.

Keech, *The Impact of Negro Voting: The Role of the Vote in the Quest for Equality* (Chicago: Rand McNally, 1968).

38. See John S. Jackson and Robert A. Hitlin, "The Nationalization of the Democratic Party," *Western Political Science Quarterly* (June 1981), 270–286.

2. Tracing the Footsteps of Blacks on the Hill

1. Because the number of black congressional representatives is still quite low, recent retirements by Augustus Hawkins (D-CA) and George Crockett, along with the resignation of Majority Whip William Gray III, all effective in 1991, drastically reduce the political influence but not the number of blacks in Congress.

2. W. E. B. Du Bois, *Black Reconstruction in America* (New York, 1935); Eric Foner, *Reconstruction, 1863–1877* (New York: Harper & Row, 1988); John Hope Franklin, *Reconstruction: After the Civil War* (Chicago: University of Chicago Press, 1961).

3. Terry Seip, *The South Returns to Congress* (Baton Rouge: Louisiana State University Press, 1983), pp. 103–104.

4. Ibid., pp. 2–3.

5. Foner, *Reconstruction*, p. 26.

6. Franklin, *Reconstruction*, p. 86.

7. Charles Vincent, *Black Legislators in Louisiana during Reconstruction* (Baton Rouge: Louisiana State University Press, 1976).

8. Foner, *Reconstruction*, p. 283.

9. Ibid., p. 282.

10. Ibid., p. 352.

11. Quoted in Francis Butler Simpkins, *South Carolina during Reconstruction* (Chapel Hill: University of North Carolina Press, 1932), pp. 123–124.

12. Senator Hiram Revels, as quoted in Maurine Christopher, *Black Americans in Congress* (New York: Crowell, 1976), p. 3.

13. James W. Garner, *Reconstruction in Mississippi* (New York: Macmillan, 1901), p. 263.

14. Governor James Alcorn, as quoted in Garner, *Reconstruction in Mississippi*, pp. 174–180.

15. Maurine Christopher, *America's Black Congressmen* (New York: Crowell, 1971); Edward Clayton, *The Negro Politician* (Chicago: Johnson, 1964), p. 32.

16. Seip, *The South Returns*, p. 20.

17. Ibid., pp. 27–29.

18. Foner, *Reconstruction*, pp. 360–361.

19. Manning Marable, *Black American Politics* (London: Verso, 1988), p. 157.

20. Franklin, *Reconstruction*, pp. 91–92.

21. Bruce Ragsdale and Joel Treese, *Black Americans in Congress* (Washington, D.C.: Office of the Historian, U.S. House of Representatives, 1990).

22. Cited in Marable, *Black American Politics*, p. 149.

23. Du Bois, *Black Reconstruction*, p. 630.

24. Senators Blanche Bruce (Mississippi) and Hiram Revels (Mississippi), and

Representatives Robert Elliot (South Carolina), John Lynch (Mississippi), Charles Nash (Louisiana), and James Rapier (Alabama).

25. Representatives Robert Cain (South Carolina), Henry Cheatham (North Carolina), Robert Smalls (South Carolina), and George White (North Carolina).
26. Representatives Henry Cheatham (North Carolina), Jeremiah Haralson (Alabama), James O'Hara (North Carolina), and George Murray (South Carolina).
27. Ragsdale and Treese, *Black Americans in Congress.*
28. Foner, *Black Reconstruction,* p. 450.
29. Marable, *Black American Politics,* p. 151.
30. Christopher, *America's Black Congressmen,* p. 147.
31. Representative Joseph Rainey, as quoted in the *Congressional Globe,* vol. 169 (Part I, 1st session, 42nd Congress), pp. 393–394. Similarly, Representative Robert Elliot asserted: "I do not wish to be understood as speaking for the colored man alone when I demand instant protection for the loyal men of the South. No, sir, my demand is not so restricted. In South Carolina alone, at the last election, twelve thousand of the working white men in good faith voted the Republican ticket, openly arraying themselves on the side of free government. . . . The white Republican of the South is also hunted down and murdered or scourged for his opinions" (quoted in ibid., p. 391).
32. Foner, *Reconstruction,* pp. 533–534.
33. George White, as quoted in Christopher, *Black Americans in Congress,* pp. 164–165.
34. George White, as cited in Clayton, *Negro Politician,* p. 37.
35. C. Vann Woodward, *The Strange Career of Jim Crow* (New York: Oxford University Press, 1974).
36. Christopher, *America's Black Congressmen,* p. 166.
37. Du Bois, *Black Reconstruction,* p. 627.
38. Seip, *The South Returns,* p. 20; Foner, *Reconstruction,* pp. 533–539.
39. Foner, *Reconstruction,* p. 112.
40. For more information about DePriest and Chicago politicians, see Harold F. Gosnell, *Negro Politicians: The Rise of Negro Politics in Chicago* (Chicago: University of Chicago Press, 1935); Dianne Pinderhughes, *Race and Ethnicity in Chicago Politics: A Reexamination of Pluralist Theory* (Urbana: University of Illinois Press, 1987).
41. Matthew Holden, "Tabulation of Bills and Proposed Resolutions Relative to Afro-Americans, the 57th–80th Congresses, 1901–1948," Matthew Holden Archives, University of Virginia, Charlottesville, 1987.
42. Christopher, *America's Black Congressmen,* pp. 174–175.
43. Nancy Weiss, *Farewell to the Party of Lincoln: Black Politics in the Age of FDR* (Princeton: Princeton University Press, 1983). Other more general works on party realignment include: V. O. Key, Jr., *Politics, Parties, and Pressure Groups,* 5th ed. (New York: Crowell, 1964); Walter Dean Burnham, *Critical Elections and the Mainsprings of American Politics* (New York: Norton, 1970); Everette Carll Ladd, Jr., with Charles D. Hadley, *Transformations of the American Party System: Political Coalitions from the New Deal to the 1970s* (New York: Norton,

1970); Kristi Anderson, *The Creation of a Democratic Majority, 1928–1936* (Chicago: University of Chicago Press, 1981).

44. Arthur Mitchell, as cited in Christopher, *America's Black Congressmen,* pp. 179–180.

45. Seven years later Powell was stripped of both his seniority and his chairmanship after having been charged with an ethics violation.

46. "Warning Shots Fired by Voters More Mood than Mandate," *Congressional Quarterly Weekly Report,* November 10, 1990, p. 3797.

47. Donald R. Matthews, "Legislative Recruitment and Legislative Careers," in Gerhard Loewenberg, Samuel C. Patterson, and Malcolm Jewell, eds., *Handbook of Legislative Research* (Cambridge: Harvard University Press, 1985).

48. Robert C. Smith, "The Black Congressional Delegation," *Western Political Quarterly* (June 1981), 209–210.

49. Charles Hayes (D-IL), with a high school education and a prior occupation of trade union president, was the exception to the norm. Nevertheless, he was clearly a member of the black middle class.

50. Seip, *The South Returns,* pp. 103–105.

51. Ralph K. Huitt, *Working within the System* (Berkeley: Institute of Governmental Studies Press, 1990), chap. 3.

52. For more information about Dawson and Powell, and a short comparison of the two, see Charles V. Hamilton, *Adam Clayton Powell, Jr.* (New York: Atheneum, 1991), pp. 480–481.

53. Ibid., pp. 216–224.

54. Gary Jacobson and Samuel Kernell, *Strategy and Choice in Congressional Elections* (New Haven: Yale University Press, 1981).

55. James Q. Wilson, "Two Negro Politicians: An Interpretation," *Midwest Journal of Political Science,* 5 (1960), 349–369.

56. Clayton, *Negro Politician,* p. 73.

57. Ibid.

58. Hamilton, *Adam Clayton Powell, Jr.,* p. 226.

59. *Brown v. Board of Education,* 349 U.S. 294, 1954.

60. In its simplest form, the prisoner's dilemma is a two-player game in which the players are confronted with a choice of cooperating or defecting. Each player must make his/her choice in ignorance of the other player. Defection always yields a higher payoff than cooperation. The dilemma occurs because mutual defection leaves both players worse off than if they had cooperated. The number of players are expanded in an *n*-person prisoner's dilemma game. See Robert Axelrod, *The Evolution of Cooperation* (New York: Basic Books, 1984), and Arthur Denzau, William Riker, and Kenneth Shepsle, "Farquharson and Fenno: Sophisticated Voting and Home Style," *American Political Science Review,* 79 (December 1985), 1117–1135.

61. Richard F. Fenno, Jr., *Congressmen in Committees* (Boston: Little, Brown, 1973), p. 130.

62. Marguerite Ross Barnett, "The Congressional Black Caucus," reprint from "Congress against the President," *Proceedings of the Academy of Political Science,* 32, no. 1 (1975), 35–36.

63. Personal communications with CBC members, January 1989.

64. Arthur Levy and Susan Stoudinger, "Sources of Voting Cues for the Congressional Black Caucus," *Journal of Black Politics*, 7 (1976), 29–46.

65. Bruce Robeck, "The Congressional Black Caucus," paper presented at the 1974 meetings of the American Political Science Association, Chicago, p. 73.

66. Charles E. Jones, "Testing a Legislative Strategy: The Congressional Black Caucus's Action-Alert Communications Network," *Legislative Studies Quarterly* (November 1987), 521–537; Augustus Adair, "Black Legislative Influence in Federal Policy Decisions: The Congressional Black Caucus, 1971–1975," Ph.D. dissertation, Johns Hopkins University, 1976.

67. Robeck, "The Congressional Black Caucus"; Barnett, "The Congressional Black Caucus," in Michael Preston, Lenneal Henderson, Jr., and Paul Puryer, eds., *The New Black Politics: The Search for Political Power* (New York: Longman, 1981).

68. Excerpt from Louis Stokes's July 1973 speech, as quoted in Barnett, "The Congressional Black Caucus," p. 39.

69. Jones, "Testing a Legislative Strategy."

70. David R. Mayhew, *Congress: The Electoral Connection* (New Haven: Yale University Press, 1974).

71. Personal communication with Alan Wheat, Kansas City, Mo., October 28, 1988.

72. Beth Donovan, "The Wilder-Dinkins 'Formula' Familiar to Blacks in the House," *Congressional Quarterly Weekly Report*, November 11, 1989, pp. 3099–3100.

73. Richard Fenno, Jr., *Home Style: House Members in Their Districts* (Glenview, Ill.: Scott, Foresman, 1978).

74. Leo Rennie, "The Congressional Black Caucus: Confronting Individual and Collective Goals," seminar paper, Princeton University, May 25, 1989.

75. David Vogler, *The Politics of Congress*, 5th ed. (Newton, Mass.: Allyn and Bacon, 1988), pp. 152–157; Raymond Wolfinger and Joan Hollinger, "Safe Seats, Seniority, and Power in Congress," in Raymond Wolfinger, *Readings on Congress* (Englewood Cliffs, N.J.: Prentice Hall, 1971), pp. 54–55.

76. Barnett, "The Congressional Black Caucus."

77. Walter Fauntroy, speech made during the Congressional Black Caucus party, Atlanta, Ga., July 1988.

78. "For Blacks Racism and Politics Mix," *New York Times*, March 11, 1983.

79. *Human Events Weekly*, January 29, 1971, p. 2.

80. Richard Cohen, "New Breed for Black Caucus," *National Journal*, September 26, 1987, p. 2432.

81. William Gray, as quoted in "The Congressional Black Caucus May Be a Victim of Success," *Washington Post National Weekly Edition*, October 12, 1987, p. 15.

82. Ibid.

83. Herbert B. Asher, "The Learning of Legislative Norms," *American Political Science Review*, 67 (June 1973), 499–513.

84. For a theoretical account of such activities, see R. Douglas Arnold, *The Logic of Congressional Action* (New Haven: Yale University Press, 1990), part 1.

3. Black Representatives of Historically Black Districts

1. Linda F. Williams, ed., *The JCPS Congressional District Fact Book*, 3rd ed. (Washington, D.C.: Joint Center for Political Studies, 1988), p. 9.
2. "19 Cities Listed for Aid to Cut Infant Mortality," *New York Times*, March 8, 1991.
3. Maurine Christopher, *America's Black Congressmen* (New York: Crowell, 1971), p. 211.
4. "Judge Caps Career in Race for House," *New York Times*, August 10, 1980.
5. "Indictments of Two Officials Darken Detroit's Mood," *New York Times*, February 13, 1991.
6. Joel D. Aberbach and Jack L. Walker, *Race in the City* (Boston: Little, Brown, 1973).
7. Ze'ev Chafets, "The Tragedy of Detroit," *New York Times Magazine*, July 29, 1990.
8. Richard Fenno, Jr., *Home Style: House Members in Their Districts* (Glenview, Ill.: Scott, Foresman, 1978), p. 188.
9. "Crockett Says He's In," *Detroit News*, April 22, 1980.
10. Interview with George Crockett, Washington, D.C., June 14, 1990.
11. *Congressional Quarterly Weekly Report*, February 17, 1990.
12. Interview with Crockett.
13. Ibid.
14. Ibid.
15. Ibid.
16. "Crockett Faces Griffin in the Thirteenth District," *Detroit News*, October 30, 1986.
17. Interview with Crockett.
18. Chafets, "Tragedy of Detroit," p. 50.
19. Interview with Crockett.
20. "Crockett Sues Reagan, Haig," *Detroit Metro Times*, May 14, 1981; "Rep. Crockett and the Volley from the Right," *Washington Post*, February 10, 1987.
21. Interview with Crockett.
22. George Crockett, "A 'Helping Hand'—Not Jail—For Drug Users," *Detroit News*, February 11, 1990.
23. "Crockett Faces Griffin in the 13th District."
24. "Rep. Crockett and the Volley from the Right."
25. Interview with Crockett.
26. Williams, *JCPS Congressional District Fact Book*, p. 28.
27. Mike Mallowe, "The North Barren," *Politics* (April 1981), 108–109.
28. Michael Barone and Grant Ujifusa, *The Almanac of American Politics, 1990* (Washington, D.C.: National Journal, 1990), pp. 1028–1033.
29. Christopher, *America's Black Congressmen*, p. 216.
30. Michael Barone, Grant Ujifusa, and Donald Matthews, *The Almanac of American Politics, 1978* (New York: E. P. Dutton), p. 723.
31. "Nix Wins 75% of Vote, Reelected to 8th Term," *Philadelphia Bulletin*, November 8, 1974.

32. "Rev. Gray to Demand Recount in Close Race against Rep. Nix," *Philadelphia Inquirer,* November 29, 1976.

33. "339 Club Boost Rev. Gray for Seat in Congress," *Philadelphia Bulletin,* December 14, 1977.

34. "Out-of-Town Endorsements Spark Nix-Gray Battle," *Philadelphia Inquirer,* May 10, 1978.

35. For more information, see Lenora E. Berson, "'The Toughest Cop in America' Campaigns for Mayor of Philadelphia," *New York Times Magazine,* May 16, 1971, p. 30.

36. "Gray Eulogizes Nix as 'the Pathfinder,'" *Philadelphia Bulletin,* May 17, 1978.

37. Alan Ehrenhalt, ed., *Politics in America: The 100th Congress* (Washington, D.C.: Congressional Quarterly Press, 1990), pp. 1285–1286.

38. "Gray-Street Racing for the Gutter," *Philadelphia Tribune,* June 11, 1982; "The Final Word—Stone Will Not Challenge Gray," *Philadelphia Tribune,* January 12, 1982.

39. Larry Eichel, "The Grudge Match," *Today: Inquirer Magazine,* p. 27.

40. Ibid.

41. "Stone Dares Gray to Prove He Lied," *Philadelphia Tribune,* February 5, 1982.

42. "The Final Word—Stone Will Not Challenge Gray."

43. Chuck Stone, "For Thornburgh and Gray and a Bright New Day," *Philadelphia Tribune,* October 30, 1978.

44. Eichel, "Grudge Match," p. 30.

45. "Philadelphians Again Looking to Rizzo," *New York Times,* May 23, 1991.

46. Gray's relationship with Bright Hope Church came under FBI investigation in 1989 because of a 1985 housing arrangement in which the church bought his Philadelphia home and allowed his family to use it rent free. Apparently the FBI became involved because the value of the rent-free house was not declared as income. There was also speculation that Gray was using the excess honoraria to pay the house payments for the church. In 1989 Gray reported earning $164,098 in 1988 in speaking fees, of which he kept $25,000 and donated $14,000 to the church: he had donated $8,100 in 1987 and $8,000 in 1986. Those amounts were substantially more than he had donated to the church in any of the previous years. He also made large donations to another organization, Kids Inc., shortly after it hired his wife to work as a fund-raiser. Although Gray denied a relationship between his mid-term resignation and lingering questions about who and what was being investigated, his financial reports showed that over a two-year period (starting in July 1989) his campaign committee paid $175,795 in legal fees. See "Rep. Gray Remains Dogged by Issue of His Ties to the Church to Which He Donated His Speaking Fees," *Wall Street Journal,* June 26, 1990; "'85 Housing Deal with Church Benefits Gray," *Washington Post,* June 29, 1989; "Decision by House Whip Gray to Leave Congress for UNCF Post Creates a Black Power Vacuum," *Wall Street Journal,* June 20, 1991; "If They Can't Call Congress a Pleasure, Some Call It a Day," *New York Times,* June 23, 1991; "Shades of Gray," *Wall Street Journal,* June 21, 1991.

47. "Pennsylvania Gray—Budgeteer, Congressman, and Minister," *Christian Science Monitor,* October 21, 1985, p. 11.

48. "U.S. Budget Battle Stirs Voters' Pride in Leadership of Philadelphia's Gray," *New York Times,* June 23, 1985.
49. I talked with Gray on several occasions. But I was never able to arrange an interview or district visit. In 1988, when I first sought to travel with Gray, I was told by key staffers that it would be nearly impossible to find him in the district for two days or more. The staffer suggested that I restrict my attention to his sermons at Bright Hope Baptist Church. I am therefore relying heavily on newspaper accounts and on interviews with other representatives and political observers from the Philadelphia area.
50. "The City's Collapsing Leadership," *Philadelphia Tribune,* June 1981.
51. "Stone Dares Gray to Prove He Lied."
52. I base these conclusions on personal communications with several members of Congress that I had shortly after Gray's denunciation of Savage's remarks.
53. "Gray Condemns Rep. Savage's 'Bigoted' Campaign Speech," *Washington Post,* March 28, 1990.
54. See Louis Farrakhan's criticisms of black politicians like William Gray III in his speech "The Danger of 'Crossover' Politicians," delivered at Mosque Maryam in Chicago on March 1, 1990.
55. "Rep. Chisholm's Angry Farewell," *New York Times,* October 12, 1982.
56. Criticisms frequently leveled against Governor Douglas Wilder of Virginia and other black leaders who have substantial white support suggest that many black voters would prefer militancy to the coalition building that could bring them more tangible benefits.
57. Ehrenhalt, *Politics in America: The 100th Congress,* p. 1284.
58. "Reps. Gray and Bonior Are Nip and Tuck in Contest for House Majority Whip," *Washington Post,* June 14, 1989.
59. Jack Anderson and Dale Atta, "Rep. Gray's Play for Caucus Post," *Washingtonian,* November 30, 1988.
60. "Gray, First Black to Join Leadership in Congress, Appears Marked by Democrats for Bigger Things," *Wall Street Journal,* December 6, 1988.
61. "Spending for 1990 Hill Races Fell," *Washington Post,* February 25, 1991.
62. "Moving to the Front," *National Journal,* April 26, 1986, pp. 989–992.
63. "Gray, First Black to Join Leadership in Congress."
64. Personal communication with a white representative from a southern district.
65. "Gray, First Black to Join Leadership in Congress."
66. Ibid.
67. Charles Bowser, as quoted in Eichel, "The Grudge Match," p. 28.
68. "Of Black and White and a Red, Red Budget," *New York Times,* May 22, 1985.
69. "The Incredible Shrinking Congressman: Invisible Bill Gray," *National Alliance,* October 24, 1986.
70. "Of Black and White and a Red, Red Budget."
71. "If They Can't Call Congress a Pleasure, Some Call It a Day."
72. Personal interviews with members of Congress.
73. Phil Duncan, *Politics in America, 1992* (Washington, D.C.: Congressional Quarterly Press, 1991), pp. 1262–1263.

74. "Decision by House Whip Gray to Leave Congress for UNCF Post Creates a Black Power Vacuum."
75. "Gray's Exit Roils Leadership as Party Seeks Stability" and "Gray Looks for 'Higher Mission' away from Capitol Hill," in *Congressional Quarterly Weekly Report*, June 22, 1991, pp. 1637–1643; "From His Pulpit, Gray Tells of 'Higher Calling,'" *New York Times*, June 24, 1991; "Race to Replace Gray as Whip in High Gear," *New York Times*, June 21, 1991.
76. Fenno, *Home Style*, p. 115.
77. For more information on how politicians view their roles, see Leonard Cole, *A Comparative Study of Black and White Elected Officials* (Princeton: Princeton University Press, 1976), pp. 83–86; the different role orientations of legislators are described in John Wahlke, Heinz Eulan, William Buchanan, and LeRoy Ferguson, *The Legislative Systems* (New York: Wiley, 1962).
78. Anonymous comment made by an incumbent black representative of several terms.
79. See Thomas E. Mann, *Unsafe at Any Margin* (Washington, D.C.: American Enterprise Institute for Public Policy Research, 1978).

4. Black Representatives of Newly Black Districts

1. Dick Kirschten, "The Delta Looks Up," *National Journal*, October 6, 1990, pp. 2382–2398.
2. For more information about the South, see V. O. Key, Jr., *Southern Politics in State and Nation* (New York: Knopf, 1949); W. J. Cash, *The Mind of the South* (New York: Knopf, 1941); Earl Black and Merle Black, *Politics and Society in the South* (Cambridge: Harvard University Press, 1987); C. Vann Woodward, *The Burden of Southern History* (Baton Rouge: Louisiana State University Press, 1968); George Brown Tindall, *The Disruption of the Solid South* (New York: Norton, 1972); J. Morgan Kousser, *The Shaping of Southern Politics* (New Haven: Yale University Press, 1974).
3. John Lynch, *The Facts of Reconstruction* (New York: Arno, 1968), p. 95.
4. Peter Boyer, "The Yuppies of Mississippi: How They Took Over the Statehouse," *New York Times Magazine*, February 28, 1988, pp. 24–27; Kirschten, "The Delta Looks Up," pp. 2382–2389.
5. Frank L. Parker, *Black Votes Count: Political Empowerment in Mississippi after 1965* (Chapel Hill: University of North Carolina Press, 1990).
6. *Allen v. State Board of Elections*, 393 U.S. 544, 1969.
7. *Connor v. Johnson*, 279 F. Supp. 619, 1966.
8. *State of Mississippi v. United States*, 444 U.S. 1050, 1052, 1980.
9. *State of Mississippi*, 490 F. Supp. at 575.
10. Interview with Mike Espy in Washington, D.C., June 14, 1990.
11. Gary Jacobson and Samuel Kernell, *Strategy and Choice in Congressional Elections* (New Haven: Yale University Press, 1981), pp. 22–23.
12. Webb Franklin, as quoted in the *New York Times*, October 14, 1982, in Alexander Lamis, "The Runoff Controversy: Implications for Southern Politics," *PS* (Fall 1984), 768.

13. Interview of Mary Coleman, "Election Aftermath—The Black Vote," *Mac-Neil/Lehrer Report*, November 4, 1982, Transcript 1854, p. 25.
14. Mary D. Coleman and Leslie Burl McLemore, "Continuity and Change: The Power of Traditionalism in Biracial Politics in Mississippi's Second Congressional District," p. 51 in Michael Preston, Lenneal J. Henderson, Jr., Paul Puryear, eds., *The New Black Politics*, 2nd ed. (New York: Longman, 1987).
15. David Bowen, as cited in Lamis, "The Runoff Controversy," p. 785.
16. Richard Fenno, Jr., *Home Style: House Members in Their Districts* (Glenview, Ill.: Scott, Foresman, 1978), pp. 54–56.
17. Coleman and McLemore, "Continuity and Change," *New Black Politics*, p. 56.
18. "Mississippi's Political Face Is Changing," *Atlanta Journal*, September 18, 1987.
19. "Pathfinder Turns Up a Landslide," *Washington Post*, November 11, 1988.
20. Paul Carton, *Mobilizing the Black Community: The Effects of Personal Contact Campaigning on Black Voters* (Washington, D.C.: Joint Center for Political Studies, 1984).
21. Interview with Robert Bush, Washington, D.C., March 16, 1988; also see Tip O'Neill's account of his political lesson from Mrs. O'Brien, a life-long neighbor, who also expected to be asked for her vote. Tip O'Neill with William Novak, *Man of the House* (New York: Random House, 1987), p. 26.
22. *National Journal*, September 26, 1987, p. 2432.
23. "Espy Was Able to Pull in White Vote," *Clarion-Ledger* (Jackson, Miss.), September 9, 1987; "Mississippi's Political Face Is Changing."
24. Alan Ehrenhalt, ed., *Politics in America: The 100th Congress* (Washington, D.C.: Congressional Quarterly Press, 1990), p. 824.
25. This discussion draws heavily from a focus group report conducted on January 25 and 26, 1988, by Barbara Kaplan of the Gene Reilly Group (and provided to me by Mike Espy's Washington office). Four focus groups were held in Greenville and Vicksburg, Mississippi. The selected groups included white women (over 45) and younger white men (under 45). All participants were high school graduates with incomes under $45,000 per year.
26. Ibid.
27. Personal communication with Mike Espy during the spring of 1988.
28. "Mississippi 2: Color It Competitive," *The Political Report*, September 4, 1987, pp. 1–3.
29. Interview with Espy.
30. Ibid.
31. "Espy Cites Increase in His White Support," *Memphis Appeal*, March 16, 1988.
32. Personal communication with black activists in the district and in other parts of the country.
33. "When a Fist Turns into a Handshake," *Insight*, June 11, 1990, p. 10.
34. Espy, in a talk in Vicksburg, Miss., on March 28, 1988.
35. Interview with Espy.
36. "When a Fist Turns into a Handshake," p. 10.
37. "Rep. Espy Fires a Round for NRA in Advertisement," *Washington Post*, January 29, 1989.

38. "Valuing a Rich Diversity, NRA Annual Meetings," *NRA Action,* vol. 4, no. 7, p. 1.
39. "U.S. Representative Mike Espy's Alliance with HUD Secretary Jack Kemp Reflects Changes," *Clarion-Ledger* (Jackson, Miss.), September 11, 1991; see also *Congressional Record,* June 6, 1991, pp. H4103–4112.
40. Interview with Espy.
41. In a study of New Jersey politicians, Leonard Cole found that black leaders frequently made statements suggesting support for black empowerment. Only 7 percent of the black elected officials, however, said that they would go with the constituents' position as opposed to their own if there were a conflict. Forty-five percent would "usually" follow personal convictions, while 23 percent "always" followed their personal convictions. Cole found that white leaders were much more likely than black leaders to take the position of their constituents. See Leonard Cole, *A Comparative Study of Black and White Elected Officials* (Princeton: Princeton University Press, 1976), pp. 83–86.
42. One of the main contributions of the literature on social choice is the introduction of issue dimensions and the freedom they give legislators. A major limitation in Anthony Downs's *Economic Theory of Democracy* is his assumption of unidimensionality. Rational choice theorists have demonstrated that legislators can move along several dimensions by emphasizing one issue over another or by introducing disequilibrium. For a review of the early literature and a discussion of its implications, see Riker, *Liberalism against Populism,* chaps. 8 and 9; Anthony Downs, *An Economic Theory of Democracy* (New York: Harper & Row, 1957), chap. 8.
43. *Pitts v. Busbee,* 395 F. Supp. 35, 40, N.D. GA, 1975; *Busbee v. Smith,* 549, F. Supp. 494, 500 D.D.C., 1981.
44. Michael Barone and Grant Ujifusa, *Almanac of American Politics, 1988* (Washington, D.C.: National Journal, 1988), p. 305.
45. See Clarence Stone, *Regime Politics: Governing Atlanta* (Lawrence: University of Kansas Press, 1989).
46. Interview with Wyche Fowler in Washington, D.C., February 27, 1991.
47. Marilyn Davis and Alex Willingham, "Taking the Fifth," *Southern Changes,* September 1986, p. 9; "How Did John Lewis Upset Julian Bond?" *New Times* (Mobile, Ala.), September 11, 1986.
48. Manning Marable, *Black American Politics* (London: Verso, 1988), pp. 22, 135; Davis and Willingham, "Taking the Fifth," pp. 7–9.
49. Davis and Willingham, "Taking the Fifth."
50. "Lewis' Upset Win in Georgia Suggests New Bloc in Atlanta," *Wall Street Journal,* September 4, 1986.
51. "How Did John Lewis Upset Julian Bond?"
52. Davis and Willingham, "Taking the Fifth," p. 9.
53. "Solidarity Is Lost Even as Black Leaders Post Gains," *Los Angeles Times,* March 31, 1988.
54. For more information see Fenno, *Home Style,* chaps. 3 and 4, on how various members of Congress present themselves to their constituents.

55. "An Underdog Stuns Atlanta's Black Elite," *New York Times*, September 4, 1986.

56. Lewis's speech dogged him even after his election. A white radio announcer stunned people during a discussion with Senator Fowler and newly elected Congressman Lewis when he stated, "I can't stand illiterates. I am not going to stand here and talk to a moron like John Lewis. I am not going to stand here and have Wyche Fowler or Ronald Reagan . . . or anybody tell me how to do the show." He went on to complain that John Lewis sounded like "Buckwheat," a character from the "Little Rascals." See "Radio Host Suspended for Insult to Lawmakers," *New York Times*, July 15, 1987.

57. Julian Bond, *A Time to Speak, a Time to Act: The Movement in Politics* (New York: Simon and Schuster, 1972).

58. Interview with John Lewis, Atlanta, Ga., April 22, 1988.

59. Ibid.

60. "Lewis' Upset Win in Georgia."

61. Personal observation at a town meeting on April 22, 1988.

62. Personal observations from several participant observations of office meetings in Atlanta, Ga., 1988–1991.

63. Interview with John Lewis, Atlanta, Ga., November 28, 1990.

64. Ibid.

65. Personal observations of Representative John Lewis during his constituency meetings in April 1988.

5. Black Representatives of Heterogeneous Districts

1. Heterogeneous districts have no single racial group large enough to constitute a majority. When districts are drawn up with a heterogeneous racial composition, the implicit assumption is that minority groups will unite to elect minority representatives. This perspective, however, ignores important differences between racial and ethnic groups and the possibility that they may have competing interests. Moreover, the plans seem to favor black over Hispanic politicians, because it takes a higher percentage of minorities to elect a Hispanic representative than it does to elect a black representative. See Bernard Grofman and Lisa Handley, "Minority Population Proportion and Black and Hispanic Congressional Success in the 1970s and 1980s," *American Politics Quarterly*, 17 (October 1989), 436–445; Kimball Brace, Bernard Grofman, Lisa Handley, and Richard Niemi, "Minority Voting Equality: The 65 Percent Rule in Theory and Practice," *Law and Social Policy*, 10, no. 1 (January 1988), 43–62; Paula D. McClain and Albert Karnig, "Black and Hispanic Socioeconomic and Political Competition," *American Political Science Review*, 84, no. 2 (June 1990), 535–545.

2. Interviews with black representatives and staffers from heterogeneous districts.

3. The description of this district is based on Michael Barone and Grant Ujifusa, *The Almanac of American Politics, 1990* (Washington, D.C.: National Journal, 1991), pp. 154–155.

4. Information on Dymally's congressional district comes from a four-day

district visit and several Washington, D.C., interviews that took place between March 1988 and October 22, 1990.

5. Interview with Mervyn Dymally, Washington, D.C., October 22, 1990.
6. Interview with Dymally's campaign manager, May 1988.
7. Interview with Dymally, October 22, 1990.
8. Ibid.
9. Ibid.
10. Gary Jacobson and Samuel Kernell, *Strategy and Choice in Congressional Elections* (New Haven: Yale University Press, 1981).
11. "Rep. Dymally's Contacts Raise Issue of Public Trust, Private Interests," *Washington Post,* January 2, 1990.
12. Phil Duncan, *Politics in America, the 100th Congress, 1989* (Washington, D.C.: Congressional Quarterly Press, 1990), pp. 187–186.
13. Interview with Mervyn Dymally, Los Angeles, April 4, 1988.
14. Interview with Dymally, October 22, 1990.
15. Ibid.
16. Glenn Simpson, "Under the Other Rainbow," *City Paper,* August 17, 1990; Mervyn Dymally, "The Rainbow Lobby and Right to Know," *Congressional Record,* May 17, 1990, pp. E1567–1569; "Inside the New Alliance Party," *Congressional Record,* May 21, 1990, pp. E1626–1627; "The Rainbow Coalition and the Rainbow Lobby," *Congressional Record,* July 26, 1989, pp. E2669–2675.
17. Glenn Simpson, "Dymally's Diamond Affair Raises Questions over Members' Ties to Non-Profit Groups," *Roll Call,* February 1, 1990.
18. Personal communications (by phone and letter) with Mervyn Dymally, December 14 and 30, 1991.
19. Glenn Simpson, "Dymally, Miffed, Cuts Ties with All Groups," *Roll Call,* June 4, 1990.
20. "Rep. Dymally in 'Toughest' Squeeze on Mx," *Congressional Quarterly Weekly Report,* May 19, 1984, p. 6.
21. "Flake Has Slight Lead in Queens House Vote," *New York Times,* June 11, 1986; "A Judge Orders Delay in Filling Addabbo's Seat," *New York Times,* June 17, 1986; "Recount Puts Waldon Ahead in Queens Vote," *New York Times,* June 18, 1986.
22. Interview with Floyd Flake, Jamaica-Queens, New York, September 7, 1990.
23. "Congressman Flake's Indictment: Good Works or Greed?" *New York Times,* August 6, 1990; "Rep. Flake's Tax Evasion, Conspiracy Trial Opens," *Washington Post,* March 12, 1991.
24. Interview with Flake.
25. Ibid.
26. Interview with one of Flake's constituents, Jamaica-Queens, New York, September 7, 1990.
27. "Representative Faces a Charge of Harassment," *New York Times,* May 13, 1988.
28. Interview with Flake.
29. Ibid.
30. Ibid.
31. Ibid.

32. Ibid.; for a similar account of constituency service, see the autobiography of Emmanuel Celler, *You Never Leave Brooklyn* (New York: John Day, 1953), p. 266.
33. Interview with Flake.
34. Ibid.
35. Phil Duncan, ed., *Politics in America: The 100th Congress, 1990* (Washington, D.C.: Congressional Quarterly Press, 1989), p. 1014.

6. Black Representatives of Majority-White Districts

1. Michael Barone and Grant Ujifusa, *Almanac of American Politics, 1990* (Washington, D.C.: National Journal, 1991), pp. 690–691.
2. Linda F. Williams, ed., *The JCPS Congressional District Fact Book*, 3rd ed. (Washington, D.C.: Joint Center for Political Studies, 1988), pp. 2–17.
3. Ibid.
4. Lyle W. Dosett, *The Pendergast Machine* (New York: Oxford University Press, 1968); Bruce Stave, *The New Deal and the Last Hurrah: Pittsburgh Machine Politics* (Pittsburgh: Pittsburgh University Press, 1970).
5. Bolling's Americans for Democratic Action (ADA) and COPE scores commonly ranged from 80 to 100 percent in support of the targeted legislation. As mentioned previously, liberal representatives tend to score high on both indicators.
6. Interview with Alan Wheat, Kansas City, Mo., October 28, 1988.
7. Ibid.
8. "Black Candidates Competing in Districts with White Majorities," *Baltimore Sun*, November 2, 1982.
9. Interview with Alan Wheat; "Black Candidates Relying on Whites," *Chicago Tribune*, November 13, 1989.
10. Interview with Alan Wheat.
11. Ibid.
12. Ibid.
13. "Alan Wheat, Our Choice," editorial, *Kansas City Call*, July 23, 1982.
14. "Coalition Provides Wheat Victory," *Missouri Times*, November 8, 1982.
15. Wheat has not used television commercials most recently because he feels that they indicate insecurity on the part of an incumbent. After noting that a colleague was running commercials, Wheat said: "X must really feel threatened."
16. "Representative Alan Wheat, Sure Thing," *Kansas City Magazine*, July 1986, pp. 42–48.
17. Interview with Alan Wheat.
18. Ibid.
19. Gary Jacobson, *The Politics of Congressional Elections* (Boston: Little, Brown, 1983), p. 37.
20. In 1984 Wheat raised $466,774 and spent $407,069; in 1986 he raised $268,786 and spent $192,612. See Alan Ehrenhalt, ed., *Politics in America: The 100th Congress* (Washington, D.C.: Congressional Quarterly Press, 1990), p. 858.

21. Richard Fenno, Jr., *Home Style: House Members in Their Districts* (Glenview, Ill.: Scott, Foresman, 1978), pp. 54–99.
22. "Flag Backdrop at Site of Speech Prompts Wheat to Explain Vote," *Kansas City Star,* July 4, 1990.
23. Phil Duncan, ed., *Politics in America, 101st Congress* (Washington, D.C.: Congressional Quarterly Press, 1990), p. 859.
24. Barone and Ujifusa, *Almanac of American Politics, 1990,* p. 691.
25. Personal observation at a Kansas City, Mo., women's forum, September 19, 1989.
26. Ibid.
27. Alan Wheat, *Kansas City Issue Forum,* September 19, 1989.
28. Ehrenhalt, *Politics in America,* p. 858.
29. "Wheat Sows Goodwill in Congress," *Globe-Democrat* (St. Louis, Mo.), May 27, 1983.
30. Barone and Ujifusa, *Almanac of American Politics, 1990,* p. 403.
31. Robert A. Catlin, "Organizational Effectiveness and Black Political Participation: The Case of Katie Hall," *Phylon,* 46, no. 3 (1985), 179–192.
32. Ibid., pp. 183–184.
33. Ibid., p. 182.
34. "Mississippi Gets a Representative from Indiana," *New York Times,* November 26, 1982.
35. Ibid.; Catlin, "Organizational Effectiveness," p. 185.
36. "Folks Back Home Speak Their Piece to Representatives," *Christian Science Monitor,* September 8, 1983.
37. "Rep. Katie Hall Facing Tough Fight in Indiana," *New York Times,* May 7, 1984.
38. Ibid.
39. Catlin, "Organizational Effectiveness," p. 192. For more information about black voting behavior, see Douglas St. Angelo and Paul Puryear, "Fear, Apathy and Other Dimensions of Black Voting," in Michael B. Preston, Lenneal J. Henderson, Jr., and Paul Puryear, *The New Black Politics: The Search for Political Power* (New York: Longman, 1982), pp. 109–129.
40. These comments came in response to the question "Why do you think Katie Hall was defeated?"
41. Several black representatives said that they took it upon themselves to advise her, even suggesting legislative initiatives. Their efforts were to no avail. Hall set her priorities in a district where George McGovern (1972) and Carter (1980) both lost their presidential bids.
42. Williams, *JCPS Congressional District Fact Book,* pp. 26–32.
43. Phil Duncan, ed., *Politics in America, 102nd Congress* (Washington, D.C.: Congressional Quarterly, 1991), p. 125.
44. Ibid., p. 116.
45. Ken Kelley, "Dellums," *East Bay Free Weekly,* vol. 11, no. 33, p. 17, May 26, 1989.
46. Ibid., p. 12.
47. "Dellums' Seat Challenged in Contra Costa," *Contra Costa Times,* October 15, 1972.

48. Ronald Dellums, "Coalition Politics in California's East Bay," *Point of View*, Spring 1988, p. 25.
49. Kelley, "Dellums," p. 17.
50. "Dellums Report," *Sun Reporter* (San Francisco), October 9, 1971.
51. "Black Politics Needed Now, Dellums Says," *Baltimore Sun*, April 4, 1977.
52. "Dellums Hits 'Divisive Politics,'" *Wilmington Journal* (Delaware), February 2, 1983.
53. Ron Dellums, speeches in Hayward and Berkeley made during Jesse Jackson's presidential bid, June 1988.
54. Edie N. Goldenberg and Michael W. Traugott, *Campaigning for Congress* (Washington, D.C.: Congressional Quarterly Press, 1984).
55. "Dellums Girds Anew against His Enemies," *Tribune* (Oakland, Calif.), May 13, 1984.
56. Personal communication with a local politician, June 1988.
57. "Dellums' Seat Challenged."
58. "Dellums' Seat Challenged"; "Dellums' Actions Meet with the Disapproval of Some Blacks," *Post Tribune*, May 29, 1971.
59. "A Rude Freshman," *News Leader* (Richmond, Va.), February 1971.
60. "D.C. Tax Exemptions for Hill Families Sought," *Washington Post*, November 10, 1989.
61. *Afro-American Press*, Washington, D.C., February 16, 1988.
62. Around the country, black Republican congressional candidates have regularly lost their election bids. Republicanism does little to enhance their electability. Black Republican candidates commonly fail to be strategic; they often challenge strong incumbents in traditionally Democratic districts. In the 1988 Maryland senatorial races, for example, Alan Keyes won the Republican nomination and sought to defeat a white liberal two-term Democratic senator, Paul Sarbanes. All the ingredients for Keyes's defeat were there. He started his campaign in late June, and he needed to raise at least a million dollars before the election. The white incumbent had PAC money on hand in a state in which Democrats outnumbered Republicans two to one. Keyes needed all the black votes and more to have any chance of winning. He lost decisively. With little money and a late start, he challenged an incumbent senator (see "GOP Candidate Seeks to Open Eyes to Tokenism," *Wall Street Journal*, September 2, 1988, p. 14).

Sometimes the party dooms black Republicans to failure by encouraging them to mount symbolic bids. In 1988 Republican party leaders endorsed a black senatorial candidate, Maurice Dawkins, who had little or no chance of defeating Virginia's former governor, Chuck Robb. The national party did not allocate many resources to the Dawkins campaign; rather, their endorsement was purely symbolic. As was expected, Dawkins lost by a wide margin. Black Republicans are at a disadvantage because they have to appeal to whites who are more conservative than one typically finds in districts with Democratic majorities. As long as black Republicans run under undesirable circumstances, they will continue to lose. Significant increases in black representation will not come from the election of black Republicans. Black conservatives are therefore unlikely to be represented by blacks.

63. Raphael J. Sonenshein, "Can Black Candidates Win Statewide Elections?" *Political Science Quarterly*, 105, no. 2 (November 2, 1990), 210–241.

7. *White Representatives of Minority-Black Districts*

1. Merle Black, "Racial Compositions of Congressional Districts and Support for Federal Voting Rights in the American South," *Social Science Quarterly*, 59 (1978), p. 438.
2. Earl Black and Merle Black, *Politics and Society in the South* (Cambridge: Harvard University Press, 1987); Jack Bass and Walter De Vries, *The Transformation of Southern Politics* (New York: New American Library, 1976), p. 62; Kenny J. Whitby, "Measuring Congressional Responsiveness to the Policy Interests of Black Constituents," *Social Science Quarterly*, 68 (1987), 367–377; Kenny J. Whitby and Franklin D. Gilliam, Jr., "A Longitudinal Analysis of Competing Explanations for the Transformation of Southern Congressional Politics," *Journal of Politics*, 53, no. 2 (May 1991), 504–518.
3. Kenny J. Whitby and Franklin D. Gilliam, Jr., "Changing Times and Changing Attitudes among Southern Congressmen," paper presented at the meeting of the Midwest Political Science Association, April 1989.
4. Earl Black, *Southern Governors and Civil Rights* (Cambridge: Harvard University Press, 1976).
5. Quoted in Bass and De Vries, *Transformation of Southern Politics*, p. 62.
6. Ibid., p. 68.
7. "Strom Thurmond: New Votes, Old Views," *Congressional Quarterly Weekly Report*, January 14, 1984, p. 70.
8. Abigail Thernstrom, *Whose Votes Count? Affirmative Action and Minority Voting Rights* (Cambridge: Harvard University Press, 1987), p. 3.
9. Interview with Robin Tallon, Washington, D.C., October 22, 1990.
10. Linda F. Williams, ed., *The JCPS Congressional District Fact Book*, 3rd ed. (Washington, D.C.: Joint Center for Political Studies, 1988), p. 14.
11. Michael Barone, Grant Ujifusa, and Donald Matthews, *The Almanac of American Politics, 1978* (New York: E. P. Dutton, 1979), p. 780.
12. Ibid.
13. See "Hill Probe of Bribery Charge Hurt by Lack of Evidence," *Congressional Quarterly Weekly Report*, February 9, 1980, pp. 323–326; "House Votes to Conduct 'Full and Complete Inquiry' in 'Abscam' Bribery Probe," *Congressional Quarterly Weekly Report*, April 5, 1980, p. 913; "Videotaped Evidence Shown at Jenrette 'Abscam' Trial," *Congressional Quarterly Weekly Report*, September 13, 1980, p. 2701; "Jenrette Is Second Member Convicted in Abscam Trial," *Congressional Quarterly Weekly Report*, October 11, 1980, p. 3103; "Representative Jenrette Resigns from the House," *Congressional Quarterly Weekly Report*, December 13, 1980, p. 3551.
14. Interview with Robin Tallon, Florence, S.C., August 26, 1988.
15. Ibid.
16. Ibid.
17. Ibid.

18. Ibid.
19. Ibid.
20. Ibid.
21. Black, *Southern Governors*, p. 337; Bass and De Vries, *Transformation of Southern Politics*, pp. 377–378; Aage Clausen, *How Congressmen Decide* (New York: St. Martin's Press, 1973).
22. District visit with Robin Tallon, August 26, 1988.
23. Interview with Robin Tallon, Washington, D.C., October 22, 1990.
24. Ibid. See note 51 on evaluation of racial composition of white representatives' staffs.
25. Ibid.
26. Ibid.
27. Ibid.
28. Interview with Marva Smalls, Florence, S.C., August 26, 1988.
29. Anonymous quote from a black representative.
30. Interview with Tallon, October 22, 1990.
31. Ibid.
32. Ehrenhalt, *Politics in America*, p. 1385.
33. Interview with Tallon, October 22, 1990.
34. Ibid.
35. Ibid.
36. Ibid.
37. It is important to realize that members can have strong civil rights and progressive voting records on domestic issues and still score high on the CC. For example, Mike Espy's high CC scores (see Chapter 4) do not designate an opposition to black-supported social and economic issues. CC scores may show ideological agreement on conservative values, for example, on the death penalty or on aid to Contras.
38. Interview with Tallon, October 22, 1990.
39. Interview with Smalls.
40. A conservative white representative would need between 75 and 80 percent of the white vote to stay in office.
41. Richard Fenno, Jr., *Home Style: House Members in Their Districts* (Glenview, Ill.: Scott, Foresman, 1978), p. 49.
42. Barone et al., *The Almanac of American Politics, 1978*, p. 629.
43. William R. Keech, *The Impact of Negro Voting: The Role of the Vote in the Quest for Equality* (Chicago: Rand McNally, 1968). He also examines Tuskegee, Alabama.
44. Although Fountain could have easily won reelection, insiders say that he did not want to campaign among Durham's liberal constituency. The redistricting hastened his retirement by pushing him from the protectionist to the expansionist stage of his constituency career. On the concept of a constituency career, see Fenno's *Home Style* and Chapter 3.
45. Interview with Tim Valentine, Washington, D.C., February 27, 1991.
46. In the infamous 1984 North Carolina Senate race between Jesse Helms and former governor Jim Hunt, the Helms forces used blatant racially polarizing techniques. After distributing pictures of Hunt and Jesse Jackson that identified Jackson as a Hunt supporter, they charged that taxpayers' money

was being used to register black voters. Continuing these tactics in his 1990 reelection bid, Helms ran an anti–affirmative action advertisement in his contest against the black candidate, Harvey Gantt. Nothing in Valentine's campaign tactics came close to Helms's techniques or Franklin's.

47. "Valentine Defeats Spaulding in House Primary," *Congressional Quarterly Weekly Report*, May 12, 1984, p. 1116; "Second District Profile," *Congressional Quarterly Weekly Report*, April 28, 1984, pp. 982–983.

48. "Two States' House Primaries Will Involve Interracial Battles," *Washington Post*, May 5, 1984.

49. "Sharpe Hits on Valentine's Racial Record," *Durham Herald*, October 27, 1990; "Durham Voters Alliance Announces Endorsements," *Raleigh News and Observer*, October 25, 1990; "Sharpe, Valentine to Square Off in 2nd District Race," *Daily Dispatch* (Henderson, N.C.), November 5, 1990.

50. Interview with Valentine, February 27, 1991.

51. In order to evaluate whether or not white members were engaging in tokenism, I examined both pay rate and job classifications for the black staffers who worked for white members during the 100th Congress. If black staffers were employed only in low-ranking jobs, such as caseworker and receptionist, I strongly suspected tokenism. At that time both Valentine and Tallon had black staffers in high-status positions. Valentine's black legislative assistant, who is no longer with him, held the second-highest position. Robin Tallon had black professionals scattered throughout his staff, and they were well paid. From this examination I concluded that for Tallon and Valentine, the hiring of black staffers did not represent tokenism. The same analysis done in 1991 would yield very different results for Valentine. The data, of course, represent racial composition of a staff at a given point in time; because of job turnover it is always difficult to evaluate the racial makeup of the staff accurately.

52. Interview with Tim Valentine, Durham, N.C., August 31, 1988.

53. Observation of Tim Valentine, August 31, 1988.

54. Interview with Tim Valentine, Washington, D.C., February 27, 1991.

55. "North Carolina Computer Draws Some Labyrinthine Lines," *Congressional Quarterly Weekly Report*, July 13, 1991, pp. 1916–1917.

56. Ibid., p. 1917.

57. "Partisans Try to Shape the Maps to Gain Control in '90s," *Congressional Quarterly Weekly Report*, December 21, 1991, p. 3711.

58. Fenno, *Home Style*, p. 188.

59. Newsletter of Representative Tim Valentine, February 1988.

60. Interview with Valentine, February 27, 1991.

61. "Sharpe Asks Valentine to Debate," *Durham Herald*, October 25, 1990.

62. Interview with Valentine, February 27, 1991.

63. Interview with Representative Charlie Rose, Washington, D.C., October 22, 1990.

64. According to a Black Caucus spokesman, Valentine sought admission to the Caucus in 1988; however, he was not permitted to join because other caucus members viewed him as a closet Republican.

65. Interview with Valentine, February 27, 1991.

66. Ibid.

8. White Representatives of Majority-Black Districts

1. Wyche Fowler was able to stave off attacks by borrowing from Dr. King and telling black Atlantians to "judge me on the content of my character and not the color of my skin." According to Fowler, he left office voluntarily to run for the Senate seat (see Chapter 4).
2. Michael Barone, Grant Ujifusa, and Douglas Matthews, *The Almanac of American Politics, 1978* (New York: E. P. Dutton, 1979), pp. 334–335.
3. "With All the Merrymaking You'd Probably Never Know New Orleans Is Falling Apart," *Los Angeles Times*, December 18, 1984.
4. Gary Clifford, "Lindy Boggs Quits Congress to Close Ranks with Her Two Remarkable Daughters, One Gravely Ill with Cancer," *People Magazine*, August 13, 1990. For Boggs's speech itself, see *The Congressional Record: The United States House of Representatives*, July 9, 1965, p. 16221.
5. Interview with Lindy Boggs, Princeton, N.J., October 10, 1991.
6. Michael Barone, Grant Ujifusa, and Douglas Matthews, *The Almanac of American Politics, 1972* (New York: E. P. Dutton, 1973), pp. 302–303.
7. *Major v. Treen*, 574 F. Supp. 325 (1983); Richard L. Engstrom, "Repairing the Crack in New Orleans' Black Vote: VRA's Results Test Nullifies Gerryduck," *Publius: The Journal of Federalism*, 16 (Fall 1986), 109–120.
8. Clifford, "Lindy Boggs Quits Congress."
9. Interview with Boggs.
10. Ibid.
11. Ibid.
12. Clifford, "Lindy Boggs Quits Congress."
13. Kim Mattingly, "Lindy Boggs Will Retire after This Term to Spend More Time with Her Daughter," *Roll Call*, July 23, 1990.
14. "Rep. Boggs, 68, Facing Her Toughest Career Challenge in Louisiana Primary," *New York Times*, September 28, 1984.
15. Engstrom, "Repairing the Crack in New Orleans' Black Vote," p. 120.
16. Michael Barone and Grant Ujifusa, *The Almanac of American Politics, 1986* (New York: E. P. Dutton, 1987), p. 557.
17. Jonathan P. Scott, "Rep. Lindy Boggs Looks Back on Half a Century of Lawmaking," *States News Service*, November 2, 1990.
18. Personal observations of Lindy Boggs and her campaign staff.
19. Interview with Boggs.
20. Ibid.
21. Ibid.
22. Scott, "Rep. Lindy Boggs Looks Back on Half a Century of Lawmaking."
23. Ibid.
24. Ibid.
25. "Cargo Bill Still Afloat on Hill," *Washington Post*, May 7, 1983.
26. Alan Ehrenhalt, ed., *Politics in America: The 100th Congress* (Washington, D.C.: Congressional Quarterly Press, 1987), p. 609.
27. Quoted in Scott, "Rep. Lindy Boggs Looks Back on Half a Century of Lawmaking."
28. Ibid.

29. This conclusion is based on conversations with black staffers, leaders, and an excerpt in *Jet* Magazine of September 1988.

30. "A Livable City? Newark. Yes, Newark," *New York Times*, June 18, 1991.

31. Ibid.

32. Barone, Ujifusa, and Matthews, *Almanac of American Politics, 1972*, pp. 535–536.

33. "Gibson's Long Struggle Ends, Newark's Continues," *New York Times*, May 18, 1986.

34. *David v. Cahill*, 342 Fed. Supp. 463, 1972.

35. Interview with Peter Rodino, Newark, N.J., January 31, 1990.

36. Ibid.

37. Ibid.

38. Ibid.

39. Ibid.

40. Ibid.

41. Ibid.

42. Ibid.

43. Interview with Donald Payne, Washington, D.C., April 25, 1990.

44. Interview with Rodino.

45. Ibid.

46. Representative Augustus F. Hawkins, "Tribute for Peter Rodino," *Congressional Record*, February 19, 1986.

47. Interview with Rodino.

48. Ibid.

49. "Black Politicians Pressure Rodino to Retire," *New York Times*, March 9, 1988.

50. Interview with Rodino.

51. Ibid.

52. Ibid.

53. Ehrenhalt, *Politics in America*, p. 965.

54. Interview with Rodino.

55. Ibid.

56. Interview with Payne.

57. Ibid.

9. *Strategies for Increasing Black Representation of Blacks*

1. Some of the more relevant literature on reapportionment and redistricting includes Nelson Polsby, ed., *Reapportionment in the 1970s* (Berkeley: University of California Press, 1971); Robert Dixon, Jr., *Democratic Representation and Reapportionment in Law and Politics* (New York: Oxford University Press, 1968); Bruce Cain, *The Reapportionment Puzzle* (Berkeley: University of California Press, 1984); Timothy C. O'Rourke, *The Impact of Reapportionment* (New Brunswick, N.J.: Transaction Books, 1980); Charles Bullock III, "Redistricting and Congressional Stability, 1962–1972," *Journal of Politics*, 37 (1975), 569–575; Keith E. Hamm, Robert Harmel, and Robert J. Thompson, "Impacts of Districting Change on Voting Cohesion and Representation," *Journal of Politics*, 43 (1981), 544–555.

2. In December 1991 the Supreme Court agreed to hear a challenge to the 1941

federal law that provides a formula for the allocation of congressional seats. A federal district court in Montana ruled that the 1941 law ignored "the goal of equal representation for equal numbers of people." If the court sustains the Montana ruling, congressional districts allocated after the 1990 census to 18 states will have to be reassigned. See "High Court to Weigh Redistricting Case," *New York Times*, December 17, 1991.

3. Q. Whitfield Ayres and David Whiteman, "Congressional Reapportionments in the 1980s," *Political Science Quarterly*, 99, no. 2 (Summer 1984), 303–314.

4. *Reynolds v. Sims*, 377 U.S. 533 (1964).

5. *Wesberry v. Sanders*, 376 U.S. 1 (1964).

6. *Kirkpatrick v. Preisler*, 394 U.S. 526, 531 (1969), *White v. Weiser*, 412 U.S. 783, 790 (1973), *Wells v. Rockefeller*, 394 U.S. 542 (1969), and *Karcher v. Daggett*, 462 U.S. 725 (1983).

7. *Kirksey v. Board of Supervisors of Hinds County, Mississippi*, 544 F. 2d 139 (1977); see also *Ketchum v. Byrne*, 740 F. 2d 1398 (1984).

8. Kimball Brace, Bernard Grofman, Lisa Handley, and Richard Niemi, "Minority Voting Equality: The 65 Percent Rule in Theory and Practice," *Law and Policy*, 10, no. 1 (January 1988), 43–62; Bernard Grofman and Lisa Handley, "Minority Population Proportion and Black and Hispanic Congressional Success in the 1970s and 1980s," *American Politics Quarterly*, 17, no. 4 (October 1989), 436–445; "Creating Black Districts May Segregate Voters," *Congressional Quarterly Weekly Report*, July 28, 1990, p. 2462.

9. Bernard Grofman, Michael Migalski, and Nicholas Noviello, "The 'Totality of Circumstances Test' in Section 2 of the 1982 Extension of the Voting Rights Act: A Social Science Perspective," *Law and Policy*, 7, no. 2 (April 1985), 199–223.

10. *Thornburg v. Gingles*, 478 U.S. 30 (1986).

11. Charles Bullock III, "Redistricting and Changes in the Partisan and Racial Composition of Southern Legislatures," *State and Local Government Review* (Spring 1987), 62.

12. "Monster Map," editorial, *Wall Street Journal*, October 18, 1991; "North Carolina Computer Draws Some Labyrinthine Lines," *Congressional Quarterly Weekly Report*, July 13, 1991, pp. 1916–1917; "Democrats' Ties to Minorities May Be Tested by New Lines," *Congressional Quarterly Weekly Report*, June 2, 1990, pp. 1739–1742.

13. Robert C. Smith provides a useful discussion of the major court cases involving blacks in his article "Liberal Jurisprudence and the Quest for Racial Representation," *Southern University Law Review*, 15, no. 1 (1988), 1–51.

14. Frank Parker, "Racial Gerrymandering and Legislative Reapportionment," in Chandler Davidson, ed., *Minority Vote Dilution* (Washington, D.C.: Howard University Press, 1984); Frank Parker, *Black Votes Count: Political Empowerment in Mississippi after 1965* (Chapel Hill: University of North Carolina Press, 1990).

15. *Wright v. Rockefeller*, 376 U.S. 52 (1964).

16. Dr. Ronald Walters, as quoted in "Changing Horizon for Black Caucus," *Philadelphia Inquirer*, September 26, 1990.

17. Bernard Anderson, as quoted in "Changing Horizons for Black Caucus."

18. See Robert C. Smith, "Recent Elections and Black Politics: The Maturation or Death of Black Politics," *PS*, 22 (June 1990), 160–162.
19. Interview with Craig Washington, Washington, D.C., October 22, 1991.
20. Ibid.
21. "Creating Black Districts May Segregate Voters," p. 2462.
22. Interview with Mike Espy, Washington, D.C., June 14, 1990.
23. "Race and Politics: A Border Clash," *Washington Post National Weekly Edition*, December 23–29, 1991, p. 13.
24. Brace et al., "Minority Voting," pp. 42–62; Grofman and Handley, "Minority Population Proportion," pp. 436–445.
25. *United Jewish Organizations v. Carey*, 430 U.S. 144 (1977), p. 166, n. 24; see also Robert Weissberg, "Collective v. Dyadic Representation in Congress," *American Political Science Review*, 72 (1978), 535–547.
26. Blacks and Hispanics are sure to fight over a new district to be drawn in the Dallas, Texas, area that will jeopardize white Democratic incumbents such as Representatives Michael Andrews and Martin Frost; see "Endangered Species: 'Anglo Democrats,'" *International Herald Tribune*, May 22, 1991.
27. See "Minority Mapmaking," *National Journal*, April 7, 1990, pp. 837–839; "Democrats' Ties to Minorities May Be Tested by New Lines"; "Maps That Stand Up in Court," *State Legislatures*, September 1990, pp. 15–19; "Mapmakers Must Toe the Line in Upcoming Redistricting," *Congressional Quarterly Weekly Report*, September 1, 1990, pp. 2786–2794; "Pushing for More Black House Seats," *National Journal*, January 5, 1991, p. 34; "Minority Poker," *National Journal*, May 4, 1991, pp. 1034–1039.
28. African Americans currently make up 20 percent or more of the voting-age population in Mississippi (31 percent), Louisiana (27 percent), South Carolina (27 percent), Georgia (24 percent), Maryland (24 percent), Alabama (23 percent), and North Carolina (20 percent). Furthermore, blacks constitute sizable minorities in New York (15 percent), Illinois (14 percent), Michigan (13 percent), New Jersey (13 percent), and Ohio (10 percent). See *Blacks and the 1988 Democratic National Convention* (Washington, D.C.: Joint Center for Political Studies, 1988), pp. 5–6; *Black Elected Officials: A National Roster*, 18th ed. (Washington, D.C.: Joint Center for Political Studies, 1989), p. 1. See also "Race and the South," *U.S. News and World Report*, July 23, 1990.
29. Bernard Grofman and Lisa Handley, "Black Representation: Making Sense of Electoral Geography at Different Levels of Government," *Legislative Studies Quarterly*, 14, (May 2, 1989), 267–268; Grofman and Handley, "Minority Population Proportion," pp. 436–445.
30. "1990s Big Winners: California, Texas, Florida; Northeast and Midwest Seen Losing Seats," *Washington Post*, February 26, 1988, p. 21.
31. David Huckabee, "House Apportionment: Preliminary Projections," *Congressional Research Service Report*, August 1988, pp. 88–567.
32. Interview with George Crockett, Washington, D.C., June 14, 1990.
33. Interview with Espy.
34. Personal communication with William Clay's district administrator, September 20, 1990.
35. Gerald D. Jaynes and Robin M. Williams, Jr., eds., *A Common Destiny: Blacks*

and American Society (Washington, D.C.: National Academy Press, 1989), pp. 140–144.

36. Ibid.
37. Carol M. Swain, "Some Unintended Consequences of the Voting Rights Act," in Chandler Davidson and Bernard Grofman, *Minority Voting: The Voting Rights Act in Twenty-Five Year Perspective* (Washington, D.C.: Brookings, forthcoming).
38. *Beer v. United States,* 374 F. Supp. 363 (D.D.C. 1974), rev'd 425 U.S. 130 (1976).
39. John Dunne, as cited in "Minority Poker," p. 1038.
40. Interview with Representative Louis Stokes, Washington, D.C., June 14, 1990.
41. Benjamin Ginsberg, as quoted in "Minority Mapmaking," p. 837.
42. Kimball Brace, Bernard Grofman, and Lisa Handley, "Does Redistricting Aimed to Help Blacks Necessarily Help Republicans?" *Journal of Politics,* 49 (1987), 169–185; Charles Bullock III, "The Election of Blacks in the South: Preconditions and Consequences," *American Journal of Political Science,* 19, (November, 1975), 727–739.
43. Ibid.
44. Interview with Washington.
45. "Democrats Court Minorities to Counter GOP's Pitch," *Congressional Quarterly Weekly Report,* May 4, 1991, p. 1104.
46. Ibid.
47. Daniel Wattenberg, "The GOP Divides to Conquer," *Insight on the News,* 7, no. 22 (June 3, 1991), 12–19.

10. The Future of Black Congressional Representation

1. See Charles Bullock III, "Racial Crossover Voting and the Election of Black Officials," *Journal of Politics,* 46 (1984), 238–251; Leonard A. Cole, *Blacks in Power: A Comparative Study of Black and White Elected Officials* (Princeton: Princeton University Press, 1976); Richard Murray and Arnold Vedlitz, "Racial Voting Patterns in the South: An Analysis of Major Elections from 1960 to 1977 in Five Cities," *Annals,* 439 (1978), 29–39. On the statewide races, see Raphael Sonenshein, "Can Black Candidates Win Statewide Elections?" *Political Science Quarterly,* 105 (1990), 219–241; Jack Citrin, Donald Green, and David Sears, "White Reactions to Black Candidates," *Public Opinion Quarterly,* 54 (1990), 74–96; Thomas Pettigrew and Denise Alston, *Tom Bradley's Campaigns for Governor: The Dilemma of Race and Political Strategies* (Washington, D.C.: Joint Center for Political Studies, 1988); Robert Staples, "Tom Bradley's Defeat: The Impact of Racial Symbols on Political Campaigns," *Black Scholar,* 13 (1982), 37–46.
2. Linda Williams, "White/Black Perceptions of the Electability of Black Political Candidates," *National Political Science Review,* 2 (1990), 45–64.
3. Janet Landa, Michael Copeland, and Bernard Grofman, "Ethnic Voting Patterns in Metropolitan Toronto," paper presented at the meetings of the Public Choice Society, Tucson, Arizona, March 16, 1990; Robert A. Lorinskas, Brett W. Hawkins, and Stephen Edwards, "The Persistence of Ethnic Voting in Rural and Urban Areas: Results from the Controlled Election Method," *Social*

Science Quarterly, 49 (1979), 891–899; Harlan Hahn and Timothy Almy, "Ethnic Voting and Racial Issues: Voting in Los Angeles," *Western Political Quarterly,* 24 (1971), 719–730; Thomas Pettigrew, "When a Black Candidate Runs for Mayor: Race and Voting Behavior," in Harlan Hahn, ed., *People and Politics in Urban Society* (Beverly Hills, Calif.: Sage Publications, 1972); Murray and Vedlitz, "Racial Voting Patterns in the South."

4. Henry Brady and Paul Sniderman, "Attitude Attribution: A Group Basis for Political Reasoning," *American Political Science Review,* 79 (1985), 1061–1077; Edward Carmines and James Stimson, *Issue Evolution: Race and the Transformation of American Politics* (Princeton: Princeton University Press, 1989).

5. The addition of significant numbers of blacks to majority-white districts could induce greater policy responsiveness. Bullock, "The Inexact Science of Congressional Redistricting," *PS* (Summer, 1982), 431–437.

6. See William R. Riker, *The Theory of Political Coalitions* (New Haven: Yale University Press, 1962); James M. Buchanan, *The Calculus of Consent* (Ann Arbor: University of Michigan Press, 1962), pp. 135–145.

7. Stokely Carmichael and Charles V. Hamilton, *Black Power: The Politics of Liberation in America* (New York: Random House, 1987), p. 87.

8. Charles Whalen and Barbara Whalen, *The Longest Debate: A Legislative History of the 1964 Civil Rights Act* (New York: New American Library, 1985).

9. Analyzing data from the 98th to the 100th Congress, I found party and region to be by far the most important influences on a representative's COPE and LCCR scores. The race of the representative and the district's black population percentage were much less important; see Carol Swain, "The Politics of Black Representation in U.S. Congressional Districts," Ph.D. dissertation, University of North Carolina at Chapel Hill, August 1989, chap. 8.

10. Interview with Andrea Turner Scott, Washington, D.C., October 22, 1990.

11. Interview with Charlie Rose, Washington, D.C., October 22, 1990.

12. "No White Candidate Need Apply," editorial, *Wall Street Journal,* May 31, 1991.

13. See "Savage: Running on the Edge," *Washington Post,* March 9, 1990; "Savage Attacks 'Racist White Press,'" *Washington Post,* March 22, 1990; "A House Member Accused of Sexual Impropriety on Trip," *New York Times,* July 20, 1989.

14. Michael Preston, "Black Elected Officials and Public Policy: Symbolic and Substantive Representation," *Policy Studies Journal,* 7 (1978), 196–201.

15. Richard Fenno, Jr., *Home Style: House Members in Their Districts* (Glenview, Ill.: Scott, Foresman, 1978).

16. The concept of "constituency" is generally used by congressional scholars to denote all who can hold the representative accountable at the ballot box. Black representatives repeatedly mention and depend on financial support from a constituency that goes beyond their district. I would propose that theories of representation be expanded to take account of such constituencies.

17. Interview with Mervyn Dymally, Washington, D.C., October 22, 1990.

18. Alan Ehrenhalt, *Politics in America: The 100th Congress* (Washington, D.C.: Congressional Quarterly Press, 1990), p. 1492.

19. Interview with Mickey Leland's district administrator, Houston, Tex., October 1988.

20. Sidney Verba and Norman H. Nie, *Participation in America: Political Democracy and Social Equality* (New York: Harper & Row, 1972), chap. 10.

21. Interview with Donald Payne, Washington, D.C., April 25, 1990.

22. Interviews with representatives and staffers from different congressional districts.

23. Bruce Cain, John Ferejohn, and Morris Fiorina, *The Personal Vote: Constituency Service and Electoral Independence* (Cambridge: Harvard University Press, 1987), pp. 41–42.

24. David Mayhew, *Congress: The Electoral Connection* (New Haven: Yale University Press, 1974).

25. The charges against Floyd Flake, for example, were not supported by strong evidence. Some black representatives, however, have been guilty of misconduct. Charles Diggs and Adam Powell were expelled from the House. Diggs was convicted of transferring payroll funds for personal use and served a prison term. Powell was indicted by the House and censured, though he was never convicted of wrongdoing.

26. "Harassment of Black Elected Officials: Ten Years Later," pamphlet, *Voter Education and Registration Act, 1987;* Mary R. Warner, *The Dilemma of Black Politics: A Report on Harassment of Black Elected Officials* (Sacramento, Calif.: National Association of Human Rights Workers, 1977).

27. John Conyers, for example, citing security reasons, refused to participate in this study. According to his aides, the Federal Bureau of Investigation once placed a "spy" on his staff. Floyd Flake, who considered the possibility that I might be an FBI agent, told me that he concluded that he had nothing to hide and, therefore, agreed to work with me. Representative Dymally told me that he thought I might be a spy for the Republicans, but that he had nothing to hide and was thus happy to help me with my research.

28. Black representatives were disproportionately represented among those members of Congress exposed in 1992 as having written overdrafts at the House bank. During the spring 1992 primaries several retirements and defeats could be directly traced to the scandal. Public anger and lessened respect for those in Congress could lead to the defeat of more incumbents in future elections. For more information, see "Panel Releases the Names of Members Who Overdrew House Bank Accounts," *New York Times*, April 17, 1992; "The House Bank," "Anger and Anxiety for Check-writing Lawmakers," *New York Times*, April 17, 1992.

29. Earl Black and Merle Black, *Politics and Society in the South* (Cambridge: Harvard University Press, 1987), chap. 14.

30. Carmines and Stimson, *Issue Evolution*, chap. 2. Thomas B. Edsall and Mary Edsall, *Chain Reaction: The Impact of Race, Rights, and Taxes on American Politics* (New York: W. W. Norton, 1991).

31. Charles V. Hamilton, "De-racialization: Examination of a Political Strategy," *First World* (March-April 1977), 3–5.

32. Joel D. Aberbach and Jack L. Walker, *Race in the City* (Boston: Little, Brown,

1973); William J. Wilson, *The Declining Significance of Race,* 2nd ed. (Chicago: University of Chicago Press, 1980).

33. The ability of David Duke to rise as a national leader and to win 55 percent of the white vote in Louisiana's 1991 gubernatorial race has been widely attributed to the frustration that white Americans feel about social welfare programs that they see as assistance for blacks at their expense.

34. Morris P. Fiorina, *Representatives, Roll Calls, and Constituencies* (Lexington, Mass.: D. C. Heath, 1974), chaps. 2–5.

35. "Bleak Outlook for an Ohio Candidate Underlines Difficulties of GOP Blacks Running for Congress," *Wall Street Journal,* August 28, 1986; "GOP Conservatives after Eight Years in Ascendancy Brood over Lost Opportunities," *Wall Street Journal,* August 17, 1988; "GOP Candidate Seeks to Open Eyes to Tokenism," *Wall Street Journal,* September 2, 1988; "A Black Congressional Hope in Connecticut," *New York Times,* August 9, 1990; "In Cincinnati House Contest, GOP Takes Aim at Elusive Goal: Victory for a Black Republican," *Wall Street Journal,* August 17, 1990. See also Chapter 6, note 62.

36. "Helms Kindled Anger in Campaign, and May Have Set Tone for Others," *New York Times,* November 8, 1990.

37. "Woman in the News; Storming the Senate 'Club': Carol Elizabeth Moseley Braun," *New York Times,* March 19, 1992.

Appendix A

1. Lewis Dexter, *Elite and Specialized Interviewing* (Evanston, Ill.: Northwestern University Press, 1970); Alexander Heard, "Interviewing Southern Politicians," *American Political Science Review,* no. 44 (December, 1950), 886–896; James A. Robinson, "Participant Observation, Political Internships and Research," *Political Science Annual,* no. 2, ed. James Robinson (Indianapolis: Bobbs-Merrill, 1970), pp. 71–100; Richard F. Fenno, Jr., *Watching Politicians: Essays on Participant Observation* (Berkeley, Calif.: Institute of Governmental Studies, 1990).

2. The black voting-age percentages of the total population were, of course, lower.

3. Shirley Hatchett and Howard Shuman, *Black Racial Attitudes, Trends and Complexities* (Ann Arbor: Institute for Social Research, 1974), p. 51.

4. David Mayhew, *Congress: The Electoral Connection* (New Haven, Conn.: Yale University Press, 1974).

5. Adolph Reed, Jr., *The Jesse Jackson Phenomenon* (New Haven, Conn.: Yale University Press, 1986), chaps. 1 and 3.

6. Richard Fenno, Jr., *Home Style: House Members in Their Districts* (Glenview, Ill.: Scott, Foresman, 1978), pp. 256–257.

Index